ALAN AYCKBOURN

Plays Two

Ernie's Incredible Illucinations

Invisible Friends

This Is Where We Came In

My Very Own Story

The Champion of Paribanou

Introduced by
the Author

faber and faber
LONDON · BOSTON

This collection first published in 1998
by Faber and Faber Limited
3 Queen Square London WC1N 3AU

Typeset by Country Setting, Woodchurch, Kent TN26 3TB
Printed in England by Mackays of Chatham plc, Chatham, Kent

Introduction © Alan Ayckbourn, 1998
This collection © Haydonning, 1998
Ernie's Incredible Illucinations © Alan Ayckbourn, 1969
first published by Alan Durband in a volume
entitled *Playbill One, a Collection of Five Plays*
Invisible Friends © Haydonning, 1991
This is Where We Came In © Haydonning, 1998
My Very Own Story © Haydonning, 1998
The Champion of Paribanou © Haydonning, 1998

A CIP record for this book
is available from the British Library

ISBN 978-0-571-19457-5

2 4 6 8 10 9 7 5 3

Contents

Introduction

I'm especially pleased that this second collection of my
plays should concentrate on my work for children. Of
the fifty plus plays I've written to date, eleven have been
aimed at a younger audience aged somewhere between
five and twelve.

Why bother? A jaded theatre writer once pointed out
to me that, generally, we all write for two reasons – to
pay the rent and to achieve critical recognition. With
children's theatre productions, thanks to low seat prices,
the royalties are negligible and national critics rarely
attend or when they do only to bring their nephew,
Daniel, aged eight and a half, to review it. ('I licked the
ice cream ladys best of all.')

Of course there are other reasons. In my case, as
artistic director of a regional theatre company, I am
anxious to try and ensure that there is a future audience
for us to play to. Secondly, and rather more altruistically,
or so I like to believe, because I want children to experience the magic and excitement of live performance;
something that no amount of film or video trickery can
ever quite match.

I'm also keen to extend that experience to the theatre
itself, not just to the drama. I want to encourage children
to come into the building. There are comparatively few
opportunities for them to do this in most theatres except
around the traditional Christmas period. Of course,
there is masses of good work being done by companies
who spend their lives on the road, fitting up in school
halls or gymnasiums at dawn, then moving on to
another venue before lunch. There are still a few good

Theatre in Education companies left. There are still dedicated, stagestruck teachers out there managing to excite their oversized classes with the theatrical thrills of story-telling and make-believe.

I applaud these. Without them all theatre would be the poorer. But I also want to show children the other magic. Not that old clap trap of the red velvet curtain (anyway I run a theatre in the round) but the magic that actors can create with seemingly nothing to help them. The magic created by the simple technologies, those of narrative and character. The magic of what you *don't* see. Of what you imagine rather than the pre-ordained and ready-to-serve.

It is a sad fact that the one or two companies who have set themselves the task of bringing theatre to children on a year-round basis – Polka Theatre for Children at Wimbledon and the Unicorn at the Arts Theatre to name but two – are desperately under-funded. Maybe, then, that is my other reason for writing such plays; namely that by adding such weight and reputation as I have to their cause, it might persuade our funding bodies and charitable institutions to take them more seriously. I am not, as they say, holding my breath.

This volume contains a cross section of my children's writing.

Ernie's Incredible Illucinations is an early piece written at the request of Alan Durband in 1969 for a published anthology of work intended for performance by children in schools. I tried to accommodate this by writing a play for a limited number of leading players and an infinitely expandable supporting cast, working on the principle that there are always three or four in any group who can do it and another fifty who just mill around eagerly but hate to be left out. Somewhat to my surprise it has turned out to be something of a success. Over the years it has received innumerable productions –

probably more than any of my plays – spanning several generations of children, including at one stage both my now extremely mature sons. Rarely does a season pass without at least one actor in my company confiding to me that *Ernie* was their starting point as an aspiring actor. It's been updated, televised, turned into countless (and totally unauthorized) musicals and even performed by an adult cast at the Unicorn Theatre for Children in London. Oddly, it is one of the few plays of mine which I've neither directed nor appeared in. It was, at the time, a rare stab for me at writing specifically for children and not a genre I was to attempt again for several years.

In fact it was 1988 when I decided, in an effort to build up a regular children's Christmas audience at the theatre in Scarborough, that I would have another shot at a Christmas Play. A year later, encouraged by the success of *Mr. A's Amazing Maze Plays* (a help-decide-the-plot, audience participation sort of show), I wrote *Invisible Friends*. It has been described as a younger version of my earlier play, *Woman in Mind*. It relies, like a lot of my children's work, upon a good deal of direct narration, this time from young Lucy who gets fed up with her own family and retreats into a fantasy world of her own. As in the adult play, her dreams appear not only to be coming true but rapidly turning into nightmares. Unlike its adult counterpart, though, it has a moral (anything's possible if you put your mind to it) and a far happier ending.

I have no hard and fast code when I write for my young audience except a determination to make sure the play opens doors of possibility and doesn't merely close them.

This Is Where We Came In and *My Very Own Story*, written within a year of each other in 1990 and 1991, are very much a pair. *This Is Where We Came In* or 'TWICCI' as it came to be known by the production team, was written initially in response to a particular set of physical circumstances. I needed a play in two halves which could be performed on alternating Saturday mornings by the permanent Scarborough company, utilizing whichever main repertoire set happened to be onstage on that particular morning. This helps to explain the play's pretext, a group of travelling players lost in a strange abstract landscape. Again, I made great use of the narrator or rather narrators but by now, encouraged by the speed of comprehension of the young audiences and their evident willingness to embrace complicated plots and sophisticated characters, the level of complexity was far greater than I had previously attempted.

It was about now that I began to stop concerning myself about what limits I should observe in children's writing and concentrated on how far I could take it.

My Very Own Story, written a year later, plays not only with space but with time, merrily hopping through the centuries as Peter, Paul and Percy in turn wrest control of the narrative from each other, appearing in each other's tales and eventually burrowing back (and sometimes forward) in time to resolve each other's story in the grandest of grand finales. One or two adults had trouble following the narrative but, as far as I know, children never did.

The Champion of Paribanou is my latest children's play. It more or less encapsulates all that I've learnt so far and am still learning about theatre for young people. It involves fantasy and magic, includes a good deal of dark passion, contains a strong narrative and I think (for its type) has quite unusual protagonists. In Murganah, I have written as tragic a heroine as I've ever achieved: a young girl who befriends a prince but is rejected, takes desperate measures to regain him by literally selling her soul. When she finally loses her lover to another, she seeks a terrible revenge. In this play the definition of good and evil is far less clearly defined. For the first time in a children's play, I've strayed into the grey area of individual choice. Are any of us ever born good or bad? Or do we only grow that way as a result of the circumstances we face and the choices we make?

Indeed, in the brief time I have been writing both types of play, I believe that now only a hairsbreadth separates my adult from my children's work.

Alan Ayckbourn
Scarborough, September 1997

ERNIE'S INCREDIBLE ILLUCINATIONS

Characters

Ernie
Mum
Dad
Receptionist
Doctor
Officer
Auntie May
First Barker
Second Barker
Third Barker
Fourth Barker
Referee
Timekeeper
Man
Woman
Kid Saracen
Second Man
Lady
Library Attendant
Girl Librarian
Lady Librarian
A Tramp
Patients, Soldiers, Crowds, Boxers, etc.

The action takes place in a doctor's waiting-room
and surgery – and elsewhere.

Time: the present.

At one side of the stage is a doctor's waiting-room. It is filled with an assortment of miserable-looking patients, coughing, wheezing, sneezing and moaning. Amongst them sit Mr and Mrs Fraser and their son, Ernie.

Ernie (*to the audience, after a second*) If you ever want to feel ill – just go and spend a happy half-hour in a doctor's waiting-room. If you're not ill when you get there, you will be when you leave.

> *A man enters, having seen the doctor. He is moaning. He crosses the waiting-room and goes out. The other patients look at him and sorrowfully shake their heads. The Receptionist enters.*

Receptionist Mr and Mrs Fraser . . .

> *Mum and Dad rise.*

Doctor will see you now.

Mum Thank you. Come on, Ernie.

> *Mum and Dad and Ernie follow the Receptionist across the stage to the Doctor who sits behind a table.*

'Morning, Doctor.

> *The Receptionist leaves.*

Doctor Ah. Ah. Mr and Mrs Fraser. Is that it?

Mum That's right. I'm Mrs Fraser – and this is my husband, Mr Fraser – and this is our son – Ernie.

Doctor Ah yes. Ernie. I've been hearing all sorts of things about you, young Ernie. Now, what have you been up to, eh?

Dad Illucinations.

Doctor I beg your pardon?

Dad Illucinations.

Doctor Oh, yes, illuci – quite, yes.

Mum What my husband means, Doctor, is that Ernie has been creating these illusions.

Doctor Ah.

Mum Well, they're more than illusions, really.

Dad I'll say.

Doctor Beg pardon?

Dad I'll say.

Mum He's been causing that much trouble. At school, at home, everywhere he goes. I mean we can't go on like this. His dad's not as strong as he was, are you, Albert?

Dad No.

Doctor What?

Dad No.

Doctor Perhaps it would be better if you told me a little more about it. When did you first notice this . . .?

Mum Ah well . . .

Dad Ah.

Mum Now then . . .

Dad Now . . .

Mum He'd have been . . . well, it'd have been about . . .
near enough . . . er . . .

Doctor Go on.

*Ernie steps forward. During his speech Mum and Dad
remain seated. The Doctor moves to the side of the
stage, produces a notebook and makes notes on what
follows.*

Ernie It started with these daydreams. You know, the
sort everybody gets. Where you suddenly score a hat
trick in the last five minutes of the Cup Final, or you
bowl out the West Indies for ten runs – or saving your
granny from a blazing helicopter, all that sort of rubbish.
It was one wet Saturday afternoon and me and my mum
and my dad were all sitting about in the happy home
having one of those exciting afternoon rave-ups we
usually have in our house.

*Ernie sits at the table in the Doctor's chair and starts
to read a book. Mum has started knitting and Dad
just sits, gazing ahead of him. There is a long silence.*

Ernie It was all go in our house.

Pause

Mum I thought you'd be at the match today, Albert.

Dad Not today.

Mum Not often you miss a game.

Dad They're playing away.

Mum Oh.

Dad In Birmingham. I'm damned if I'm going to
Birmingham. Even for United.

Ernie Meanwhile – while this exciting discussion was in progress, I was reading this book about the French wartime resistance workers and of the dangers they faced – often arrested in their homes. I started wondering what would happen if a squad of soldiers turned up at our front door, having been tipped off about the secret radio transmitter hidden in our cistern – when suddenly . . .

The tramp of feet, and a squad of Soldiers comes marching on and up to their front door.

Officer Halte! (*He bangs on the door.*)

Pause.

Dad That the door?

Mum What?

Dad The door.

Mum Was it?

Officer Open zis door. Open the door! (*He knocks again.*)

Mum Oh, that'll be the milkman wanting his money. He always comes round about now. Albert, have you got ten bob . . .?

Dad (*fumbling in his pockets*) Ah . . .

Officer (*shouting*) Open zis door immediately. Or I shall order my men to break it down! (*He bangs on the door again.*)

Mum Just a minute. Coming.

Dad Should have one somewhere . . .

Officer We know you're in there, English spy! Come out with your hands up . . .!

Mum What's he shouting about? Oh, I'd better ask him for three pints next week, if Auntie May's coming . . .

Officer Zis is your last chance. . . (*He knocks again.*)

Mum Oh, shut up . . .

The Officer signals his men. Two of them step back, brace their shoulders and prepare to charge the door.

I'm coming – I'm coming.

Ernie I shouldn't go out there, Mum . . .

Mum What?

Ernie I said don't go out there.

Mum What . . .?

Ernie It's not the milkman. It's a squad of enemy soldiers.

Mum Who?

Ernie They've come for me . . .

Mum Who has?

Ernie The soldiers. They've found out about the radio transmitter.

Mum What radio?

Dad Hey, here, that's a point. Have you paid our telly licence yet, Ethel? It might be the detector van.

Mum Oh, sit down, Albert. Stop worrying. It's just Ernie. Shut up, Ernie.

Ernie But Mum . . .

Dad I think I'll take the telly upstairs. Just in case . . .

The Soldiers charge at the door. A loud crash.

9

Ernie Don't go out, Mum.

Mum Shut up!

Dad (*picking up the television, struggling with it*) Just take it upstairs.

Ernie (*to Mum*) Don't go!

Mum I can't leave him out there. The way he's going he'll have the door off its hinges in a minute . . . (*She moves to the door.*)

Dad Mind your backs. Out of my way . . .

Ernie Mum . . .

> *Mum opens the door just as the two Soldiers are charging for the second time. They shoot past her, straight into the hall, collide with Dad and land in a heap with him. Dad manages to hold the television above his head and save it from breaking.*

Mum Hey . . .

Dad Oy!

> *The Officer and the other Soldiers enter. Ernie crouches behind the table.*

Officer Ah-ha! The house is surrounded.

Mum Who are you?

Officer Put up your hands. My men will search the house.

Dad (*feebly*) Hey . . .

Officer (*shouting up the stairs*) We know you're hiding in here, you can't get away . . .

Dad Hey – *hey* – HEY!

Officer Ah-ha. What have we here?

Dad Oh. It's the telly. The neighbour's telly. Not mine.

Officer Ah-ha.

Dad Just fixing it for him, you see . . .

Officer Outside.

Dad Eh?

Officer You will come with me.

Dad What, in this? I'm not going out in this rain.

Officer Outside or I shoot.

Dad Here . . .

Mum Albert . . .

Ernie Hold it! Drop those guns!

Officer Ah, so . . . (*He raises his gun.*)

Ernie Da-da-da-da-da-da-da-da-da-da-da.

The Soldiers collapse and are strewn all over the hall.
Mum screams. Then there is a silence

Mum Oh, Ernie. What have you done?

Ernie Sorry, Mum.

Dad Oh, lad . . .

Mum Are they – dead?

Dad Yes.

Mum screams again

Steady, steady. This needs thinking about.

Mum What about the neighbours?

Dad Could create a bit of gossip, this could.

Mum What about the carpet? Look at it.

Dad Hasn't done that much good.

Mum What'll we do with them?

Dad Needs a bit of thinking about.

Ernie steps forward. As he speaks and during the next section, Dad and Mum carry off the bodies.

Ernie Well, Mum and Dad decided that the best thing to do was to pretend it hadn't happened. That was usually the way they coped with all emergencies . . .

The Doctor steps forward.

Mum (*struggling with a body*) We waited till it got dark, you see . . .

Doctor Yes? And then . . .?

Dad We dumped 'em.

Doctor I beg your pardon?

Dad We dumped 'em. Took 'em out and dumped 'em.

Doctor Dumped them? Where, for heaven's sake?

Dad Oh – bus shelters – park benches . . .

Mum Corporation car-park.

Dad Left one in the all-night cafeteria.

Mum And one in the Garden of Rest.

Dad Caused a bit of a rumpus.

Doctor I'm not surprised.

Mum We had the police round our way for days – trying to sort it out . . .

Dad They never did get to the bottom of it, though.

Doctor Extraordinary. And then?

Ernie (*stepping forward*) And then – Auntie May arrived to stay. I liked my Auntie May.

Auntie May enters. The Doctor steps back again.

Auntie 'Ullo, Ernie lad. Have a sweetie.

Ernie Ta, Auntie. And Auntie May took me to the fair.

The stage is filled with jostling people, barkers and fairground music. The Barkers speak simultaneously.

First Barker Yes, indeed, the world's tallest man! He's so tall, madam, his breakfast is still sliding down him at tea time. Come along now, sir. Come inside now . . .

Second Barker Ladies and gentlemen. I am prepared to guarantee that you will never again, during your lifetimes, see anything as unbelievably amazing as the Incredible Porcupine Woman. See her quills and get your thrills. Direct from the unexplored South American Jungle . . .

Third Barker Try your luck, come along, madam – leave your husband there, dear, he'll still be there when you come back – tell you what – if he isn't, I can sell you a replacement – five shots for sixpence – knock 'em all down and pick up what you like . . .

Ernie Can I have a go on that, Auntie?

Auntie Not now, Ernie.

Ernie Oh go on, Auntie May.

Auntie I want a cup of tea.

Ernie Have an ice-cream.

Auntie I've had three. I can't have any more. It'll bring on my condition . . .

Ernie What condition, Auntie?

Auntie Never you mind what. But I should never have had that candy floss as well. I'll suffer for it.

Fourth Barker Just about to start, ladies and gentlemen. A heavyweight boxing bout, featuring the one and only unofficial challenger for the heavyweight championship of the world – Kid Saracen. The Kid will be fighting this afternoon for the very first time, a demonstration contest against the new sensation from Tyneside, Eddie 'Grinder' Edwards. In addition, ladies and gentlemen, the Kid is offering fifty pounds – yes, fifty pounds – to any challenger who manages to last three three-minute rounds. . .

Ernie Oh, come on, Auntie. Let's go in and watch.

Auntie What is it?

Ernie Boxing.

Auntie Boxing? I'm not watching any boxing. I don't mind wrestling but I'm not watching boxing. It's blood-thirsty.

Ernie Auntie . . .

Auntie Nasty stuff, boxing . . .

Fourth Barker Come along, lady. Bring in the young gentleman. Let him see the action . . .

Auntie Oh no . . .

Fourth Barker Come along. Two is it?

Ernie Yes please. Two.

Fourth Barker Thank you, son.

Auntie Eh?

Ernie This way, Auntie.

Before Auntie May can protest, she and Ernie are inside the boxing-booth. The crowd have formed a square around the ring in which stand Kid Saracen, Eddie Edwards and the Referee.

Referee Ladies and gentlemen, introducing on my right, the ex-unofficial challenger for the World Heavyweight Championship – KID SARACEN . . .

Boos from the crowd.

And on my left, the challenger from Newcastle upon Tyne – EDDIE EDWARDS . . .

The crowd cheers

(*to the boxers*) Right, I want a good, clean fight, lads. No low blows and when I say 'break' – stop boxing right away. Good luck.

Timekeeper Seconds out.

The bell rings The crowd cheers as the boxers size each other up. They mostly cheer on Edwards – 'Come on, Eddie', 'Murder him, Eddie', etc. The boxers swap a few punches.

Auntie Oooh. I can't look.

The man next to her starts cheering.

Man Flatten him, Eddie!

Auntie peers out from behind her hands in time to see the Kid clout Eddie fairly hard.

Auntie Hey, you stop that!

Man Get at him, Eddie . . .!

Auntie Yes, that's right, get at him!

Man Hit him!

Auntie Knock him down!

Man Smash him!

Auntie Batter him! (*She starts to wave her arms about in support of Eddie, throwing punches at the air.*)

Man That's it, missis. You show 'em.

Auntie I would, I would.

Man Give 'em a run for their money, would you?

Auntie I'm not that old . . .

Man Eddie!

Auntie Come on, Eddie!

Ernie Eddie!

In the ring the Kid throws a terrific blow which brings Eddie to his knees.

Referee One – two – three –

Man Get up, Eddie . . .

Auntie Get up . . . get up . . .

Referee – four . . .

Eddie rises and blunders round the ring. The Kid knocks him clean out. The Referee counts him out. The crowd boos wildly. The Kid walks smugly round the ring, his hands raised above his head in triumph.

Auntie You brute.

Man Boo. Dirty fight . . .

Auntie Bully . . .

Referee (*quietening the crowd*) And now, ladies and gentlemen, the Kid wishes to issue a challenge to any person here who would like to try his skill at lasting three rounds – any person here. Come along now – anybody care to try . . .

Muttering from the crowd.

Auntie (*to the Man*) Go on then.

Man Who, me?

Auntie What are you frightened of, then?

Man I'm frightened of him . . .

Referee Come along now. We're not asking you to do it for nothing. We're offering fifty pounds – fifty pounds, gentlemen . . .

Auntie Go on. Fifty quid.

Man I'd need that to pay the hospital bill . . .

Auntie Go on . . .

Man It's all right for you, lady – just standing there telling other people to go and get their noses broken.

Auntie All right, then. I'll go in myself. Excuse me . . . (*She starts to push through the crowd towards the ring.*)

Man Hey . . .

Ernie Auntie, where are you going?

Auntie Out of my way . . .

Man Hey, stop her – she's off her nut . . .

Ernie Auntie!

Auntie (*hailing the Referee*) Hey, you . . .

Referee Hallo, lady, what can we do for you? Come to challenge him, have you?

Laughter from the crowd.

Auntie That's right. Help me in.

Referee Just a minute, lady, you've come the wrong way for the jumble sale, this is a boxing-ring.

Auntie I know what it is. Wipe that silly smile off your face. Come on then, rings out of your seconds . . .

The crowd cheers.

Referee Just a minute. Just a minute. What do you think you're playing at . . .?

Auntie You said anyone could have a go, didn't you?

Woman That's right. Give her a go, then.

Referee (*getting worried*) Now, listen . . .

Kid Saracen Go home. There's a nice old lady . . .

The crowd boos.

Auntie You cheeky ha'porth.

Second Man Hit him, grandma.

The crowd shouts agreement.

Referee Tell you what, folks. Let's give the old lady fifty pence for being a good sport . . .

Auntie I don't want your fifty pence . . . Come on.

Woman Get the gloves on, granny.

Auntie I don't need gloves. My hands have seen hard work. I was scrubbing floors before he was thought of . . .

Woman That's right, love.

18

Ernie (*stepping forward*) And then suddenly I got this idea. Maybe Auntie May could be the new heavyweight champion of the world . . .

The bell rings. Auntie May comes bouncing out of her corner flinging punches at the Kid, who looks startled. The crowd cheers.

Auntie Let's have you.

Kid Saracen Hey, come off it!

The Referee tries vainly to pull Auntie May back but she dances out of reach.

Kid Saracen Somebody chuck her out.

The Kid turns to appeal to the crowd. Auntie May punches him in the back.

Auntie Gotcher!

Kid Saracen Ow!

Auntie May bombards the Kid with punches

Ernie (*commentator style*) And Auntie May moves in again and catches the Kid with a left and a right to the body and there's a right-cross to the head – and that really hurt him – and it looks from here as if the champ is in real trouble . . . as this amazing sixty-eight-year-old challenger follows up with a series of sharp left-jabs – one, two, three, four jabs . . .

The Kid is reeling back.

And then, bang, a right-hook and he's down . . .!

The Kid goes down on his knees. The crowd cheers.

Auntie (*to the Referee*) Go on. Start counting.

Crowd One – two – three – four – five – six . . .

The Kid gets up again.

Ernie And the Kid's on his feet but he's no idea where he is – and there's that tremendous right uppercut – and he's down again . . .!

The crowd counts him out. Auntie May dances round the ring with glee. The crowd bursts into the ring and Auntie May is lifted on to their shoulders.

The crowd go out with Auntie May, singing 'For She's a Jolly Good Fellow'. The Referee and the Kid are left.

Referee Come on. Get up – Champ.

Kid Saracen Ooooh. (*He staggers to his feet.*)

The Kid goes out, supported by the Referee. Ernie, Dad, Mum and the Doctor are left.

Doctor (*still writing, excitedly*) Absolutely incredible!

Mum Terrible it was. It took it out of her, you know. She was laid up all Sunday.

Dad And we had all those fellows round from the Amateur Boxing Association trying to sign her up to fight for the Combined Services.

Mum So I told his dad on the Monday, seeing as it was half-term, 'Take him somewhere where he won't get into trouble,' I said. 'Take him somewhere quiet.'

Dad So I took him down to the library.

The Doctor retires to the side of the stage again. Dad, Mum and Ernie exit.

The scene becomes the Public Library. It is very quiet. Various people tip-toe about. At one end sits an intellectual-looking Lady with glasses, reading; at the

other, an old Tramp eating his sandwiches from a
piece of newspaper. One or two others. A uniformed
Attendant walks up and down importantly. The Lady
with glasses looks up at the lights. She frowns.

Lady Excuse me . . .

Attendant Sssshhh!

Lady Sorry. (*mouthing silently*) The light's gone.

Attendant (*mouthing*) What?

Lady (*whispering*) I said the light's gone over here.

Attendant (*whispering*) What?

Lady New bulb.

The Attendant shakes his head, still not understanding.

(*loudly*) UP THERE! YOU NEED A NEW BULB – IT'S
GONE. I CAN'T SEE!

People Sssshhhh!

Attendant (*whispering*) Right.

Lady (*whispering*) Thank you.

The Attendant tip-toes out as Dad and Ernie tip-toe in.

Dad (*to Ernie*) Sssshhhh!

Ernie nods. They tip-toe and sit.

Ernie (*to the audience*) I didn't really think much of this
idea of my mum's . . .

People Sssssshhhh!

Ernie (*whispering*) I didn't really think much of this idea
of my mum's. It was a bit like sitting in a graveyard only
not as exciting. The trouble is, in library reading-rooms
some bloke's pinched all the best magazines already and

you're left with dynamic things like *The Pig Breeder's Monthly Gazette* and suchlike. I'd got stuck with *The Bell Ringer's Quarterly*. Which wasn't one of my hobbies. Nobody else seemed to be enjoying themselves either. Except the bloke eating his sandwiches in the corner. I reckoned he wasn't a tramp at all, but a secret agent heavily disguised, waiting to pass on some secret documents to his contact who he was to meet in the library and who was at this very moment lying dead in the Reference Section, a knife in his ribs. Realizing this, the tramp decides to pick on the most trustworthy-looking party in the room – my dad!

> *The Tramp gets up stealthily and moves over to Dad. As he passes him he knocks his magazine out of his hand.*

Dad Hey!

Tramp Beg pardon, mister. (*He bends to pick up the magazine and hands it back to Dad. As he does so, he thrusts his newspaper parcel into Dad's hands.*) Sssshhhh. Take this. Quickly! They're watching me. Guard it with your life.

Dad Eh?

> *The Tramp hurries away. A sinister man in a mackintosh gets up and follows him out.*

Who the heck was that?

Dad (*examining the parcel*) What's all this, then?

Ernie Dunno.

Dad I don't want his sandwiches. Spoil my dinner. (*as he unwraps the parcel*) Hey!

Ernie What is it?

Dad Looks like a lot of old blue-prints and things. Funny. This anything to do with you?

Ernie (*innocently*) No, Dad.

The Attendant enters with a step-ladder. He places it under the light. A Girl Librarian who has entered with him steadies the step-ladder. The Attendant produces a bulb from his pocket and starts to climb the step-ladder.

(*watching the Attendant*) And now, as Captain Williams nears the summit of this, the third highest mountain in the world never before climbed by man . . .

Wind noises start.

He pauses for a moment through sheer exhaustion . . .

The Attendant, feeling the effects of the wind, clings to the stepladder for dear life. It sways slightly.

Attendant (*shouting down to the Librarian*) More slack. I need more slack on the rope . . .!

Librarian (*shouting up to him*) More slack. Are you all right?

Attendant I – think – I can – make it.

Librarian Be careful. The rock looks treacherous just above you.

Attendant It's all right. It's – quite safe – if I – just aaaaaahhh! (*He slips and holds on with one hand.*)

Lady Captain! What's happened?

Attendant Damn it. I think I've broken my leg . . .

Lady Oh, no.

Librarian How are we going to get him down?

Dad rises.

Ernie And here comes Major Fraser, ace daredevil mountaineer to the rescue.

Dad Give me a number three clambering-iron and a hydraulic drill-lever, will you? I'm going up.

Librarian Oh no, Major.

Dad It's the only way.

Lady Don't be a fool, Major.

Dad Someone's got to go. Give me plenty of line . . . (*He starts to climb.*)

Librarian Good luck.

Lady Good luck.

A sequence in which Dad clambers up the ladder, buffeted by the wind.

Dad Can you hold on?

Attendant Not – much – longer.

Dad Try, man, try. Not much longer . . .

Lady Keep going, man.

Dad reaches the Attendant. People cheer. The two men slowly descend the ladder.

Ernie And here comes the gallant Major Fraser, bringing the injured Captain Williams to safety . . .

Dad and the Attendant reach the floor. More cheers and applause from the onlookers. The Attendant is still supported by Dad with one arm round his neck. There is a general shaking of hands. The wind noise stops.

Attendant (*coming back to reality, suddenly*) Hey, hey! What's going on here? (*to Dad*) What do you think you're doing?

Dad Oh.

Attendant Let go of me.

Dad Sorry, I . . .

Attendant Never known anything like it. This is a public building, you know . . .

Dad Ernie . . .

Ernie Yes, Dad?

Dad Did you start this?

Ernie (*innocently*) Me, Dad?

Dad Now listen, lad . . .

A Second Librarian enters, screaming.

Second Librarian Oh, Mr Oats, Mr Oats . . .

Attendant What's the matter, girl? What's the matter?

Second Librarian There's a man in the Reference Section.

Attendant Well?

Second Librarian He's dead.

Lady Dead?

Second Librarian Yes. I think he's been killed. There's a knife sticking in his ribs . . .

The First Librarian screams. The Attendant hurries out, followed by the others. Ernie and Dad are left.

Dad Ernie!

Ernie Sorry, Dad.

The Doctor moves in. Mum joins them.

Doctor Incredible.

Dad Embarrassing.

Doctor Yes, yes.

The scene is now back to where it was at the beginning, with the four in the Doctor's room on one side and the waiting-room full of patients on the other.

Mum Can you do anything, Doctor?

Doctor Mmmm. Not much, I'm afraid.

Mum No?

Doctor You see, it's not really up to me at all. It's up to you. An interesting case. Very. In my twenty years as a general practitioner I've never heard anything quite like it. You see, this is a classic example of group hallucinations . . .

Dad Illucinations, yes.

Doctor Starting with your son and finishing with you all being affected . . .

Mum All?

Doctor All of you. You must understand that all this has happened only in your minds.

Dad Just a minute. Are you suggesting we're all off our onions?

Doctor Off your . . .?

Dad You know. Round the thing. Up the whatsit.

Doctor No . . .

Dad My missis as well?

Doctor No. No.

Dad Then watch it.

Doctor I was just explaining . . .

Dad You don't need. It's Ernie here, that's all. He imagines things and they happen.

Doctor Oh, come now. I can't really accept that.

Dad Why not?

Doctor It's – impossible. He may *imagine* things . . .

Dad He does.

Doctor But they don't really happen. They *appear* to, that's all

Dad Is that so?

Doctor Of course.

A slight pause.

Dad Ernie.

Ernie Yes, Dad.

Dad Imagine something. We'll see who's nutty.

Ernie What, Dad?

Dad Anything, son, anything. Just to show the doctor.

Mum Nothing nasty, Ernie. Something peaceful . . .

Dad How about a brass band? I like brass bands.

Mum Oh dear. Couldn't it be something quieter? Like – a mountain stream or something . . .

Dad Don't be daft, Ethel. The doctor doesn't want a waterfall pouring through his surgery. Go on, lad. A brass band.

Ernie Right, Dad. (*He concentrates.*)

A pause.

Doctor Well?

Dad Give him a chance.

A pause.

Mum Come on, Ernie. (*Pause.*) He's usually very good at it, Doctor.

Dad Come on, lad.

Ernie It's difficult, Dad, I can't picture them.

Doctor Yes, well, I'm afraid I can't afford any more time just now, Mr and Mrs Fraser. I do have a surgery full of people waiting to see me – (*He calls.*) – Miss Bates! – so you will understand I really must get on.

The Receptionist enters.

Receptionist Yes, Doctor?

Doctor The next patient, please, Miss Bates.

Receptionist (*going*) Yes, Doctor.

The Receptionist exits.

Doctor (*getting up and pacing up and down as he speaks*) What I suggest we do is, I'll arrange an appointment with a specialist and – he'll be able to give you a better diagnosis – (*His steps become more and more march like.*) – than I will. I'm quite sure – that – a – few – sessions – with a trained – psychiatrist – will – be – quite – sufficient – to – put – everything – right – right – left – right – left – left – left – right – left . . .

The Doctor marches to the door of his room, does a smart about-turn and marches round his desk.

The Patients from the waiting-room enter and follow him, some limping, some marching and all playing, or as if playing, brass instruments.

L-e-e-e-ft . . . Wheel . . .

After a triumphal circuit of the room everyone marches out following the Doctor, who has assumed the rôle of drum major.

Ernie (*just before he leaves*) It looks as though the Doctor suffers from illucinations as well. I hope you don't get 'em. Ta-ta.

Ernie marches out jauntily, following the band, as – the curtain falls.

INVISIBLE FRIENDS

Characters

Lucy Baines
Gary, her real brother
Joy, her real mother
Walt, her real father
Zara, her invisible friend
Chuck, Zara's invisible brother
Felix, Zara's invisible father

Scene: The Baines home. Real and imaginary.

Invisible Friends was first performed at the
Stephen Joseph Theatre in the Round, Scarborough,
on 22 November 1989. The cast was as follows:

Lucy Baines Emma Chambers
Joy Doreen Andrew
Walt Bill Moody
Gary Ian Dunn
Zara Jennifer Wiltsie
Felix Robin Bowerman
Chuck Sean Chapman

Director Alan Ayckbourn
Design Juliet Nichols / Geof Keys
Lighting Jackie Staines

Act One

The Baines house. 5.00 p.m. Visible are a ground-floor
living area, and the kitchen leading off that. Stairs up
lead to a corridor with bedrooms leading off it. The
visible rooms are Lucy's room, small and tidy. She is
that exception to the rule, a young teenage girl with an
excessive love of orderliness. Besides the bed, it has a
small desk/work table, an easy chair and a wardrobe/
cupboard. A notice board filled with her private lists
and favourite sayings and quotations. Next to hers is her
older brother Gary's room. By complete contrast this
room is a tip. Clothes strewn everywhere, an unmade
bed, cluttered tables and chairs. Prominent among all
the clutter is Gary's pride and joy, his hi-fi equipment.
At the start, Gary is lying on his bed atop a mound of
clutter that he hasn't bothered to move, listening to
something loud and aggressive. Something, fortunately,
that we're unable, as of now, to hear. Gary, in appearance, almost exactly matches his room.

Downstairs is the living area, drab and also rather
untidy. Walt, Gary's and Lucy's father, lies slumped fast
asleep in an armchair, facing the TV which has on an
early-evening news programme. We can't, at present,
hear this either. Looking at Walt, we can understand
who Gary takes after. Overweight and unkempt, Walt
asleep is almost as unprepossessing as Walt awake.

In the kitchen, Joy, wife and mother, is preparing tea.
She does this, as she does everything in life, with a great
sense of sorrow. Seldom can anyone have been more
unsuitably named. She sighs to herself as she moves
about the kitchen. We hear none of this though, for we

37

are as yet still outside the house. Lucy now appears from along the street, carrying her school bag. She stops as she reaches her house. Faint traffic and perhaps a little urban birdsong.

Lucy (*to the audience*) It all started the Friday I came home from school to tell my family some exciting news. By the way, my name's Lucy Baines. That's my mother there in the kitchen. And my father pretending he's watching the telly but actually he's fast asleep. And that one upstairs, that's my older brother – known usually as Grisly Gary. Anyway, you'll meet them soon enough because unfortunately they all feature in this story I'm going to tell you. As soon as you have met them, you're immediately going to wish you hadn't met them. I mean, they're all right. I suppose. Sometimes. Very, very, very occasionally. Like every fifth Christmas in June, they're all right. It's not that they're cruel to me or anything. I think they actually do love me, really, though you'd never know it most of the time. They're just so – gloomy and glum. Like you know that saying: 'Eat, Drink and Be Merry for Tomorrow We Die'? Well, my Dad's version of that is, 'Tomorrow We Die, So What Are You Looking So Cheerful About?' I mean, I don't expect them to leap about laughing all day long but, well, on a day like this for instance, when I came home on this particular Friday with this terrific news – it would have been nice to have had a really warm welcome. (*She goes through the front door. Calling as she goes*) Mum! Mum!

Joy (*immensely cheerily*) Lucy, you're home at last! How lovely to see you!

Lucy Hallo, Mum.

They embrace.

Joy Oh, you're looking so bonny. Have you had a good day at school? Tell me all about it.

Lucy Wonderful, I've had a wonderful day. I have to tell you, Mum, it's so exciting – I've been chosen for the school swimming team.

Joy (*with a cry of delight*) You haven't!

Lucy I have! The relay and the 200 metres backstroke.

Joy Backstroke! Oh, that's just wonderful. We must tell your Dad. Dad!

Lucy Oh, don't wake him up . . .

Joy No, I must. He'll want to know. Walt! Walter!

Walt (*waking up cheerfully*) What's that? What's all this?

Joy Dad, listen to this, listen to this news . . .

Walt (*playfully*) Did I doze off? I must have dozed off.

Joy (*affectionately*) Yes, you did, you know you did, you old devil. And now you're awake you can just listen to Lucy's news.

Walt News? What news is this? Come on, out with it, young Lucy.

Joy Tell him your news.

Lucy I will when you'll let me get a word in. Dad, I've been picked for the school swimming team . . .

   Walt stares at her, speechless.

(*shrugging modestly*) That's all.

Walt The school swimming team?

Lucy Yes.

Joy Backstroke and relay.

Walt (*rather overcome*) Backstroke and relay?

Lucy Yes.

Walt moves to Lucy and hugs her fiercely. He is obviously deeply moved.

Walt I'm so proud, girl. I'm so proud of you. This is the proudest day of my life.

Joy And mine, Dad. And mine.

Walt Where's that lad Gary, then? We must tell Gary.

Joy Oh, yes. We must tell Gary. (*calling*) Gary!

Walt (*calling*) Gary!

Gary, at the sound of their voices, springs off his bed and starts downstairs eagerly.

Lucy Oh, don't disturb him.

Joy No, he'll want to know . . .

Walt The lad'll want to know . . .

Joy (*calling*) Gary!

Walt (*calling*) Gary!

Gary (*having come downstairs*) Yes? What is it? (*overjoyed*) Hallo, Lucy! Are you home from school already?

Lucy Hi, Gary.

Gary Did somebody call? What can I do for you?

Joy Tell him your news, then.

Walt Tell him your news.

Lucy I've been picked for the school swimming team.

Joy Two hundred metres backstroke . . .

Walt And the relay.

A fractional pause, then Gary steps forward, picks up Lucy and whirls her in his arms.

Gary (*as he does this*) YIPPEEE!

A huge crowd starts cheering.

Joy Hooray!

Walt Bravo!

The briefest burst of vigorous brass-band music. Before festivities can get under way, Lucy disengages herself from the riotous group and steps back outside the house again. Under the next, the others quietly resume their original starting positions.

Lucy (*as she moves*) I mean, I didn't expect them to behave quite like that. But, you know, they could have at least said 'good' or something. 'Well done', even. But anyway, on this particular day, I came home from school – this is my house by the way – Number 162 Sycamore Street – it's just past the traffic lights and before you get to the zebra crossing, I don't know if you know Sycamore Street at all but – (*breaking off again*) Sorry, I'm rambling again. On this Friday I came home full of excitement, with my fantastic news about the school swimming team.

As Lucy enters the house, the traffic sounds disappear and are replaced by the noises inside. The TV drones on throughout and upstairs, faintly, the thud of Gary's music.

Mum!

Joy (*without stopping her tasks*) Shh! Your father's asleep.

Lucy (*whispering*) Sorry! Mum, guess what?

Joy Your dad's had a terrible day. His van broke down again, miles from nowhere . . .

Lucy I've got this amazing news . . .

Joy . . . he had to walk five miles . . .

Lucy . . . go on, guess what happened to me today.

Joy . . . by the time he'd phoned the AA and then walked five miles all the way back again, someone had stolen his front wheels . . .

Lucy Shall I tell you?

Joy Left his van standing on six bricks. I mean, I don't know what the world's coming to, I really don't.

Lucy I'll tell you, shall I?

Joy Stealing people's front wheels. I mean, what if your dad had been a pensioner? What if he'd been disabled . . .?

Lucy I've been picked for the school swimming team.

Joy They should bring in stricter laws and stop all this vandalism in one fell swoop. I mean, the way we're going at the moment, none of us will be able to sleep securely in our beds . . .

Lucy Two hundred metres backstroke. And the relay.

Joy I mean, look at old Mrs Hadron. Those lads rode their bike right through her back garden. Ruined her bird table, cut up her lawn . . .

Lucy Isn't that great news?

Joy I mean, they should have been locked up. She's got no husband and her little dog's poorly . . . You see, if this council worried less about putting up new band-stands and building multi-storey car parks and a little more on making the streets safe from vandals and layabouts . . .

Lucy holds a conversation with herself.

Lucy (*under this last*) 'Tremendous news, Lucy. Absolutely fantastic. You're brilliant, I don't know how you do it . . .' 'Oh, it was nothing, Mum, really . . .'

Joy (*stopping as she sees Lucy*) What are you going on about there?

Lucy Nothing.

Joy What were you saying?

Lucy Nothing. Just talking to myself, Mum. (*under her breath*) As usual.

Joy (*suspiciously*) You haven't got that friend of yours back, have you?

Lucy What?

Joy That – invisible friend of yours? I hope you're not starting all that again?

Lucy No.

Joy You know how that annoys your dad.

Lucy Yep. (*She moves away.*)

Joy Where're you going?

Lucy Upstairs. Put my things away.

Joy Well, come straight down again. It's nearly tea-time. You can give me a hand.

Lucy Right.

Joy I've been on my feet all day, I've not had a minute's break since I got up, it's all right for the rest of you . . .

Joy's stream of complaining drops to a low mutter as Lucy moves out of earshot. She moves to where Walt is sitting asleep in front of the TV. As she nears him the TV fades up a little.

TV Voice And finally . . . more sobering economic news as the pound slumped lower still against a basket of other currencies. On top of that, inflation, as we heard earlier, is also up and indications are, according to the latest forecasts, that it will rise still further over the next three months. Later on this evening, in *Newsnight*, we shall be showing a special programme in which seven European economic experts will be giving their verdict: Is Britain's Economy a Sinking Ship? That'll be on *Newsnight* at 10.30 tonight. But now it's time to go over to Bert Cod at the London Weather Centre for the latest picture.

Lucy watches this for all of two seconds and scowls.

Lucy (*to audience*) Even the TV's depressing in our house. We're only allowed to watch the programmes he wants to watch. And they're all dead boring. This is my father. Who's the current *Guinness Book of Records* twenty-four-hour sleeping champion. (*loudly*) Whey-hey, Dad!!

Walt (*snorting awake*) Whah!

Lucy Sorry, Dad, did I wake you?

Walt (*drowsily*) Not just at the moment, love, I want to watch the news . . . (*He falls asleep again.*)

Lucy (*to audience*) That was the extremely rare glimpse of my father awake. Would that we'd had a camera team here to capture that moment. No, I don't want to be too mean about Mum and Dad, but really . . . I don't honestly know why they're still together, if you want the truth.

These days they don't even seem to like each other . . .
I mean, don't get me wrong, I don't want them to start
getting all lovey-dovey and daft . . .

*Walt springs up from his armchair and faces Joy with
adoration all over his face. She does likewise. They
sing a brief excerpt from* The Beggar's Opera.

Walt (*singing*) 'I would love thee ev'ry day . . .'

Joy (*singing*) 'Ev'ry night we'd kiss and play . . .'

Walt (*singing*) 'If with me you'd fondly stray . . .'

Joy and Walt (*together*) 'Over the hills and far away . . .'

They swiftly resume their original positions again.

Lucy I wouldn't want anything like that, for heaven's
sake. Yuk!

Joy (*calling from the kitchen*) Lucy, are you coming to
help me, or not?

Lucy Yes, Mum.

TV Voice (*under all this*) Well, as to the weather picture,
I'm afraid it's another gloomy one tomorrow as far as
most of the country's concerned.

Lucy With heavy rain mostly situated over Number 162
Sycamore Street . . .

TV Voice As you can see there from our radar chart,
this large area of low pressure here continues to sit over
most of northern Europe. And that, of course, is causing
those outbreaks of thunder we've been experiencing in
certain areas, together with that virtually non-stop sleet
and heavy rain which has also been affecting most
regions during today. Tonight, well, it's going to get a
good deal colder over most of the country, particularly
up here in the north-east. Widespread frost, especially

inland, with temperatures getting down in one or two places to as low as minus two or even three centigrade in some sheltered areas. And that promises to be more or less the picture over most of the country during the next day or so . . .

During this, Lucy starts upstairs. As she moves away from the TV the sound fades down. Simultaneously, the rock music from Gary's room gets a little louder.

Lucy (*as she goes upstairs, to audience*) Come with me, if you will. Upstairs. If you listen very carefully you can just hear the distant sounds of the greater spotted Grisly Gary, my unbelievably talkative brother. Grisly Gary is doing a building course at the technical college, training to be a bucket. (*She reaches the door of Gary's room. The music is louder now.*) Here we go. I'll just have a quiet word with him. Cover your ears.

Lucy opens Gary's door. The heavy-metal music comes up to a deafening level. Lucy, when she speaks, is quite inaudible. Gary, lying on the bed with his eyes closed, fails to notice her at all.

(*mouthing, swiftly*) Hallo, Grisly. It's your loving sister, Lucy. Just to tell you I've been picked for the school swimming team. Thought you'd like to know. Bye, Grisly. (*Lucy closes the door again. The music goes down to a lower level.*) I enjoyed that chat. (*She opens the door of her own room and goes inside.*) This is my room. No one's allowed in here, except me. I'm a very tidy sort of person. Which is a bit extraordinary in this house. I think I must be a freak. I actually like to know where I've put things. This is my bed. That's my desk. And up there on the shelf. Those are my special, most favourite books.

The music pounds through the wall.

Actually, one of the reasons I keep it tidy is because my very, very best friend, Zara, also likes things tidy. Oh yes, I ought to explain to you about Zara. You may have heard my mum talking about my invisible friend. Do you remember? Well, that's my invisible friend, Zara. (*introducing her*) This is Zara. I want you to meet Zara. Zara, say hello. That's it. Will you say hello to Zara, my invisible friend? I invented Zara – oh, years ago – when I was seven or eight. Just for fun. I think I was ill at that time and wasn't allowed to play with any of my real friends, so I made up Zara. She's my special friend that no one can see except me. Of course, I can't really see her either. Not really. Although sometimes I . . . It's almost as if I could see her, sometimes. If I concentrate very hard it's like I can just glimpse her out of the corner of my eye. (*She is thoughtful for a second.*) Still. Anyway. I've kept Zara for years and years. Until they all started saying I was much too old for that sort of thing and got worried and started talking about sending for a doctor. So then I didn't take her round with me quite so much after that. But she's still here. And when I feel really sad and depressed like I do today, then I sit and talk to Zara. Zara always understands. Zara always listens. She's special. Aren't you, Zara? (*She listens to Zara.*) What's that? Yes, I wish he'd turn his music down, too. I've asked him, haven't I? (*mimicking Gary*) 'How can I hear it if I turn it down, I can't hear the bass then, can I?' I used to have pictures in here but every time he put a disc on they fell off the walls. (*Pause. The music continues.*) I mean, don't get me wrong. We like loud music, don't we, Zara? We love loud music. Sometimes. (*yelling*) BUT NOT ALL THE TIME. (*Pause.*) Why doesn't he ever listen to quiet music? Just once. Wouldn't that be nice?

The music changes to a delicate piece of Bach, just

*for a second. Gary sits up in an attitude of deep
appreciation, eyes still closed. Then the music resumes
as before and he lies back down again.*

But if he did that, he wouldn't be Grisly Gary then, would
he? (*Pause.*) Oh, Zara, did I tell you I've been picked for
the school swimming team? Isn't that exciting? Yes.
Thank you. I'm glad you're excited, too. Good. (*Pause.*)

(*shouting*) IF ANYONE IS INTERESTED AT ALL, I
WAS PICKED FOR THE SCHOOL SWIMMING
TEAM TODAY. WHAT ABOUT THAT, FOLKS? (*She
listens. No reply.*) Great. Thanks for your support,
everyone. (*tearful*) They might at least . . . They could
have at least . . . Oh, Zara . . . I know you're always
here, but sometimes I get so . . . lonely . . .

*She sits on her bed, sad, angry and frustrated.
Downstairs, Joy has come to the foot of the stairs
and now calls up to Lucy.*

Joy Lucy, I told you to come straight down, do you
hear me?

Lucy (*calling*) Yes, Mum.

Joy Well, hurry up, then. And tell your brother tea's
nearly ready.

*Joy goes back into the kitchen. Lucy comes to a
sudden decision.*

Lucy All right, then. Come on, Zara. I don't care what
they say. Today you're coming downstairs to tea. If they
won't listen to me I'll invite someone who will listen.
Come on, Zara, down to tea.

*Leading Zara by the hand, Lucy goes first into Gary's
room. A burst of loud music as she enters. Gary lies
as before.*

(*yelling*) Gary! Tea-time! Gary!

Gary doesn't hear her.

Gary!

She picks up a spray can of shaving foam from among the junk and sprays him with it. Gary sits up, indignantly.

Gary Oy!

Lucy Tea-time.

Gary (*swinging off the bed*) I'll get you, you . . .

But Lucy, with a laugh, is out of the room before he can catch her, slamming the door behind her. She now leads Zara downstairs. Gary ruefully mops himself down and in a moment switches off his sound gear and puts on his Walkman. He then goes off to the bathroom.

Lucy (*to audience, as she goes downstairs*) Once, Zara used to come everywhere with me. I never left her behind for a minute. She used to sit with me at school and she came on holiday one year. And we even had to pack her a special suitcase. Dad was wild.

As Lucy passes Walt, still asleep in his armchair, we hear a brief excerpt from a gardening programme. This fades as Lucy reaches the kitchen.

TV Voice . . . and there's a very wide species of these. Some of them are evergreen and some deciduous. So make sure you get the right sort. They've lovely bright flowers and fruits. Like this chap here. There, who can ask for anything more colourful? And the good thing about *Berberis* is that he's not too fussy about the soil . . .

Lucy Here we are.

Joy (*suspiciously*) Here who are?

Lucy Me.

Joy At last. Where have you been? Never mind. You can lay the table, it's nearly ready.

Lucy OK. (*to Zara, still holding her hand*) Come on then, Zara.

Joy What?

Lucy Nothing.

Joy What's the matter with your hand?

Lucy Nothing.

Joy Have you hurt it?

Lucy No.

Joy Well, don't be so silly and lay the table.

Lucy Yes, Mum.

> *During the next Lucy lays the table with five places and also brings up an extra chair. Joy doesn't notice, she is so busy preparing the meal.*

Joy (*as they do this*) I saw Mrs Hedges today in the street. She was just coming back from the doctor's. She's no better. And her Ted's legs are going. He can barely take his weight on them now. Only a matter of time. And her Arthur's hand's still useless. She doesn't know which way to turn, I can tell you. Not that she can turn at all, poor woman, not with her back the way it is.

Lucy Mum . . .

Joy She was in agony just talking to me. Tears of agony. She shouldn't have been out except she can't bear to stay in. Not now her Tom's gone.

Lucy Mum . . .

Joy And then I met Mrs Bracewell – don't interrupt me, I'm talking, Lucy – she's had a chapter of accidents, too. Just got over her poorly foot and then her son rings up to say he'd broken both his legs skiing. So I don't know who she's going to get to lift her Maureen out of bed . . .

Lucy (*to audience*) As you see, conversation is very much a one-way business in this house . . .

Joy . . . and all that on top of her dog going. I mean, I don't know how she keeps cheerful, I don't. (*She pauses briefly.*)

Lucy (*seizing the opportunity*) Mum . . .

Joy Oh, yes, and talking of that, old Mr Perkins, you remember him, he used to give you barley sugars, well, he's passed on at last. I saw his daughter, Mrs Clarke, with the hip, in the supermarket. She said it was a great relief to them all. Mind you, I don't know how Mrs Perkins will cope now without him. She's very feeble these days and all.

Lucy Never mind, Mum. On the brighter side . . .

Joy Have you called your brother?

Lucy Yes. A really good thing happened to me today . . .

Joy Call your father then. I can hear all that later.

Lucy Right.

Joy I'll hear it later.

Joy moves back to the kitchen.

Lucy Yes. (*to herself*) I bet. (*to Zara*) Come on, then.

She crosses to Walt who is still asleep. As she does so, we hear more of the gardening programme.

TV Voice . . . the real question of course is how much to cut off. Well, if you look at any branch of a shrub, like this one here, you'll see that the tip is soft and green. Now if you look from there back towards the main stem, you'll see a ring marking the end of last year's growth – just there, you see? There's your old wood. And there's your new wood. Now, you want to cut back, almost to your old wood, just about – there. Like so. And that's where your new shoots will be. And that's where your flowers are going to grow. Now, that's your winter or early-spring varieties. There's nothing mysterious about pruning. All it takes is good old-fashioned common sense and a little tiny bit of know-how . . .

During the next, Gary comes downstairs with his Walkman on. He is in a world of his own. He goes to the table and sits nodding to the silent music.

Lucy Dad! Dad! (*She shakes him.*) Tea-time.

Walt (*snorting awake*) Just a minute, love, I'm watching this.

Lucy Tea's ready.

Walt I'm watching this, love.

Lucy (*to audience*) Why's he watching this? It's a gardening programme and we haven't even got a garden.

They watch for a moment.

Joy (*to Gary*) Will you be out tonight, Gary? (*louder*) Gary?

Gary (*lifting one earphone*) What's that, Mum?

Joy I'm saying, are you going out tonight?

Gary Yes, I'll be out with Ronnie and Billy and Jimmy and Tel.

Joy Oh, that'll be nice.

Lucy (*to audience*) Ronnie and Billy and Jimmy and Tel are Gary's special mates. From the tech. Also training to be buckets. Except Tel, who's studying to be a pile of sand.

Walt What's all this we're watching?

Lucy I don't know. You had it on.

Walt I don't want this. Who put this on?

Lucy You did.

Walt I wanted the film. I'm missing the film. (*Walt jabs the remote control. TV changes to western music. A little dialogue. A lot of gunshots.*)

That's better.

Lucy (*to audience*) Oh no. Westerns. I hate westerns . . .

Joy brings a casserole dish to the table. A burst of country music. The lights change.

Joy Here y'are, boys. Y'eat this up while it's still good and hot, y'hear?

Gary Yahoo, Maw. Is that a clam bake ah spy theyur?

Joy Nope. This'n just plain old bacon 'n' beans, boy. You get them down inside you.

Walt Better get your vittals, son. We got a long hard, dusty ride tomorrow, boy . . .

Gary Yippie! Yeah, Paw. Yee-haw!

The music stops. The lights revert to normal.

Lucy No. I think I prefer things the way they are, really . . .

Joy brings the casserole dish to the table.

Joy It's on the table.

Walt (*keeping his eyes glued on the TV set*) Right.

Walt sits at the end of the table, turned half away, watching the TV. Gary sits jigging to his music. Lucy sits next to the additional chair. Joy returns with four bowls. She starts to serve. Lucy gets up and crosses to the kitchen cupboard.

Joy Where are you going, Lucy? Sit still and have your tea.

Lucy Just getting an extra plate, Mum.

Joy I've got enough here.

Lucy No, we've got – (*indicating the extra place*) Look.

Joy (*realizing*) Oh, no.

Lucy Zara's here.

Joy Oh, no, she isn't.

Lucy She is. Promise.

Joy Well, I'm not serving extra food to her . . . I'm not going through all that again. She's not having any, I'm sorry.

Lucy All right, she can have mine.

Joy Lucy! I'm warning you.

Lucy I'll share mine with her . . .

Joy Walt! Walter . . .

Walt Just a second, love. I'm just watching this.

Joy Tell this girl. You tell her. I'm not having this again. I'm not going through all that. Double meals. Double

54

loads of washing . . . Double baths . . . I'm not starting all this again . . .

Walt (*to the TV*) Yeah!

Joy Walter!

Walt What's that? I'm sorry, love, what's the problem?

Joy Tell this girl I'm not having that so-called friend of hers back here again.

Walt Back where?

Joy (*indicating Zara's place*) There!

Walt Friend? I can't see any friend.

Joy No, her invisible friend. That one. That Sarah.

Lucy Zara.

Walt Oh, no. We're not having that, Lucy. We've had quite enough of her, thank you very much.

Lucy Zara's got to eat . . .

Walt Well, I'm sorry. Not at my table. You clear that place right away, do you hear me?

Lucy Then she'll starve, won't she?

Walt (*sharply*) I said, clear it away. At once, Lucy!

Joy There! That's your dad telling you that, do you hear?

Lucy gets up and starts to clear the place away to the kitchen.

Lucy It'll be your fault if she dies of starvation.

Walt Damn good job if she does. The sooner the better.

Joy Oh now, Walter . . .

Walt What?

Joy You mustn't talk like that. Even about . . .

Walt Even about what?

Joy Well, even about invisible people. I don't think that's right. You mustn't wish them dead.

Walt What are you talking about, she's not even alive.

Joy Well, maybe she isn't alive, I don't know. But you still shouldn't wish her dead, it's not right.

Lucy returns to the table.

Walt Rubbish. (*to Lucy*) And you can put that extra chair back as well.

Lucy (*indignantly*) You mean Zara has to *stand* all through the meal, as well?

Walt (*fiercely*) DO AS YOU'RE TOLD! You'll get no tea in a minute.

Joy You hear that, Lucy? You'll get no tea.

Lucy (*muttering*) I don't want any tea.

Walt You won't get any tea at this rate.

Lucy I don't want any tea.

Joy Now, now, that's enough of that, just come and eat your tea.

Lucy I've said, I don't want any tea.

Walt You do as your mother tells you, girl, and eat your tea.

Joy You hear that, Lucy? That's your dad telling you that.

Lucy returns the extra chair.

I thought you'd grown out of all this, Lucy. (*to Walt*)
I thought she'd grown out of it. I mean, most children
grow out of it by this age. I mean, they do, don't they?
How old is she now?

Walt (*back to the TV*) Just a minute, love. I just want to
watch this . . .

*Lucy rejoins the table. A silence. Joy serves them with
stew. Gary suddenly drums vigorously on the table, in
time to his tape.*

Gary Ter-rer . . . ter-rer-ter-rer . . .

Joy Don't do that, Gary. Not at the table.

Gary (*loudly*) Great track, this one, Mum.

Joy Yes.

Gary (*beating time*) Even you'd like it. Tung . . . tung . . .
tung . . . tung . . . tung . . .

They eat in silence. Walt eats, half turned away.

Lucy (*after a pause, to audience*) Another exciting meal
time with the Baines family. (*A burst of gunfire from the
TV.*) Be great, wouldn't it, if one of those gunmen on the
TV shot Grisly Gary. (*A gunshot. Gary clutches his chest
and falls off his chair.*) No, I didn't mean that. Not
really.

*Gary gets up off the floor and resumes his seat,
looking slightly puzzled.*

I mean, don't get me wrong, I'm not saying that our
meals should consist of endless, boring, meaningless
small talk like this . . .

*The other three immediately turn to face one another
and burst into very animated, very loud simultaneous
conversation.*

Joy (*very smart*) . . . and I caught sight of this dress in the window and I just had to dash in and buy it, that very instant. I said to Walter, 'I don't care what the cost is. If necessary, I'll mortgage my *soul* to have it.' It's just divine . . .

Walt (*simultaneously, equally smart*) . . . and the thing about these westerns is, of course, that they're basically morality tales. The age-old battle between good and evil, that's what they boil down to . . . Which is what I find so absolutely fascinating about them . . .

Gary (*simultaneously, equally smart*) . . . I mean, yes, I know, I know, this sort of music is only a basic essential outlet for youthful aggression. But look at it this way. Better aggression channelled thus than through expressions of violent, anti-social, much more public actions, surely . . .?

Lucy cuts them off dead with a gesture. The meal continues as normal.

Lucy (*to audience*) . . . I'm not saying they should carry on like that. Not at all. But it would be nice to have a *little* conversation. If only, 'Pass the salt, please.' Is it any wonder I have to invent invisible friends? Can you blame me?

She turns to Zara, apparently standing beside her.

(*whispering*) You all right just standing there, are you, Zara?

Joy (*looking up from her meal*) What's that, dear?

Lucy Nothing. (*whispering again*) Come on. Come and sit here with me. There's plenty of room. (*She slides to the edge of her chair to make room for Zara.*) That's better . . .

Joy What are you doing now, Lucy?

Lucy Nothing.

Joy Well, sit properly. And eat your tea.

Walt (*watching the TV*) Whey-hey. He's marvellous, this one.

Lucy (*to Zara, whispering*) Are you hungry, Zara? Would you like some of mine? Would you?

> *Lucy holds out a forkload of food to Zara's imaginary mouth, somewhere near her shoulder. Neither Walt nor Joy notices her doing this. Gary though, looking up momentarily from his plate, does. He stares at Lucy in amazement.*

(*unaware Gary is watching her*) Come on then, Zara, come on. Open wide, that's it. One big mouthful, that's it. Open wide.

Gary (*loudly*) What's she doing?

> *Lucy hastily stops and swallows the food herself.*

Joy (*looking up*) What?

Walt (*looking round*) What's who doing?

Gary Her. She was sticking her food in her ear.

Joy What were you doing, Lucy?

Walt Were you sticking your food in your ear?

Lucy No.

Gary Yes, she was. I saw her.

Lucy I wasn't.

Walt What were you doing?

Lucy Nothing.

Walt (*fiercely*) What were you doing, girl?

Lucy I was . . . (*muttering*) I was – just giving some food to Zara.

Gary To who? Who's she talking about?

Walt Right. That's it. That's enough of that. I'm not having any more of that. Upstairs. Do you hear me? Upstairs.

Gary (*rising*) I haven't finished my dinner yet . . .

Walt Not you, you lunkhead. Her.

Gary sits again.

Joy Oh now, Walter . . .

Walt No arguments. UPSTAIRS!

Lucy (*leaving the table*) Right.

Walt And you stay up there till you learn to behave yourself.

Lucy Suits me.

Walt And don't you argue with me, girl.

Lucy I'm not arguing.

Walt Oh yes, you are.

Lucy I'm not, I'm agreeing.

Walt (*shouting*) What're you doing now if you're not arguing?

Lucy (*shouting back*) I'm agreeing.

Walt Don't argue with me, you're arguing, girl. And don't walk away when I'm talking to you either. Come back here.

Lucy (*returning and sitting again*) Right. Make up your mind.

Joy Now, now, now, now, now, now, now . . .

Gary (*rising*) What's everyone arguing about?

Walt (*savagely*) You, shut up!

Gary (*sitting*) Right.

Walt (*to Lucy*) Upstairs!

Gary (*rising again*) Right.

Walt Not you. Her.

Gary (*sitting*) Right.

Lucy (*rising*) Right.

Walt And don't come down until you're ready to apologize, do you hear?

Joy That's your father talking, Lucy. Are you listening to him?

Lucy I can't help listening to him, can I, he's screaming at me. Come along, Zara. Say good night to everyone. Say good night to Zara . . .

Walt UPSTAIRS!

   Lucy starts upstairs.

Oh . . . oh . . . Sometimes, I could . . .

Joy Now, Dad.

Walt She can thank her lucky stars she's – she's who she is. (*to Gary*) If she'd been you, lad, I'd have walloped her.

Gary Eh? What's that, Dad?

Walt Doesn't matter. Doesn't matter.

Gary Can I have Lucy's tea, Mum?

Joy You might as well, she's not going to eat it.

Walt Give it him. Before he starts eating the table.

Gary (*grabbing her plate*) Ta!

Joy He needs his food, Gary's a growing lad.

Walt Well, I only hope his brain catches up with the rest of him, that's all.

Gary What's that, Dad?

Walt Eat your tea, genius.

> *Lights fade on the trio downstairs. Lucy is slowly entering her bedroom. She still holds Zara's hand. Under the next, they finish their tea downstairs. Joy quietly clears the table. Gary, where he is, listens to his music. Walt watches TV. Lucy sits sadly on her bed.*

Lucy (*to audience*) So, I came upstairs again with Zara. Feeling even more depressed. Because I knew that, partly anyway, that had all been my fault. I knew what would happen if I brought Zara downstairs. I knew Dad would go mad. He always does. I think, in a funny way, they get like that about Zara because she frightens them. Well, the idea of her frightens them. Because they don't understand about her at all. But then people are always frightened of what they don't understand. They didn't understand why I needed her. Let's face it. They didn't understand, full stop. So I sat up in my room with no supper and I talked to Zara. Because she did understand.

> *Under the next, Walt and Joy come upstairs and go off to their bedroom.*

And finally we stopped talking and Zara curled up on the end of my bed and fell asleep like she often did – and maybe I fell asleep, too, I don't know. And when I woke up I could hear Dad and Mum going up to their room to bed. And I thought about going in there and saying I was sorry to them both – and then I thought, 'No, why should I?' So instead, I switched off my light so they'd think I was asleep – (*She does this.*) Though I knew that really I should have gone and said sorry to them. That's what I should have done. Then none of what happened next would have happened. But it did.

Gary has started upstairs, too. He goes into the bathroom. Wind and rain sounds start under.

And then I heard it start to rain, and I went to the window, being careful not to disturb Zara, and I looked out – and it was a really dark night. The sort of night that makes you glad that you're safe and snug indoors. No stars, no moon, just the street lamps and this rain and wind lashing at the window. It looked like there was going to be a storm. And I was glad Zara was sleeping with me because – no, it doesn't matter.

Gary comes out of the bathroom in his pyjamas. Under the next he gets into bed under all the junk and goes to sleep.

And then I heard Gary coming to bed next door. And I hoped that tonight he wouldn't snore. Because when he snored it was almost as loud as his music. The walls in this house are made of old newspaper. And then I think I did sleep for just a few moments.

The house is now in darkness. Just a little street light on Lucy through her window, where she is sitting. She closes her eyes. A second's pause. Wind and rain rise. A clap of thunder. Lucy jolts awake.

63

It was the thunder that woke me. There was a terrible
storm outside now and I suddenly felt rather frightened –
and I turned to look for Zara but she wasn't on the bed
any more. She'd gone. Zara had gone. (*Lightning*.) And
now there was lightning . . . (*Thunder*.) And more
thunder. And I went to turn on my light. (*She tries her
light switch*.) Only it wasn't working. For some reason
the lights weren't working. It must have been the storm.
And I opened my door to go and see Mum and Dad . . .
(*She does this*.) But as I did this, above the storm, I
heard something – someone moving downstairs. And
I thought at first it might have been Gary – he's always
getting up in the night for a sandwich – but I listened at
his door –

She does so. Gary snores a little. Lightning.

And I heard him snoring. (*Thunder*.) It would take more
than a storm to wake Gary. (*A creak from the kitchen*.)
And I heard the sound again, coming from what
sounded like the kitchen. And I knew then it must be
Zara. Zara was down there. And I knew she wanted me.
And I knew she might be frightened, too. (*She gropes her
way to the stairs*.) And I felt my way to the stairs in the
dark, trying not to wake anyone. (*calling softly*) Zara!
Zara! Where are you? Zara! It's me, Lucy. Don't be
frightened. (*to audience*) And then it happened. I was
halfway down the stairs when –

Bright lightning and thunder in quick succession.

(*over this, quickly*) There was this tremendous flash of
lightning and this huge clap of thunder and I must have
caught my foot on the stairs in the dark because the next
thing I knew I was falling . . . falling . . . (*She falls
downstairs. As she does so, with a cry*) ZARA!

She lands in a heap at the bottom of the stairs. Quick

blackout. Then quite soon the lights return, brightening as Lucy regains consciousness. Zara, a visible solid version now, stands looking down at her.

Zara (*concerned, her voice coming at first from a distance*) Lucy . . . Lucy . . .

Lucy (*groggily*) Wah – wha – wha . . .?

Zara (*gently*) Lucy . . .

Lucy Who're you . . .? Who're you . . .?

Zara Are you all right?

Lucy Yes, I . . . Who are you . . .? What are you . . .?

Zara (*helping her up*) Here. Come and sit down for a second.

She guides Lucy to the armchair.

You'll be all right. You just knocked your head when you fell.

Lucy (*as she sits*) Who are you? What are you doing in our house?

Zara Don't you know?

Lucy I've never seen you before in my life.

Zara Oh yes, you have, you know . . .

Lucy You'd better tell me who you are at once or I'll call my parents . . .

Zara Can't you guess who I am, Lucy?

Lucy I'll call my brother. Gary's very strong . . .

Zara No, he's not. Gary's a weed, Lucy.

Lucy Don't say that . . .

Zara You said it yourself. You said it to me. 'Gary's a weed,' you said once . . .

Lucy I've never even spoken to you –

Zara Lucy, you talk to me all the time. You tell me everything. Your deepest secrets. I know everything there is to know about you, Lucy.

Lucy You can't. Nobody does.

Zara I know how you cried when Tracy Taylor said she wasn't going to be your friend any more because she said you'd cheated in French. Which you did. And you pretended you didn't care but afterwards you went and hid in the changing rooms on your own and you cried.

Lucy I did not. That's a lie . . .

Zara You did, I saw you . . . And the next day you brought some scissors to school that you took from the bathroom cabinet because you were going to cut up her French exercise book just to teach her . . .

Lucy I did not. I never did that.

Zara No, not in the end, you didn't. But that was only because you got too scared to go through with it.

Lucy How do you know all this? Nobody knows this.

Zara I do. Do you want me to tell you what happened at Peter Garforth's parents' house when you went to his birthday party?

Lucy No. . .

Zara You wanted to use the toilet only it was busy so you went in his bath instead . . .

Lucy (*with a wail*) I did not.

Zara I saw you, Lucy. I was there.

66

Lucy You couldn't have been. Who are you? The only person who could possibly know that is . . . is . . .

Zara Yes.

Lucy Zara. (*incredulously*) Zara?

Zara Hallo, Lucy.

Lucy Zara. You can't be Zara. She's invisible. You're invisible.

Zara I still am.

Lucy But I can see you.

Zara Only you. Nobody else can. I'm still invisible to everyone else.

Lucy Then how can I see you? What's happening?

Zara If you believe anything strongly enough, it can happen. You believed in me, Lucy. You believed in me so much that I'm here. I've come to stay with you.

Lucy Forever?

Zara If that's what you'd like.

Lucy Oh, yes. Oh, yes, yes, yes! Please.

Zara Then I'll stay.

Lucy Oh, Zara . . . (*She hugs her.*) I've been so unhappy, you see. So lonely.

Zara I know.

Lucy No one's interested in me – No one listens to me . . .

Zara I know. I know. It's all right. I'm here now. I'm with you, now. You must get some sleep. We'll talk again in the morning.

Lucy Yes. OK.

Zara helps Lucy to her feet. They start for the stairs.

Will you stay here tonight?

Zara I'll be here. Don't worry. I'll never be far away.

Lucy I still can't believe it. I can touch you. You're real, aren't you?

Zara As real as you are.

Lucy But how –? I still don't see . . .

Zara I've told you. Believe in anything and it can happen. It's up to you. We don't ever use most of our brains. If we used them properly, we could see things, do things, go to places, make things happen that we've only dreamt about. You can do almost anything, if you put your mind to it . . .

Lucy Anything?

Zara Almost.

Lucy Like what?

Zara Well, you could do little things like this . . . Look. See the vase, on the table there. You could do this, for instance.

The vase moves several inches along the table, apparently of its own volition.

Lucy (*awed*) Gosh! Could I do that?

Zara With a little practice. Concentration. Just put your mind to it, that's all. Come on.

They go upstairs. During the next, Lucy goes into her room and lies on the bed. Zara follows and stands in the bedroom doorway.

Lucy (*to audience*) And at that moment, I felt the happiest I had ever been in my whole life. At last I had a real friend. At last I had someone to talk to. Someone who really understood. Someone who knew. The moment my head touched the pillow, I must have fallen asleep. I don't remember. (*yawning, drowsily*) I remember Zara standing in the doorway and I remember thinking . . . I must remember . . . thinking . . . to ask her in the morning . . . if . . . if . . . Mmmmm . . .

She falls asleep. The lights fade again. A second's blackout. Then they snap up again very bright. Zara has gone. Joy is busy in the kitchen getting breakfast. Gary is still asleep. There is no sign of Walt.

(*sitting up, abruptly*) And the next thing I knew it was morning. But I could no longer see Zara. Zara? Maybe I had dreamt it all. I don't know. Oh, please God I didn't dream it. Zara! But she was nowhere. And suddenly I was wide awake and I had to find her. I just had to find Zara. (*Lucy leaps off the bed and runs out of her room.*)

(*calling*) Zara! Zara!

Gary, in his bedroom, wakes up with a start.

Gary (*startled*) Wah! Whassat?

Lucy (*yelling*) Zara!

Joy (*calling from the kitchen*) What's that?

Lucy runs downstairs. Under the next Gary gets up and goes into the bathroom.

Lucy Zara!

Joy What on earth's the matter, Lucy? What are you shouting about, girl?

Lucy (*looking around, dismayed*) She's gone.

Joy Who's gone?

Lucy Zara.

Joy Oh, now, I'm warning you – if you're starting that again –

Lucy She was here. Zara was here, Mum, I saw her.

Joy Now, you'd better stop this before your dad gets back, that's all. Because you know what'll happen if he hears you. He'll go completely off his trolley . . . Now, come and help me at once.

Lucy (*muttering*) She was here.

Joy (*sharply*) Lucy! That's your last warning. I'm not saying it again. (*thrusting cutlery into Lucy's hand*) Lay the table and do as you're told.

    Lucy reluctantly starts to do so.

Lucy (*muttering to herself*) I'll show her. I'll show them. (*Her eye lights upon the vase on the table. An idea*) Yes. What was it Zara said? You can do almost anything if you put your mind to it . . . (*She stares at the vase and concentrates. Frowning with effort*) Come on then. Move. Come on, move, won't you? Move!

Joy (*noticing her*) Lucy, what are you doing now?

Lucy I'm trying to move the vase.

Joy The vase?

Lucy Yes.

Joy I see. Well, I'll give you a little tip, shall I? If you want to move something you get hold of it, you see, like this, and then you wrap your fingers round it, like this, and then you lift it, like that, and then you move it to where you want to put it, like this, and then you put it down again, like that. It's a wonderful invention the human hand and God's been very generous and given you two of them, all right? Now get on with it. I think you're going barmy, girl. They'll lock you up for good one of these days.

Lucy Very funny! (*She starts to lay the table. After a second, having checked that Joy isn't looking, she tries again to move the vase. Softly*) Come on!

Suddenly the vase moves very slightly but quite perceptibly.

(*with a cry*) I did it! I did it!

Joy Did what?

Lucy I moved it. I just moved the vase.

Joy Did you? Well done. Now try putting the knives and forks down on the table. Practise doing that next, will you?

Lucy Oh, Mum.

Joy We're going to have to call the van out for you, I can see that.

Walt comes in through the front door. He has a newspaper with him.

Walt (*as he enters*) Breakfast ready then, is it?

Joy It will be. As soon as Flash Gordon here lays the table.

Walt What's she doing now?

Joy Moving the vase. That took her ten minutes.

Walt Get a move on. Stop annoying your mother.

Lucy Morning, Dad. Nice to see you, too.

Walt That's enough of that. You're not too old, you know.

Lucy Too old for what?

Walt Too old for – for you know very well.

Joy You know what he means. You listen to your dad.

Lucy (*muttering*) I don't know what he means . . .

Walt turns on the TV, sits in the armchair and reads the paper. In a moment, the sound comes up. A technical lecture.

TV Voice (*under the next*) The phenomena associated with the flow of electricity in metallic conductors can be explained with the aid of the interaction of the elementary electric charge of the electron with the atoms of the metals. For convenience, the electrons are assumed to have a spherical shape. A metal very widely employed for the conduction of electricity is copper. It has a crystalline structure as we see here in this diagram. The nucleus of the copper atom contains twenty-nine positive elementary charges, which are neutralized by twenty-nine negatively charged electrons. The twenty-ninth (outermost) electron is only very loosely connected to the atomic nucleus. Even at room temperature the thermal energy is great enough to enable the copper atoms to perform vibrations about their position of rest in the crystal lattice. As a result, these loosely connected electrons are, as it were, shaken off and thus become available as free carriers of negative electric charge for the conduction of electricity. These electrons are what we term 'quasi-free', that is they are repeatedly captured and released again. In the crystal lattice they behave rather like a gas in a container; for this reason the term 'electron gas' is sometimes employed as we see here. When a potential difference is applied between the ends of a conductor, electrons go from the negative to the positive pole. We see this illustrated here. The flow of electrons thus moves in the direction opposite to that of the current as conventionally defined . . .

The speech continues under until Zara finally switches it off.

Joy Come on, Lucy. Put these out as well.

Lucy fetches some more items and continues to lay the table for breakfast. While her back is turned, Zara enters unexpectedly and sits at the table. Lucy turns and sees her. Zara puts her finger to her lips. Lucy gasps and drops what she's carrying in surprise.

What are you doing now, girl? Pick them up at once.

Walt Pick them up, you heard your mother.

Joy Pick them up. Do as your dad tells you.

Lucy opens her mouth to argue, thinks better of it and picks the items up.

Zara (*mimicking, as Lucy does so*) Clumsy!

Lucy What –?

Joy What?

Walt What?

Lucy Nothing.

Zara Shh! Careful. They can't hear me, but they can hear you.

Lucy (*moving to the table, in a whisper*) Can they see you?

Joy at this moment brings something to put on the table. Zara gets up and stands in front of Joy waving her arms and calling.

Zara Yoo-hoo!

Joy doesn't react. She puts down what she is carrying and returns to the kitchen.

Apparently not.

Lucy (*whispering*) Where have you been, Zara? I thought you'd left.

Zara I was around. I told you. I'll always be around, somewhere. Don't worry. You'll never be alone again.

Gary comes out of the bathroom. He is now dressed. He starts downstairs. He has his Walkman on, as usual.

Lucy (*still whispering*) I moved the vase. Just now. I moved it with my mind.

Zara I know. I saw you. Well done.

Gary comes into the sitting room. He stops behind his father and reads the paper over his shoulder.

Joy Ah, Gary, just in time. It's on the table.

Gary doesn't hear.

(*louder*) Gary! Lucy, tell your brother his breakfast is ready.

Lucy crosses to Gary and lifts one earphone from his head.

Lucy (*bawling into Gary's ear*) YOUR BREAKFAST IS READY, GRISLY!

Gary and Walt both jump.

Gary (*alarmed*) What you doing?

Walt Stop that! You stop that at once or you know what'll happen to you.

Lucy No. What'll happen to me?

Walt Never you mind. You know perfectly well what'll happen, I'm telling you.

Joy There, Lucy. That's your father telling you what'll happen to you. It's on the table, Dad.

Walt Right.

Walt gets up. He puts the paper down. Gary picks it up. Walt gets intrigued by what's on the TV screen. Gary takes the paper to the table and starts to read it as he goes. He is about to sit in the chair that Zara is occupying.

Lucy (*softly, to Zara*) Zara, look out.

Zara swiftly rises from the chair.

Zara Whoops! Excuse me!

She bows as Gary goes to sit in the chair. She pulls it from under him at the last minute. Gary sits on the floor. Lucy is amused. Zara laughs.

Gary Wah!

Joy (*alarmed*) Gary, are you all right?

Gary (*loudly*) I missed my chair.

Joy Oh, dear.

Walt (*to Lucy, suspiciously*) Was that anything to do with you?

Lucy No.

Walt You behave yourself.

Gary I don't know how I missed my chair. I don't usually miss my chair.

They start to help themselves to cereal. Zara hovers round the table watching them. The TV voice drones on.

Joy Have you got the TV on for a reason, Walter?

Walt No, I'm waiting for the boxing. Satellite.

None the less he seems fascinated with the current programme and gives little attention to the table, keeping his eyes glued to the TV screen. Gary, too, is absorbed in the newspaper.

Joy Oh, that'll be nice. Cornflakes?

Walt No, I'll have the Krispies.

Joy (*to Lucy*) There you are. Pass your father the Krispies, Lucy. (*shouting*) Do you want Krispies, Gary? Krispies?

Gary No, I'll have Cornflakes, Mum.

Joy Pass your brother the Cornflakes, Lucy.

Lucy does so. A pause. The adults are immersed; Joy in her food, Walt in the TV, Gary in the paper. Gary shakes a few Cornflakes into his bowl. Walt shakes a few Krispies into his. They pause just long enough for Zara to give Lucy a smile and switch the bowls over. Walt is about to resume filling his bowl. He looks into it and stops.

Walt Hang on.

Joy What?

Walt I've got Cornflakes here.

Joy No, you haven't.

Walt Yes, I have.

Joy No, you've got Krispies. Those are Krispies. Look at the packet.

Walt It may say Krispies on the packet. But they aren't. (*indicating bowl*) Look. These are Cornflakes.

Joy That's odd. What's Gary got then?

Walt (*looking*) He's got Krispies.

Joy He doesn't want Krispies. He wanted Cornflakes. He didn't want Krispies.

Walt No, I'm the one who wanted Krispies.

Joy That's odd. They must have put Krispies in a Cornflakes packet.

Walt And Cornflakes in a Krispies packet.

Joy Yes.

Gary (*waking up to the situation*) Hey. I got Krispies here.

Walt Yes, we know. We know.

Gary I wanted Cornflakes.

Walt Yes, I know. Here, have these.

Gary Ta.

Walt Give me yours.

Gary Right.

They exchange bowls.

Walt Hey, you'd better give me your packet and all.

Gary No, these are fine. I wanted Cornflakes.

Walt I know you did. But those aren't Cornflakes, those are Krispies.

Gary Are they? It says Cornflakes on the packet.

Walt Yes, I know it says Cornflakes on the packet, but they're not Cornflakes, they're Krispies. Now give them to me. You can have these.

He gives Gary the Krispies packet and takes the Cornflakes from him.

Gary I don't want these, I wanted Cornflakes.

Walt Those are Cornflakes.

Gary Are they? It says Krispies on the packet.

Walt I know. But they're not Krispies, they're Cornflakes. The Cornflakes are in the Krispies packet and the Krispies are in the Cornflakes packet. Those are not Krispies, those are Cornflakes. And these are not Cornflakes, these are Krispies. Look. (*He shakes some Cornflakes on to his Krispies.*)

Gary Those are Cornflakes.

Walt Cornflakes? How did they get in there?

Gary It's a Cornflake packet. (*He shakes some Krispies over his Cornflakes.*)

Walt Those are Krispies, those are. How did they get in there?

Gary In where?

Walt In the Krispies packet? What the hell are the Krispies doing in the Krispies packet?

Gary I don't know. Is that not right, then?

Joy Can I help at all, Dad?

Walt No, you can't.

Joy Do you want me to scrape those Cornflakes off your Krispies?

Walt No, I don't.

Gary (*offering the Krispies packet*) Do you want these back?

Walt (*angrily*) No, I don't. I don't want anything. I'll just have some toast. I'm going to write and complain about this.

Joy (*to Lucy*) Pass your father the toast, Lucy.

Lucy (*doing so*) Dad?

Walt (*to Lucy*) Was that anything to do with you?

Lucy No. (*She suppresses a giggle.*)

Walt If I catch you smirking you'll go straight upstairs.

Lucy (*injured*) What have I done now?

Walt You know, you know. You don't need to be told.

Joy You know. You don't need telling.

> The TV drones on. Gary carefully picks the Krispies off his Cornflakes and eats what remains. Zara has wandered over and is idly sitting on the edge of the armchair, half watching the TV.

Zara This programme's extremely boring, isn't it?

Lucy (*unthinking*) Yes.

Walt What?

Joy What?

Lucy Nothing.

Walt Well, don't suddenly say 'yes' like that for no reason.

Lucy No.

Walt looks at her suspiciously.

Zara Oh, I've had enough of this programme.

Zara holds up her hand, cocks her thumb, lines it up, squinting at the screen, and operates it like a remote-control button. The TV programme changes abruptly to some loud pop music.

Walt Oy!

Joy What's happened?

Walt The programme's changed. That's odd. (*He locates the remote control. He returns the programme to what it was.*) That's better. That's better.

Zara changes it back again.

(*angrily*) What's going on here? Something's wrong with the set now.

Walt changes it back again. Zara changes it again. They to and fro between channels for a bit.

(*wrestling with the control*) Damn thing . . .

Zara (*finally losing patience*) Oh, I've had enough of this.

She gestures rather more emphatically at the screen. There is a loud bang from the TV set. A silence.

Joy Oh, goodness.

Walt Now look what's happened.

Gary (*lifting one earphone*) What's happened?

Joy The telly blew up.

Gary (*uninterested*) Oh.

Walt (*to Lucy*) Have you been monkeying around with that set?

Lucy No.

Walt I wouldn't put it past you. Well, that's that. I've missed the boxing now, haven't I? Missed it.

Zara Well, it might be an idea if we all sat and talked to each other, just for a change.

Lucy Great.

Walt What do you mean, 'great'?

Joy Don't say that, Lucy. Your father's missed his programme.

Zara Good. Boxing's stupid, anyway.

Lucy Extremely stupid.

Joy Lucy!

Walt Who are you calling extremely stupid?

Zara Two grown men battering each other senseless . . .

Walt Who are you referring to?

Zara I ask you what would you rather do?

Walt Lucy?

Joy Lucy?

Zara Watch boxing or talk to me?

Walt I'm asking you a question.

Zara Me or boxing?

Walt Answer me! Who were you calling stupid?

Zara Boxing or me, Lucy?

Walt Who?

Lucy (*confused*) You!

Walt Right, that does it. Upstairs, this minute.

Lucy What?

Walt (*yelling*) UPSTAIRS!

Joy You heard your father.

Lucy (*rising*) I can't help hearing him.

Walt You stay in your room till you're ready to apologize. I'm not having a daughter of mine calling me stupid under my own roof.

Zara Let's go out in the garden and call him stupid.

Lucy giggles despite herself.

Walt And don't you start laughing, my girl, or you will be in trouble. Upstairs.

Joy Upstairs . . .

Lucy Dad, I didn't mean to –

Walt (*fiercely*) Upstairs.

Zara Come on, upstairs.

Lucy Oh. . .

Gary (*looking up*) Where's she off to?

Joy Upstairs.

Gary Oh.

Lucy and Zara go upstairs together.

Lucy (*to audience*) At that moment, I was so angry –
I was really so angry – I mean, it was just unfair. They
blamed me for everything. Just everything. It was unfair.
So I got angry, you see. I mean, that's the reason I agreed
to . . . I didn't mean to hurt them, any of them . . .
(*lamely*) I just got angry, that's all.

She and Zara are now in the bedroom.

(*to Zara*) I hate them sometimes. I really hate them.

Zara Well. If you really hate them that much . . .

Lucy What?

Zara Why don't you – get rid of them?

Lucy Get rid of them?

Zara Why not? If you hate them?

Lucy Get rid of them? How? You mean kill them?

Zara No, no. Nothing like that. Just make them
invisible.

Lucy Invisible? How?

Zara The same way you made me visible. The power of
the mind, Lucy. Remember?

Lucy I could do that? Really?

Zara Oh, yes. Easily.

Lucy Just put my mind to it? Would it . . .? Would it –
hurt them?

Zara No. Not really. They wouldn't even know about it.
They'd just disappear. That's all. No fuss. No mess. No

questions. Just vanish like that. It's easy. Remember how you moved that vase? You did that. You just have to concentrate, that's all.

Lucy That's all.

Zara Try it. Go on. Just close your eyes and concentrate.

Lucy does so.

Now try and picture them. Can you do that?

Lucy Yes.

Zara Picture your father . . .

Lucy Yes . . .

Zara Picture your mother . . .

Lucy Yes . . .

Zara Picture your brother. Can you see them?

Lucy Yes, I can see them.

Zara Right, now imagine them gone. Picture the empty table . . .

Lucy Yes.

Zara Empty the picture. Can you do that?

Lucy I'm trying. Can't you help me?

Zara No, you have to do it, Lucy. It has to be you. Come on, you can do it . . .

Lucy Yes. . .

A strange eerie sound of a wailing, rushing wind, slowly approaching and gathering volume.

Zara That's it! It's working, Lucy, it's working. Come on . . .

Lucy Yes . . .

Zara Make them go, Lucy . . .

Lucy Yes . . .

Zara Make them vanish . . .

Lucy Yes . . .

Zara Vanish!

Lucy (*loudly*) Vanish!

Zara (*louder still*) Vanish!

Lucy (*still louder*) Vanish!

Zara (*shouting*) Vanish!

Lucy (*with a great scream over the furore*) V-A-A-N-I-I-I-S-H-H!

> *Quick blackout. Silence. When the lights return the breakfast table downstairs is empty. Walt, Joy and Gary have all disappeared.*

(*in a whisper*) Have they gone? Are they invisible?

Zara Go down and see for yourself.

> *Lucy, rather nervously, starts for the stairs. As she descends, frightened of what she might see, she calls out her family's names rather tentatively. Zara follows her.*

Lucy (*descending the stairs, calling*) Mum! . . . Dad! . . . Gary! Mum!

> *They enter the living area.*

(*looking at the empty table*) Mum . . . Dad . . .

> *A silence.*

They've gone. They've really vanished. How long will they be gone for? How long?

Zara They'll be gone – till you really want them back. For ever if necessary.

Lucy moves to the table.

Lucy (*a little nervously*) I may . . . I may want them back, sooner or later.

Zara That's up to you.

Lucy I mean, even if I hate them – I'll probably miss them, too. A bit. Fairly soon. I mean, I know you're here, Zara, but it might still get a bit lonely. Mightn't it?

Zara (*smiling*) Oh, no.

Lucy No?

Felix Oh, no.

Chuck Oh, no.

As if from nowhere, Felix and Chuck have appeared. They are a part of Zara's 'invisible' family and have, like her, a pristine unreality about them. They stand smiling at Lucy.

Lucy (*startled*) Who are –?

Zara Lucy, I want you to meet my family. This is my father, Felix. And that's my brother, Chuck . . . Say hello, Lucy.

Lucy (*weakly*) Hallo.

Felix Hallo, Lucy.

Chuck Hallo, Lucy. We've come to stay with you. Isn't that nice?

Felix Isn't that nice?

Zara Isn't that nice?

Lucy (*weakly*) Lovely. (*to audience*) And how I came to live with my new family – and how I got my own family back again, I'll tell you in a little while. (*She looks at the others, nervously. To audience*) See you soon. Don't leave me for long, will you?

Blackout.

Act Two

The same. Lucy comes on, looking very happy.

Lucy (*to audience*) Right. Let me tell you the rest of this story. Are you ready? Well, the next few hours were the happiest in my whole life. My real family had completely vanished – and though at first I felt – well, a bit guilty – because I wouldn't have wanted them to be hurt or anything – Zara told me that they were perfectly OK. They weren't suffering or anything. The way she explained it, they were just in another plane, like in another universe, practically the same as the one we're in, only running alongside it. But quite separate. It's difficult to explain. Zara made it sound all very simple but then she's brilliant sometimes.

During the next, Zara, then Chuck and Felix come on. They all sit at the table and start to play Snakes and Ladders.

Anyway, we all settled down to live happily together in the house – Zara and me and Zara's brother Chuck who was just great and her father Felix who was also very nice. We just laughed and played games a lot and sometimes just talked. Or rather I talked and they sat and listened. It seemed they really wanted to hear what I had to say. Unlike some people I could mention.

Felix Come on, Lucy, it's your go.

Zara Lucy, come on . . .

Chuck (*resignedly*) She'll win again. She always does.

Lucy (*to audience*) We played all sorts of stupid games, too. Like Snakes and Ladders.

Lucy joins them at the table. She starts to shake the dice.

Zara Cheer up, Chuck. She can't win this time, she's miles behind.

Chuck Bet you she does . . .

Lucy (*to audience*) They weren't very good at games, though. (*She throws. To the others*) Six!

Felix Another go . . .

Lucy moves her counter and makes to throw again.

Zara Get a one, go on get a one, then you'll go down the snake . . .

Chuck She won't get a one. She'll get a six.

Lucy throws again.

Lucy Six!

Felix Another six . . .!

Chuck (*disgustedly*) I told you. I don't believe it.

Zara Well done! Another turn, Lucy.

Lucy moves her counter and makes to throw for a third time.

Chuck Well, she can't get possibly get another six. Not possibly.

Zara Don't be too sure. Lucy's the champion, remember?

Felix Come on, champ.

Lucy throws.

Chuck Oh, no . . .

Lucy, Felix and Zara (*together*) Six!

Lucy I won! I won! I won!

Chuck Again! I don't believe it!

Zara Poor old Chuck. You must let him win sometimes, Lucy.

Lucy (*laughing and hugging Chuck*) Sorry, I'm sorry, Chuck. Don't be angry with me, please don't be angry.

Chuck No, I'm not really. It's just that every game we play, you seem to win it.

Felix Well, I don't know about the rest of you but I think it's my bedtime. Chuck, you're the loser tonight. Loser tidies up, there you are . . . (*He indicates the Snakes and Ladders.*)

Chuck Oh, not again!

Zara Loser tidies up!

Lucy Loser tidies up!

Chuck All right! All right!

Chuck starts to clear the table. Felix heads for the stairs.

Felix By the way, I saw in the paper tonight there was a funfair in town. I thought we might go to that tomorrow, if you'd like to.

Zara Oh, great . . .

Chuck You bet!

Felix Just a minute, just a second, you two. Does Lucy want to go, that's the point? It's up to Lucy, isn't it?

Zara Yes, sorry. Of course.

Chuck Sorry.

Felix Let's ask Lucy. Shall we go to the funfair, Lucy?

Zara Oh, say 'yes', Lucy.

Chuck Please say 'yes'.

Lucy OK. We'll go to the funfair.

Zara Terrific!

Chuck Yes!

Felix All right. Funfair it is. Lucy has spoken. See you in the morning. I'll sleep in the front bedroom, if that's OK, Lucy?

Lucy (*with a twinge of guilt*) Mum and Dad's bedroom. Yes, sure.

Felix Thank you. (*to Chuck and Zara*) And you two, remember to ask Lucy which rooms she wants you both to use. Remember it's her house and we're her guests and she's in charge. All right?

Zara Yes, of course.

Chuck Sure.

Felix Goodnight, then.

Zara Night!

Lucy Night!

Chuck Goodnight.

Felix goes up and off into Walt's and Joy's bedroom.

Well, where are you going to put me, Lucy?

Lucy Well, there's my brother's room. Gary's room, I suppose.

Chuck Would that be OK?

Lucy It's a bit untidy.

Chuck Oh, I'll soon tidy it up.

Zara Chuck's great at tidying.

Lucy OK, I'll show you.

They start for the stairs.

It's next to mine. I think, Zara, you'll have to share with me . . .

Zara Sure. . .

As they go, Chuck turns and, with a wave, switches off the downstairs lights.

Lucy We've got a small folding bed. It isn't very comfortable, I'm afraid.

Zara That'll be fine.

Chuck Zara can sleep anywhere.

Lucy That's my room and then here – this is Gary's room. You'll see what I mean by untidy. (*She switches on the light and steps back to allow Chuck to see the disarray.*)

Chuck Oh, dear. Yes, this is a big job.

Lucy Shall we help you . . .?

Chuck No, that's OK.

Zara Chuck will do it. He's good at tidying.

Chuck Just a second.

Chuck frowns in concentration. The room 'tidies' itself. Objects shoot under the bed and back into cupboards. In the space of a few seconds, everything is clear.

Lucy (*in disbelief*) Christmas!

Chuck That's better. Right. See you in the morning. Night. Sleep well.

Zara Night.

Lucy (*still dazed*) Night.

> *Chuck closes the door and lies on the bed, eyes closed as if in meditation.*

(*in a whisper to Zara*) How did he do that?

Zara I've told you. If you want something enough, you can make it happen. All you need to do is put your mind to it.

Lucy But it just tidied itself.

Zara No, Chuck tidied it. Chuck can do all sorts of things like that.

Lucy Well . . . I'll find that bed for you, hang on.

Zara Wait, there's no need for that –

Lucy What?

Zara We'll do what Chuck did just now.

Lucy How do you mean?

Zara Come on. Just concentrate.

Lucy Concentrate?

Zara (*closing her eyes and frowning*) What do we want to do? We want the folding bed that's in the cupboard along the passage there, we want to unfold it and put it up in your bedroom. OK?

Lucy Yes, but –

Zara Come on then. Concentrate on doing just that. Are you ready? Close your eyes . . .

They both close their eyes.

Both together. And . . . one . . . three . . .

A brief blackout. When the lights return there is an additional small bed in Lucy's room.

Lucy Did anything happen?

Zara See for yourself.

Lucy cautiously opens her bedroom door.

Lucy (*seeing the extra bed*) Zara, it worked. The bed's in here. It worked. We did it.

Zara Of course we did. (*She sits on the bed.*) Oh, it's quite comfortable. This'll be fine.

She lies on her bed. Lucy does the same.

Lucy What else can you do then? I mean, just with your mind?

Zara I've told you. Practically anything. The more practice you have the better. Chuck can do much more than me because he's older. And as for my father – well, Felix is brilliant.

Lucy What else can Chuck do?

Zara Oh, masses. He drives cars with no petrol in. He always makes it snow at Christmas. He was awful at school. He once drained the school swimming pool and filled it up again with red ink.

Lucy Did he get into trouble?

Zara You bet. The P.E. teacher was swimming in it at the time. He was stained bright pink for months.

They laugh.

94

Lucy I'm glad you're here, Zara. I mean, really here, not just imaginary here.

Zara I'm glad, too. (*yawning*) Oh, I'm tired. Go to the funfair tomorrow, eh?

Lucy Yes.

Zara That'll be good. Want the light out?

Lucy Yes. I'll –

She makes to get up.

Zara No, no . . . Not like that.

Lucy No, of course.

She closes her eyes and concentrates fiercely. Nothing happens.

Zara No?

Lucy I can't do it.

Zara You will in time, don't worry. (*She waves her hand. The bedroom light goes out. There is still light through the window.*) You'll soon get the knack of it.

Lucy I hope so. (*Pause.*) Zara . . .

Zara Mmmm?

Lucy If – if Chuck is so good at – making things happen – like doing things with cars and swimming pools and so on . . . well, how come he can't win at board games? Like when he shakes the dice – he only throws ones and twos – never fives or sixes. Why does that happen? He should be able to throw any number he wants, shouldn't he?

Zara (*sleepily*) I don't know. You'd better ask Chuck.

Lucy (*half to herself*) It's odd, that. Very odd . . .

*She lies awake, puzzling. Zara, apparently, is asleep.
In the next room, Chuck laughs softly to himself.
Lucy doesn't hear him. The lights change and it is
morning. Lucy is asleep. Zara bounds off her bed and
runs out of the door. She shakes Lucy as she passes.*

Zara Wakey, wakey!

Lucy (*awaking with a jolt*) Oh!

*Zara runs along the hall and downstairs. Simul-
taneously, Chuck leaves his bedroom and follows
her, under the next. They, in turn, are joined by Felix.
All three sit at the table downstairs and wait.*

(*to audience*) The following morning, everybody seemed
to get up at dawn. Everyone but me, that was. It was
about now that things started to go wrong – just very
slightly at first and then worse and worse – until it all
became a real nightmare. I got up and went downstairs.
(*She does so, during the next.*) Actually, I felt a bit rough.
I hadn't been able to get to sleep for ages. Probably
because the house had been so quiet. I never thought
I'd say this, but I think I actually missed the sound of
Gary's snoring.

*She reaches the sitting room. The others are all sitting
at table. They look at her expectantly.*

(*to the others*) Good morning.

Felix, Chuck and Zara (*in unison, cheerfully*) Good
morning!

Lucy What are you all doing?

Felix Are we glad to see you!

Chuck You bet.

Zara About time.

Lucy Why?

Felix We were getting hungry.

Chuck Starving.

Zara What's for breakfast?

Lucy Breakfast?

Felix Well, it's half-past six.

Lucy (*appalled*) Half-past six!

Chuck Six thirty-two, actually.

Lucy In the morning?

Zara Six thirty-three now.

Felix Any chance of something to eat, Lucy? I don't want to rush you. It's just that we really are starving. Aren't we?

Zara and Chuck (*together*) We certainly are!

Lucy Oh. Yes. Well, couldn't you have . . .? I mean, why didn't you help yourselves? There's probably food there. Mum usually has – had . . . food in . . . If you – If you –

Felix Oh, no. We couldn't do that.

Chuck We couldn't help ourselves.

Zara That wouldn't be right.

Felix After all, we are guests.

Chuck We couldn't go barging around in someone else's kitchen, could we?

Zara That would be terribly rude.

Lucy (*uncertainly*) Yes. OK. I'll see what we – I mean,

I'm not very good at cooking . . . What would you . . .?
Anything you'd like? Especially?

Felix Oh. Not really. Just a few eggs.

Lucy Eggs. Right.

Chuck Bacon, perhaps?

Lucy (*starting to hunt*) Bacon, yes. I'll see if we . . .

Zara Sausages?

Lucy Sausages, I'm not sure . . .

Felix Fried bread, possibly.

Chuck Grilled tomatoes.

Lucy Tomatoes, yes.

Zara Mushrooms.

Lucy Mushrooms.

Felix Any black pudding . . .?

Lucy Black pudding? No, I don't think we've . . .

Chuck Bit of fillet steak . . .

Zara Smoked haddock.

Felix Kippers.

Chuck Kidneys.

Zara Kedgeree . . .

Felix Caviare . . .

Chuck Smoked salmon . . .

Zara *Pain perdu* . . .

Lucy (*loudly*) Just a minute. Just a minute. We haven't got all this stuff. Caviare? We haven't got that. You'll just have to have what we've got here.

Felix Yes, of course, Lucy.

Chuck We'll have what you've got.

Zara Of course.

Felix What have you got?

Lucy We've got . . . (*She looks in the fridge.*) We've got . . . one . . . two . . . three . . . four . . . five fish fingers.

Chuck Five fish fingers?

Zara Yuk!

Felix Nothing else?

Lucy Er . . . Some deep-frozen sprouts.

Chuck Deep?

Zara Frozen?

Felix Sprouts?

Chuck For breakfast?

Lucy (*indignantly*) Well, I didn't know you'd want breakfast, did I? I mean, I don't do the shopping. My mother does the shopping. Only my mother . . . isn't here. (*pathetically*) I don't do the shopping. How am I expected to know?

Zara It's all right. It's all right, Lucy. We'll help you, won't we?

Felix Oh yes.

Chuck You bet.

Zara We'll all go shopping with you this morning and

show you what to buy. All right?

Lucy Yes, OK.

Zara So you'll know in future. And by tomorrow, you'll have everything you need and you'll be able to cook us a really huge breakfast.

Lucy Am I going to have to cook it every morning?

Felix Why? Is that a problem?

Lucy Well . . .?

Chuck Are you busy doing something else, then?

Lucy Well . . . I have to go to school, you know.

Zara Not till later, surely?

Lucy Well, at eight fifteen, I do.

Felix Oh, we'll have finished breakfast by then, won't we? We like to eat early. Six thirty at the latest.

Lucy But I'll have to get up at five or something to cook it.

Zara I'll wake you. I'm always up by then.

Lucy Then if you're up, why don't you cook it?

Zara It's not my house. I couldn't cook breakfast in someone else's house. It would be terribly rude. I mean, if you came to stay at our house we'd never expect you to cook.

Lucy Where is your house?

Zara We haven't got one.

Chuck Come on. Enough of this chat. What are we going to eat?

Felix Well, I think we're going to have to forget breakfast, Chuck. We're going to have to wait for lunch.

Chuck Lunch? What's for lunch then?

Zara What have you got us for lunch, Lucy?

Lucy Lunch? Nothing. I haven't got you anything.

Felix Nothing?

Lucy Nothing. Five fish fingers and deep-frozen sprouts.

Chuck What again? Fish fingers and sprouts? Do you have that for every meal?

Lucy No . . .

Chuck Doesn't it tend to get a bit boring?

Lucy No, of course we don't. I'm just telling you, that's all we've got, that's all. That's all we've got in the house to eat.

Chuck Oh, lord.

Felix Oh, dear.

Zara Oh, heavens.

Chuck I must say this is very depressing.

Felix Awful.

Zara Dreadful.

They all sit very dejectedly. Lucy looks at them, alarmed.

Lucy I'm sorry. Don't be sad. It wasn't my fault. Please. Don't be like that. We were having such a lovely time. Tell you what, would you like to play a game?

Pause. They look at her.

You'd like to play a game, wouldn't you?

Felix (*suspiciously*) What sort of game?

Lucy I don't know – Snakes and Ladders?

Chuck No. You always win at that.

Lucy Ludo?

Zara No. It's too complicated.

Lucy Happy Families?

Felix Hardly suitable at the moment, is it?

Lucy I know. What about Snap? That's easy. Snap. Look, I've got some cards here. Let's all play Snap. (*She finds the cards.*)

Chuck How do you play this Snap?

Lucy Oh, you must know Snap. It's the easiest game in the world. Look, I'll show you. We deal out all the cards like this – (*She does this as she speaks.*) – only you mustn't look at them – and then we take it in turns to put one down in front of us from our own pile face upwards – and when you see two cards that are the same, you shout out snap. And the first person to call it out, wins and takes all the cards on the table. And the person with all the cards at the end wins.

Chuck Sounds very complicated.

Lucy Look, I'll show you. We'll have a go. I'll put a card down first. (*She does so.*) Like that. Now you, Zara. You do the same.

Zara Right. (*She plays a card.*)

Lucy Now, Felix. Your turn.

Felix Yes. (*He plays a card.*)

Lucy Now you, Chuck.

Chuck (*playing a card*) Snap!

Lucy No, it isn't. You have to have two cards the same, before you shout snap. If you shout out snap when you shouldn't the cards should really go in a pool.

Chuck In a pool?

Lucy Yes.

Chuck Won't they get a bit damp?

Lucy No, not a real pool . . . it's a . . . Oh, it doesn't matter. My turn. (*She plays another card.*)

Zara Now me?

Lucy Yes.

   Zara plays a card.

Felix And me. (*He plays a card.*)

Lucy And snap. There's two cards the same, you see?

Felix Oh, yes.

Zara Oh, yes.

Chuck Is there? Oh, yes, so there are.

Lucy I win. So I take all these cards.

Chuck She's won again, what did I tell you?

Lucy So now I start.

   Lucy plays a card. Zara plays a card. Felix plays a
   card. Chuck plays a card. Lucy plays another card.
   Zara plays another card.

And snap!

Felix (*belatedly*) Snap – oh, yes. Too late. Very good. Well done, Lucy. Good game this.

Zara Very good.

Chuck Yes, I'm getting the hang of it now.

Lucy It's not that difficult.

Felix No. Tell you what. Shall we play with the cards the other way up? Would that be more fun?

Zara Oh, yes, let's.

Lucy The other way up?

Felix Yes.

Lucy How do you mean, the other way up?

Zara With the cards the other way up, you know.

Lucy But then you won't be able to play.

Chuck Why not?

Lucy Because you won't be able to see the cards. You can't play Snap if you can't see the cards.

Zara Why not?

Lucy Because you won't know what they are.

Felix You can guess what they are though, can't you?

Lucy Guess?

Chuck Yes.

Lucy That's stupid.

Chuck No, it's not.

Lucy It is. What's the point of that?

Felix Come on, Lucy. Let's try it. We can give it a try.

Zara Let's give it a try.

Chuck Give it a try.

Lucy (*muttering*) I don't see the point. It's completely and utterly stupid.

Felix We'll see. Your go, Lucy.

Lucy puts down a card, face down. Zara does likewise. So does Felix. So does Chuck.

Lucy This is stupid. You can't see them.

Zara Your go, Lucy.

Lucy plays a card.

Felix (*knowingly*) Ah ha!

Zara plays a card.

Chuck (*thoughtfully*) Oh ho!

Felix plays a card.

Zara (*pensively*) Hee hee.

Lucy (*exasperatedly*) What are you all doing?

Chuck plays a card.

Felix, Zara and Chuck (*almost together*) Snap!

The family laughs.

Chuck Who was first? Was it you, Zara?

Zara No, it was Felix. Felix was first.

Felix Me, was it? Was it me first, Lucy?

Lucy I've no idea. I don't know what you're all doing. How could you know it was snap?

Zara Because Chuck played the same as you did, Lucy. Those are the rules, aren't they?

Lucy How do you know his card's the same as mine?

Felix Because it is.

Chuck It's obvious. Look. (*He turns over his card.*

Zara Now look at your card.

Lucy does so. Hers and Chuck's are the same.

You see?

Lucy How did you know that?

Felix We guessed.

Chuck We're all frightfully good guessers. Whose go?

Zara Felix's. Come on, Lucy. You can guess, too.

Lucy It's a ridiculous way to play.

Felix plays a card. Chuck plays a card. Lucy plays a card.

(*sulkily*) Snap, then!

Felix Oh, no. Come on.

Zara No, no, no.

Chuck Play properly.

Felix That's just being silly, Lucy. Be sensible.

Zara She didn't mean it. It was a mistake.

Lucy Yes, I did. I meant it. Let me see your cards.

Lucy, Felix and Chuck turn over their cards. None are the same.

Well, they might have been.

Chuck No way. Carry on, Zara.

Zara plays a card. Felix plays a card. Chuck plays a card. Lucy plays a card. Zara plays a card. Felix plays a card. Chuck plays a card. Lucy plays a card. As she does so, the other three let out a great roar.

Felix, Chuck and Zara (*together*) SNAP!!!

Again, the three laugh delightedly. Lucy gets up from the table angrily.

Lucy That's it! I'm not playing any more. You're just cheating, all of you. It's not fair! (*She throws her cards down on the table. Silence.*)

Felix Well, I don't think I want to sit here and put up with behaviour like that.

Chuck No.

Zara (*unhappily*) No.

Felix I think I'll just get my coat from upstairs. Might go for a walk. It's a lovely morning.

Chuck Good idea.

Zara Fine.

They move to the stairs. Lucy watches them.

Felix Loser clears up, I think. Doesn't she, Lucy?

Lucy glares. Felix and Chuck go upstairs and off. Zara lingers behind.

Zara Come on, Lucy. I'll help you. Lucy?

Felix (*calling*) Zara!

Zara Yes, Felix.

Felix Here a second.

Zara Coming. (*to Lucy*) I'll be back. Start clearing up, there's a love. Don't spoil the day.

Zara goes upstairs after Felix and Chuck. Lucy stands miserably.

Lucy (*to audience*) I tidied away the cards. (*She starts to do so.*) But I was still angry. It wasn't fair, it really wasn't. I mean, fancy playing cards and cheating like that. Just because they could do things I couldn't. I was very upset indeed. Not even my brother, Grisly Gary, would have behaved like that. So, later on when they all came down again . . .

Felix, Chuck and Zara all come down in their coats.

Felix Lucy, we thought we'd stroll along to the funfair. Do you want to come with us?

Lucy (*sulkily*) No, I don't.

Zara Oh, come on, Lucy.

Lucy I don't want to go, thank you.

Chuck Lucy . . .

Lucy You go.

Felix Oh well, suit yourself. Bye, then.

Chuck Bye, then.

Zara Bye.

They all go out of the front door and off.

Lucy (*to audience*) I don't know why I said 'no'. I really wanted to go to the funfair. I think I just said 'no' to upset them. Only I didn't upset them at all, of course. I just upset me even more. They were gone for ages, too.

And I sat around feeling very sorry for myself. And then I thought, 'Well, I'll try and do something to make up for it.' Maybe – give them a surprise when they get back – that's it. And I hunted around in the kitchen. And I found this cookery book. (*She finds the book in question. Reading*) *Quick and Easy Cake-Making* by Elizabeth Spatula. And then I had this great idea. While they were out, I'd make them this delicious cake – just to say I was sorry for losing my temper. I'd never made a cake before – as I said, I'm not very good at cooking – but it said easy on the cover and quick – so it must be true or they wouldn't have been allowed to print it. (*She lays the book on the table.*) Now then. (*reading*) 'Ingredients. Self-raising flour.' (*She hunts for each ingredient in turn. Finding a labelled tin*) Self-raising flour. Here we are. (*reading*) 'Margarine.' I know we've got that. (*She finds the margarine from the fridge.*) 'Sugar.' (*hunting*) Sugar – sugar – sugar . . . (*She finds the sugar.*) Right. (*reading*) 'Mixed dried fruit.' Oh, now . . . more difficult . . . (*She locates a withered orange, a black banana and a shrivelled lemon*) These look pretty dried. I'll mix these up. What else? (*reading*) 'Two eggs. Milk.' Well . . . (*She hunts again. At the fridge*) Oh yes, eggs, here we are. Great. Didn't know we had these. And milk. Right. (*She comes across another packet.*) Hey! Here's some prunes. They're dried fruit. I'll put those in as well. Good. So, those are the ingredients. Off we go. Now what? (*reading*) 'Heat the oven.' Heat the oven. (*She switches on the oven. Checking*) Is that lit? Oh, yes. It lights itself. (*reading*) 'Grease a cake tin.' (*hunting*) Cake tin . . . (*She finds an ordinary cake tin with a lid and CAKE written on it.*) Cake tin . . . Now, grease . . .? Oh, yes. I know. There's that stuff Dad used on our back gate when the hinges squeaked . . . (*She locates a can of grease under the sink.*) This should do. Grease the tin. I wonder why you have to do this? (*She greases the tin on the outside.*) I mean, all it does is make it slippery to pick up. Stupid. Perhaps it's to stop the lid squeaking. Yuk! Now I'm all greasy. What's next? (*reading*) 'Large mixing bowl.' Yes. We've got one of those somewhere. (*She finds the mixing bowl. Reading*) 'Put the ingredients into a mixing bowl and beat well.' Right. Here goes. (*She puts everything into the bowl – whole eggs, unpeeled fruit and pours the sugar, flour and milk liberally over the lot.*) Lucy Baines, Master Cook. There! It's dead easy this cake-making. (*reading*) 'Beat well . . .' (*She finds an electric hand-held egg-beater.*) Yeah! Great! This'll do. (*She activates the whisk in the bowl. A lot of flour flies about.*) That's it. (*reading*) 'Pour into tin.' Right. (*She does this. Reading*) 'Bake in oven for one hour.' That's all there is to it. Don't know why Mum makes such a fuss about cooking. Anyone can do it. (*She puts the cake in the oven. To audience*) All I had to do then was to sit and wait. I hoped my cake would be ready before they all came back from their walk. I wanted to surprise them. It was while I was sitting there, waiting for it to cook, that I heard the voices. I may have dozed off but I don't think I did.

>   *The distant, disembodied voices of her 'real' family are heard.*

Walt Loooooo . . . cy!

Joy Looooo . . . cy!

Gary Loooo . . . cy!

Lucy (*startled*) What's that?

Walt Loooo . . . cy!

Lucy Who is that? Where are you?

Joy Lucy! Come back to us. Come back.

Lucy Mum? Where are you?

Gary Come back, Lucy. We're sorry.

Lucy Gary? I can hear you but I can't see you . . .

Walt I'm ever so sorry, love. We didn't mean to make you unhappy . . .

Lucy Dad? Why can't I see any of you?

The voices start to recede.

Walt Looo . . . cy!

Joy Loooo . . . cy!

Gary Looooo . . . cy!

Lucy (*calling after them*) Mum? Dad? Gary? Come back! Come back!

Felix, Chuck and Zara appear at the front door, unexpectedly.

Felix We're back.

Chuck It's all right.

Zara Don't worry.

Lucy (*a little disappointed*) Oh.

Felix Well, try and look a bit pleased to see us.

Lucy Yes. Hallo.

Zara The funfair was great. Wasn't it?

Chuck Wonderful.

Felix Terrific.

Lucy Yes, I expect it was.

Zara Sorry you didn't come. You'd have loved it. Wouldn't she?

Chuck She certainly would. You should have come.

Felix You should have done. Pity you didn't.

Lucy (*muttering*) Yes. (*to audience*) I wish they wouldn't go on about it.

Felix And what have you been doing, Lucy? You look as if you've been busy.

Lucy Yes, I was . . . I've made you a surprise . . .

Chuck A surprise!

Zara Wonderful! How exciting!

Lucy Wait! I think it's ready. You have to close your eyes. All of you, close your eyes . . .

Felix We will.

Chuck All right.

Zara OK.

The three close their eyes while Lucy gets her cake from the oven (in a duplicate tin). She picks the tin out with a cloth, takes it to the table and tips the cake out.

Lucy And lo and beho – Oh.

Her 'cake' is a solid uneven misshapen ball. Very heavy and solid. Dotted with prunes, a whole eggshell sticks out of one side, a lemon from the other. From the top, protrudes the black banana. The other three open their eyes.

Oh, dear.

Felix Oh.

Chuck Ah.

Zara Mm.

Chuck What's the point of this game? Are we supposed to try and guess what it is, is that the idea?

Lucy No . . .

Felix I know, it's a piece of sculpture . . .

Lucy No . . .

Chuck No, it's the head of a yeti . . .

Lucy No . . .

Zara A Martian football . . .?

Lucy No, it's a cake . . .

Felix A what?

Lucy It's meant to be a cake.

Chuck A cake?

Zara A cake. Well . . .

Felix Well, a cake. I'd never have guessed that in a hundred years. Well done, Lucy. Good game.

Lucy It didn't come out like it was supposed to.

Chuck Never mind. Perhaps Felix will make us a cake.

Zara Oh, yes. Make us a cake, Dad.

Felix All right. I'll make a cake.

> *Under the next, Felix prepares to make his cake. He finds a covered dish from a cupboard – actually one with a false lid. He lifts the lid off to reveal the empty dish. He sprinkles a little of the remaining flour on the dish with his finger and thumb, the merest drip of milk and sprinkling of sugar. The others watch him as they speak.*

Lucy You can't. There's nothing left to make it with. I've used up all the ingredients.

Felix Oh, never mind about that.

Chuck He doesn't need ingredients.

Zara He's just brilliant. He makes cakes out of thin air.

Lucy Thin air?

Zara Yes.

Lucy Cakes?

Zara Yes.

Lucy (*sceptically*) Oh yes?

Zara Just you watch.

Lucy There's not going to be much of it, is there?

Felix Tell you what, Lucy. I'll have a bet with you. If I fail to make a delicious cake – big enough for all of us – I'll do all the cleaning up for you. That a bargain?

Lucy Right!

Felix But if I do manage to make a cake, you do the clearing up. All right?

Lucy All right.

Zara (*to Lucy*) Better get the broom out . . .

Felix finishes his preparations. He re-covers the dish again.

Felix Right, then.

Lucy Is that it?

Felix That's it.

Lucy How long does it take to cook?

Felix Oh, just a second or two. And – (*He breathes on the dish.*) Just warm it up a little . . .

Lucy (*muttering*) Stupid.

Felix And – *voilà*! (*He lifts the lid to reveal an iced cake.*)

Chuck (*in approval*) Yeah!

Zara Bravo!

Felix Not bad, not bad. Turned out quite well.

Lucy (*stunned*) How did you do that?

Zara I told you. He's really good at cake-making.

Chuck Can we have a piece now?

Felix Of course. Zara, fetch three plates.

Zara Three plates, right.

Lucy (*dismayed*) Three?

Felix None for you till you've cleaned up, Lucy. Remember our bargain?

Lucy (*unhappily*) Oh. Yes.

She starts to tidy up the kitchen, throwing her own cake away and wiping down the table. Zara has found three side plates and a knife for the cake.

Zara Here we are.

Felix Splendid.

Chuck Yummy.

Felix cuts the cake into four.

Felix Zara . . .

Zara Thank you . . .

Felix Chuck . . .

Lucy Save some for me . . .

Felix And this piece for me. (*Felix takes the base with the remaining piece of cake on it, re-covers the dish and crosses to a cupboard.*) Lucy, I'm going to put your piece in the cupboard here. Now, I'm trusting you to keep our bargain. You mustn't eat it until you've finished cleaning the whole house. All right?

Lucy The *whole* house?

Felix The whole house.

Lucy What, *all* of it?

Felix Yes. Including the attic.

Lucy The *attic*?

Felix And the cellar. It's your house, after all.

Chuck You'd better get going, hadn't you?

Zara Or your cake will get stale.

Lucy That isn't fair at all.

Felix No cheating, now.

Chuck No cheating.

Zara No cheating.

> *The three sit to enjoy their cake. Lucy scowls and tidies a little more.*

Lucy I was beginning to get a bit fed up with these three. I mean, this is my house. I'll do what I like in it. (*She crosses to the TV. Sarcastically*) If no one has any objections, I'd like some music whilst I'm working, if you don't mind. Thank you very much. (*She switches on the TV. The test card appears. Loud pop music*) All right? Thank you very much.

Lucy returns to her kitchen – tidying. Felix motions at the set with his finger and thumb. The music changes to something gently classical. Lucy stamps back to the set.

Excuse me. I preferred the music that was on before. (*She snaps the TV set switch back on to the pop music.*) Thank you very much.

She returns to her work. She has scarcely got back to work before Chuck has effected another channel change back to the classical music. Zara laughs.

(*returning, furiously*) Will you kindly leave this television set alone?

Zara Nobody's touched it.

Lucy switches the set back to the pop music, glares at them, and makes to go back to the kitchen area. She has not gone two feet before Zara has again altered the channel back to the classical music.

(*screaming at them*) Look, will you all stop doing this? Will you stop it. STOP IT!

She seizes the TV knob altogether too roughly. It comes away in her hand. She is left holding the knob, which is attached to a long spring and a mass of loose wires. The TV makes a strange warbling sound, gurgles and dies.

(*tearfully*) Now look what you've made me do. Look what you've made me do.

Slight pause. They stare at her.

Felix I think if you'll all excuse me, I'm going to finish my cake upstairs. It's just a bit too noisy down here. (*He rises.*)

Chuck (*rising too*) It certainly is. I'll join you.

Zara (*also rising*) Yes, I will too. Lovely cake, Felix.

Chuck Terrific. Thank you.

Zara leads the way upstairs, followed by Chuck and then Felix. Lucy glares at them.

Lucy Well, I'm going to have my piece now, so there. I'm going to eat my piece. I don't care. (*Lucy marches to the cupboard, opens the door, takes out the dish and sets it on the table. She lifts the lid. Her piece of cake has gone. In its place is half a brick with a candle in it.*) What –?

Felix (*as he goes*) Now, I did warn you, Lucy. I warned you.

He goes upstairs, laughing as he does so. The other two join in the laughter and sing a quick burst of 'Happy Birthday to You'. During the next, Zara goes into Lucy's room and lies on Lucy's bed. Chuck goes into Gary's room and does the same. Felix goes off to Joy's and Walt's room. Lucy clears away the cake dish as she speaks. The kitchen by now is back to normal.

Lucy (*to audience*) I was beginning to get a little bit nervous, I don't mind saying. They seemed to be taking over the house, me, everything. And there didn't seem to be much I could do to stop them.

Distant voices are heard, faintly and briefly.

Joy, Walt and Gary (*in unison*) Looooo . . . cy!

Lucy (*calling softly*) Mum? Dad? Are you there? Gary?
Can you hear me? Mum? (*She listens.*) But I must have
imagined them again. They won't come back – ever.
They've gone. (*slightly tearful*) And I made them go.
I was all alone. How will I ever get them back? What
did Zara say? Anything's possible, if you put your mind
to it. Come back, Mum! Come back Dad! Oh, it's no
use. I sat downstairs for ages. I didn't really want to go
upstairs. Not even to see Zara. Once she'd been my
friend, my very best friend in the world – but not any
more. She'd changed.

The lights have dimmed.

But as it got later and I got tireder and tireder I thought,
'No, why shouldn't I sleep in my own bed?' It was my
bed. This is my house. (*Slight pause. Determinedly*) I'm
going upstairs.

*Lucy goes up to her room. She opens the door to find
Zara lying on her bed.*

Zara (*casually*) Oh, hi!

Lucy What are you doing?

Zara Mmm?

Lucy That's my bed, get off my bed. That's your bed,
there.

Zara No, I think we take it in turns, Lucy, that's only
fair.

Lucy Get off! I want my bed.

Zara That's your bed, there.

Lucy No, it isn't.

Zara (*colder*) It is tonight.

Lucy You get off my bed or I'll . . . or I'll . . .

Zara (*sitting up and staring at her, dangerously*) Or you'll what?

Lucy (*nervously*) You'd better be careful, that's all.

Zara I think you're the one who has to be careful, Lucy. Very, very careful indeed.

Zara smiles nastily. She looks up at Lucy's bookshelf. The books start to jump off the shelf, one by one. Lucy tries to save them. Zara laughs.

Lucy Stop it! Please, please, stop it. Stop it!

The books stop falling. Lucy gathers them up protectively.

Zara Now get into bed like a good little girl.

Lucy thinks about replying but doesn't. She returns the books to the shelf and lies on the folding bed.

Lucy (*as she does so*) Ooh! Ow! This is a terrible bed. I'll never sleep on this.

Zara Ssssh! Go to sleep. (*She gestures and the lights go out in the bedroom.*) Goodnight.

Lucy (*to audience*) It was all very well for her to talk but I couldn't get to –

Zara (*fiercely*) Shhh!

Lucy (*in a whisper*) . . . I couldn't get to sleep at all. The bed had so many – struts and – pointed bits. It was like trying to sleep in the – bottom of a – rowing boat. Ow!

Zara Lucy! You are making a noise. Shut up.

Lucy This is uncomfortable. I can't sleep on this.

Zara Then go and sleep somewhere else.

Lucy Where?

Zara I don't know. On the floor, somewhere.

Lucy I'm not sleeping on the floor. I want my bed back. Give me my bed.

The lights come on. Zara sits up, looking menacing. She extends her arm; seemingly, Lucy is gripped by an invisible force.

Zara I'm warning you, Lucy. One more sound and I'll make sure you never sleep again. I'll glue your eyelids open for ever.

She releases her. Lucy swallows.

Goodnight.

The lights go out again. After a second, Lucy tosses and turns uncomfortably.

Lucy Ooof! Eeee! Aaaa!

Zara (*growling*) Lucy!

Lucy gets up off the bed.

Lucy I'm sorry. I'm sorry. Don't glue my eyelids, please! All right. All right. You win. I'll go and sleep somewhere else, then. But I'm having my bed back tomorrow night, so there.

Zara We'll see.

Lucy (*snatching up her blanket*) We certainly will.

Lucy goes out of her bedroom, closes the door and lies down on the landing.

(*muttering to herself*) I'll sleep here then. Good as anywhere else. It's my house, I don't see why I have to sleep on the landing. Why doesn't somebody else sleep

on the landing? Why has it got to be me? It's not fair.
It's not fair . . .

*During this last, Chuck has got off his bed and opens
the door.*

Chuck I say, do you have to lie out here making all that
din?

Lucy I wasn't making a din.

Chuck You were, you were making the most terrible
racket. Now, if you want to do that, I'd rather you didn't
lie outside my door to do it. Go and lie somewhere else,
all right?

Lucy I can lie where I like, this is my house.

*Chuck reaches out a hand and practically lifts Lucy
off the floor with an invisible force.*

Chuck Now don't get me angry, please. Just remember
how good I am at tidying things away. Be careful, or
I might decide to tidy you away. Permanently. OK?

He 'drops' her back on the floor with a thump.

Lucy (*getting up hurriedly*) Where do I sleep then?

Chuck What about downstairs? Go on. Get off
downstairs.

*Chuck goes back into Gary's room and closes the
door. Lucy goes downstairs, clutching her blanket.*

Lucy (*muttering again*) Don't see why I have to go
downstairs. Why do I have to sleep down here? It's not
fair. It's my house. Why doesn't somebody else sleep
down here, that's what I want to know. (*She sits in the
armchair and wraps the blanket round her.*) Aah! This is
even more uncomfortable than the floor. I can't sleep in
this chair. Mum! Dad! Please come back. I'm sorry.

Please come back. Just put your mind to it, Lucy, just put your mind to it. I won't be rotten about you ever again. I won't even be rotten to Gary. Well, maybe just a bit, but not as much. Mum! Just put my mind to it . . .

Felix has appeared on the stairs.

Felix Lucy!

Lucy (*startled*) Who's that?

Felix Please try not to make quite so much noise. People are trying to sleep.

Lucy So am I. I'm trying to sleep.

Felix Well, do it a little more quietly, like everyone else.

Lucy (*wailing, loudly*) It's all right for them, they've got beds. I haven't even got a bed. Why can't I have a bed!

Zara		(*from upstairs*) Be quiet!
Chuck	} (*together*)	(*from upstairs*) Shut up!
Felix		(*fiercely*) Lucy!

Slight pause. Felix reaches out his arm and seemingly grips Lucy by her nose. Lucy reacts.

Felix (*quietly*) Lucy, you are a noisy, untidy, bad-mannered, dirty, smelly, ignorant, thoroughly unprepossessing lump of a girl.

Lucy (*in pain*) Ow, by dose . . .

Felix I don't want to hear another sound from you, is that clear? Now goodnight.

He releases Lucy. She falls to the ground. Felix goes off to his room.

Lucy (*in a whisper*) I am not smelly. I bath – lots of times. Every other – time I can. I'm not a lump either.

(*slightly louder*) I am not a lump. I'm in the school swimming team. I couldn't swim if I was a lump, could I? (*reflecting*) I was in the school swimming team, anyway. Mum! Oh, Mum! Just put your mind to it . . .

There is a soft knocking at the front door. Lucy stops and listens.

What's that?

The knocking is repeated, softly.

Mum? Is that you? Mum? (*Lucy creeps to the door, still clutching her blanket, and listens.*) Dad? Gary? Who's out there? (*opening the front door cautiously*) Hallo? Anybody here?

She ventures outside a little way, very cautiously. She looks up and down the street. Suddenly the front door closes behind her.

Hey! (*She tries the door but it is locked.*) Oh, no. Now I'm locked out.

Knocking on the door.

Somebody. I say. Hallo! Hallo!

Down the street a dog barks. Then a baby starts crying.

Oh! It's freezing out here. (*shouting*) Help! Help!

From up the street an angry voice shouts: 'Be quiet down there!'

(*indignantly*) Be quiet yourself. I'm locked out! Oh. (*She puts her mouth to the letter box. Shouting through it*) Hallo! Hallo! (*giving up*) Oh, this is hopeless. I must get someone to hear me or I'll freeze to death. Zara! I'll see if I can wake her up. If I throw some small stones at the window, she might hear.

She gathers a handful of gravel and throws it at the window. Sounds as it hits the window. Zara sits up in bed.

(*calling softly, as she throws more gravel*) Zara! Zara!

Zara comes to the window and looks out.

Zara (*crossly*) What is it? What do you want?

Lucy Help me. Can you help me?

Zara Why?

Lucy I'm locked out. Can't you see, I'm locked out?

Zara Yes, I know you are.

Lucy You knew? Then why didn't you –?

Zara Because I locked you out, Lucy.

Lucy (*hurt*) Why? Why did you do that?

Zara Because we don't want you here any more. We don't want you living with us.

Lucy Why not? Zara! You used to be my friend. My best friend. My invisible friend. Why are you doing this? What have I ever done to you?

Zara Felix told you, Lucy. He's already told you. You are noisy. You are untidy. You don't know how to behave properly. You're just not someone that nice people want to live with, that's all. Goodnight. (*She makes to go inside again.*)

Lucy Zara!

Zara What?

Lucy Do you think I'm smelly as well?

Zara Oh yes. Most definitely. Very, very smelly. Goodbye.

Zara withdraws her head through the window. The house is in darkness. Lights only on Lucy in the road. During the next, both Zara and Chuck go off unseen.

Lucy (*wailing*) What am I going to do now? I can't stay out here all night. Where am I going to go?

A car passes. Lucy waves into the headlights but it speeds on past and into the night.

(*as it passes*) Hey! Hey! I say. (*dejected*) Oh. (*a sudden thought*) I know. There might be a window open some-where. If I could climb in without them hearing me . . . I could get a few things together. My money's all in my desk. Yes, that's it. Get some money. I need money. Then maybe I can catch an all-night bus – or even a taxi to Auntie Gertie's. I can't stand Auntie Gertie, her and her big fat budgie, but anything's better than freezing to death out here. (*looking up at the house*) Yes, I think I could, climb up there without them hearing me. It's worth a try. Here goes. Wish me luck. (*to audience*) Ssshhh!

A sequence where Lucy climbs up to an upstairs window. The more tension and thrills the better. At one point at least, she nearly falls. Finally she reaches her bedroom, either via that window or another first-floor window.

(*looking round the room*) Zara's not here. Odd. Now, quickly. Money. (*She rummages in her desk drawer.*) Where is it? I wish I could turn the light on, but I daren't risk it. Have to be so quiet too. Chuck's next door and he hears everything. Ah, here we are. My whole fortune. Seven pounds fifty-two p. Terrific. Go to Hong Kong for that. If I walked. Right. (*looking at the window*) Not going back that way. I'll risk the stairs. (*She tiptoes out of her room and along the landing. She starts to descend the stairs. Whispering*) Shh! Quietly! One of these creaks. I can never remember which one.

Loud creak as she treads on a stair.

Whoops! That's the one. Nearly there . . . Nearly there!

Suddenly, Zara appears at the bottom of the stairs.

Zara Gotcha!

Lucy (*startled*) Ah!

Zara What are you doing in our house?

Lucy Me?

Zara What are you doing here?

Lucy This isn't your house.

Zara Oh, yes, it is.

Lucy This is my house.

Zara Not any more it isn't. You're trespassing. You're breaking and entering. You should be locked up and put in prison . . .

Lucy Nonsense.

Zara You've even stolen money from us, haven't you?

Lucy I have not.

Zara Seven pounds fifty-two pence. Don't lie, I even know how much was there . . .

Lucy So do I. I knew how much was there, too. It's my money.

Zara Prove it, then.

Lucy I don't have to prove it.

Zara Tell me the number of the note. Do you know the number on that five-pound note?

Lucy No, of course I don't.

Zara Ah, but I do, you see. RE59 778752. Did you know that?

Lucy No.

Zara There you are then. That proves it must be mine.

Lucy How do you know that's the number?

Zara Because I'm a very good guesser, that's why. (*starting to advance on her*) Thief! You'll go to prison for years, you will. Do you know the date on the fifty-pence piece, then?

Lucy (*retreating from her up the stairs*) No.

Zara Thief! What's the date, thief?

Lucy (*desperately*) I don't know! I don't know!

> *Chuck appears at the top of the stairs. Felix also appears.*

Chuck Nineteen-eighty.

Lucy (*jumping, as she sees them*) Wah!

Zara She didn't know that.

Felix Because she's a thief.

Chuck Thief!

Zara Thief!

Felix What about the two-p piece? Going to tell us the date of that, are you?

Lucy I don't know. (*Desperately trying to look at the coins in her hand.*) I can't see it, it's too dark.

Felix Come on, it's easy.

Zara Easy!

Felix Easy!

Lucy I don't know.

Felix, Chuck and Zara (*together*) Nineteen eighty-three! Thief!

> *Felix and Chuck begin to advance upon Lucy during the next. Also, under the next, the voices of Walt, Joy and Gary are heard, as before disembodied and distant but steadily increasing in volume.*

Walt, Joy and Gary (*together, a repeated cry*) Lucy! Lucy!

Felix Thief!

Chuck Thief!

Zara Thief!

Lucy I'm not . . .

Felix and Chuck (*together*) Thief! Thief!

Lucy Stop it!

Felix, Chuck and Zara (*together*) Thief! Thief! Thief!

Lucy (*with a great cry, over the increasing hubbub*) STOP IT! STOP IT! STOP IT! ZARA . . .!

> *Lucy, intent on retreating from Felix and Chuck, loses her footing on the stairs and topples down them, mirroring the fall she had earlier in the play. She lands at Zara's feet. A quick blackout. Felix's, Chuck's and Zara's chant stops but the other from the real family continues. Felix and Chuck exit in the blackout. Joy, Walt and Gary enter and gather with Zara around*

129

Lucy. The calls of 'Lucy' are now taken up live. Zara is also calling her name gently. The lights come up on an anxious group, waiting for Lucy to regain consciousness. Zara has changed her appearance just fractionally. Maybe a pair of glasses. She is adjusting the blanket around Lucy. Later, we will see that the whole house is back as it was before Lucy's first fall. Gary's bedroom, for instance, has 'untidied' itself again.

Zara (*gently*) Lucy! Lucy! Come on. Lucy!

Joy Lucy!

Walt Lucy!

Gary Lucy!

Lucy groans.

Zara It's all right. She's coming round.

Joy Is she going to be all right, Doctor?

Zara She may have a slight concussion. But I'm sure she'll be fine. Nothing seems to be broken anyway.

Joy Oh, thank God. Thank God.

Lucy (*drowsily*) Mum! Mum!

Joy I'm here, love, I'm here.

Lucy (*relieved*) Mum?

Joy It's all right, love. Talk to her, Dad, talk to her.

Walt Hallo then, Lucy. It's your dad here speaking, Lucy.

Lucy Dad!

Joy That's your dad speaking, Lucy. And here's Gary. You remember Gary.

Gary Hallo, Lucy.

Lucy Oh, hello, Grisly. (*She tries to sit up.*) If you put your mind to it, you can . . . You can . . .

Zara No, don't sit up. Just lie still.

Lucy (*seeing her for the first time*) Who are . . .? Who are . . .? Zara? What are you doing here? Zara?

Zara That's the name she was saying before.

Lucy Zara?

Zara (*to Joy*) Who's Zara, do you know? Is it a friend of hers?

Joy Oh. That'll be her invisible friend, Doctor.

Walt Like imaginary, in her head, you know.

Zara Oh, yes. I understand. A lot of children have those.

Walt Do they?

Joy Fancy.

Lucy Zara?

Joy I think she thinks you're Zara, Doctor.

Zara Yes. Possibly.

Joy This is Doctor Ziegler, love. From down the road. Your dad went out and telephoned her. You were lying so still, we thought you were dead.

Lucy You're not Zara.

Zara No. I'm a doctor, Lucy. You've had a bit of a fall. You're going to feel a bit bruised and dizzy for a while but you're going to be fine. The ambulance is here. The men are just fetching a stretcher for you. Just try and lie still till it comes.

Lucy (*alarmed*) Ambulance?

Zara I want you to go into hospital overnight, Lucy. Just so they can keep a proper eye on you.

Lucy I don't want to leave here. I can't leave here.

Zara Just overnight.

Lucy I'll get locked out. They'll lock me out again if I go.

Walt We're not going to lock you out, love. This is your home. We won't lock her out, will we?

Gary No, we wouldn't lock her out. Probably.

Joy Gary! (*to Zara*) Does she have to go in, Doctor? I mean, we could keep an eye on her. Couldn't we?

Walt Oh yes.

Gary Yes.

Zara Well, I can't force her to go to hospital, but I really would prefer it.

Joy I thought we'd lost her, you see. I really thought we'd lost her. I mean, if I thought we'd lost her – well, I don't know what I'd have done if I thought we'd lost her . . . (*grasping Lucy emotionally*) Oh, my baby. Oh, my baby.

Lucy Ouch! Mum, steady on!

Zara Careful!

Walt Careful, Joy.

Gary Careful, Mum.

Joy (*weeping now*) Oh, we're so glad you're back with us, love. We're so grateful you were spared. We'll take care of you. I promise you we'll take special care of you.

Lucy (*to audience*) She's a very emotional woman my mother, once she gets going. (*to Joy*) Thanks, Mum. I'm in the school swimming team. Did I tell you?

Joy Oh, that's wonderful. Did you hear that, Walt? She's in the school swimming team. Isn't that wonderful?

Walt Oh, that's wonderful, love. Did you hear that, Gary? She's in the school swimming team. Isn't that wonderful?

Gary Wonderful. Dog-paddle team, is it?

Joy You shut up. Or I'll burn your headphones.

The 'ambulance men' arrive at the front door, with the stretcher. They are, of course, Felix and Chuck, now in uniform.

Felix (*cheerfully*) Here we are, back again. How is she then?

Zara She's regained consciousness. She seems all right.

Chuck (*to Lucy, gently*) Now, love. We're just going to lift you on to this, all right. Don't try and do it yourself, just relax . . .

Lucy (*recognizing him*) Chuck?

Felix Chuck? No, we won't chuck you, love, I promise. We'll just lift you.

Lucy Felix!

Chuck Come on, then. Upsidaisy.

Lucy No, get away. Mum! Don't let them touch me! Don't let them touch me!

Chuck and Felix back off, startled at her vehemence.

Felix It's all right. It's all right. We're not going to hurt you.

Joy It's all right, Lucy.

Walt It's all right.

Chuck (*aside, to Zara*) Concussion, is it?

Zara (*softly, to Chuck*) She's obviously had quite an emotional shock. Maybe it's better if we don't try to move her. Not immediately. She may be better if she stays here in familiar surroundings.

Felix Come on. We're only going to lift you on to this, that's all.

Lucy Get away, Felix, get away from me.

Joy Lucy! It's only the ambulance man . . .

Felix My name's George, love. And him there's Harry. (*to the others*) Felix. She thinks I'm a cat.

Chuck Doctor thinks maybe we should leave her, George.

Felix Leave her?

Zara Might be better. On second thoughts.

Felix Right, you're the doctor. (*He starts to fold up the stretcher again.*)

Zara Sorry to have called you out.

Chuck That's all right. All in a night's work. (*mock sternly to Lucy*) Just you go carefully on those stairs in future. All right? Worried everyone to death, you have.

Lucy (*meekly*) Sorry.

Felix Goodnight, all.

Chuck Goodnight, all.

All Goodnight.

Felix and Chuck leave.

Zara Now, are you strong enough to sit up, Lucy?

Lucy Yes, I think so.

Joy Carefully, love.

Walt Careful.

Gary Carefully.

Zara That's it. Now I want you to take your weight on me and try and walk as far as that chair. Are you ready?

Lucy Yes.

Zara And one, two, three – up . . .

Lucy lifts herself to her feet with Zara's help. Once up, she sways uncertainly.

Lucy Ah!

Zara Help her someone!

They all rush forward together, nearly knocking Lucy over again in their eagerness to help.

Joy Here!

Walt Here!

Gary Here!

Zara Carefully, now. Just one of you will do.

Joy Sorry.

Walt Sorry.

Gary Sorry.

They all step back again. Somehow Zara gets Lucy to the chair unaided, where she sits her down.

Zara There! Well done, Lucy. Clever girl. (*turning*) Now. For the next day or so, she is not to be left alone. Not for a single minute. Is that understood?

Joy Yes.

Walt Yes, Doctor.

Gary Yes.

Zara (*sternly*) I shall pop round to see her regularly but in between times I don't want her moving unnecessarily for any reason at all. She must have complete rest. Complete quiet. First sign of any stress or over-exertion and she goes straight into hospital, no arguments. Understood?

Joy Yes, Doctor.

Walt Yes.

Gary Yes, Doctor.

Zara (*scrawling on her pad*) First thing in the morning, you get these from a chemist. They're to be taken four-hourly over twenty-four hours. Understood?

Joy Yes.

Walt Yes, Doctor.

Gary Yes.

Zara Good. Goodnight, Lucy. Try and get some sleep.

Lucy Can I have my bed back?

Zara Yes, of course you can have your bed.

Lucy Thank you.

Zara I'll look in again in the morning.

Joy Thank you, Doctor.

Walt Thank you.

Gary Thank you, Doctor.

Zara (*as she goes*) Goodnight.

Joy Goodnight.

Walt Goodnight, Doctor.

Gary Goodnight.

Zara goes out through the front door.

Joy Right. Now what can we get you, love? You just say the word. We're all here to look after you. Aren't we?

Walt Yes.

Gary Oh, yes.

Joy What can we get you, love?

Lucy I'm a little bit cold.

Joy Cold, she's cold. Gary!

Gary Yes, Mum.

Joy Fetch your sister another blanket. Quickly.

Gary Yes, Mum.

Joy And a pillow. Fetch her a pillow. Quickly.

Gary Yes, Mum. (*He sprints upstairs.*

Joy Walter. Put the kettle on, make her a hot-water bottle. Quickly.

Walt Right. (*He goes to do this*)

Joy I'll make you some hot chocolate. Would you like that?

Lucy Lovely. Thank you, Mum.

Joy goes to do this.

(*to audience*) The next few days were great. They were all running all over the place for me. Nothing was too much trouble. I lived like a princess. Mum brought me hot meals in bed every two hours. Gary stopped playing his music. And Dad only had the TV programmes on that I wanted to watch. More important still, they all started actually *talking* to me. It was amazing. A miracle.

Simultaneously, Gary arrives with a second blanket and a pillow from upstairs. Walt arrives with a hot-water bottle, Joy brings her a mug of chocolate. They all fuss around her, arranging pillows and tucking in rugs, etc. They all move away from her again under the next, leaving Lucy alone.

Of course, it couldn't last for ever. But it was great while it did. I mean, I'd love to be able to tell you that after that we were all tremendously happy for ever like the end of some romantic movie – you know . . .

A burst of romantic music. Pretty lights.

Walt (*to Joy, with great emotion*) Darling. Oh, my darling.

Joy Oh, my darling darling . . .

Walt Oh, darling . . .

Gary Hallo, darlings . . .

Walt and Joy (*together*) Darling!

They all embrace each other.

Lucy Hallo, darlings. It's me.

All Darling!

The music stops, the lights revert. Everyone resumes their former positions. The family exit, under the next.

Lucy But it wasn't like that. Then things never are, not in real life. But I think we'd all learned something. We did try to get on with each other a bit more. Mum, Dad and Gary – they each made an effort, in their own way. (*She gets up from the chair.*) As for me – well, I made an effort, too. And I steered well clear of any more invisible friends, I can tell you. Enough of that. Still, all in all, life's a great improvement. So if there's anything to be learnt from what occurred, it's this: if you put your mind to it – you can make practically anything happen for you. Anything. Like this. (*She points to the vase, back on the table.*) Everybody – concentrate and when I tell you, think of the word 'move' very hard. Are you ready? After three then. One . . . two . . . three . . . and MOVE . . .

The vase fails to move.

No? Try again. Think harder this time. And . . . one . . . two . . . three . . . and MOVE . . .

Still nothing happens.

No. We can't be thinking hard enough. One last time. We can do it. One . . . two . . . three . . . and MOVE!

This time the vase moves all along the table.

(*triumphantly*) YES!!! Didn't I tell you? Anything's possible! Anything! Bye.

She waves to the audience and goes off.
Blackout.

THIS IS WHERE WE CAME IN

Characters

Fred

The Players
Nell
Bethany
Talitha
Jenkin
Albert

The Storytellers
Great Aunt Repetitus
Uncle Erraticus
Uncle Oblivious

with

Kevin on Keyboards

This Is Where We Came In was first performed at the
Stephen Joseph Theatre in the Round, Scarborough,
on 4 August 1990. The cast was as follows:

Fred Danny McGrath
Nell Kate Rhodes James
Bethany Clare Clifford
Talitha Cecily Hobbs
Jenkin Robert McCulley
Albert Timothy Kightley
Great Aunt Repetitus Antonia Pemberton
Uncle Erraticus Gordon Reid
Uncle Oblivious Guy Nicholls
Kevin on Keyboards John Pattison

Director Alan Ayckbourn
Musical Director John Pattison
Design Juliet Nichols
Lighting Jackie Staines

Part One

Somewhere or other.
   *Fred, a young man, waits by a sign that says, 'STORIES
TOLD HERE TODAY AT 10.30 A.M.' Or whenever. His
clothes, though not of the same period as the other
characters, should seem neutral and timeless.*

Fred (*to no one in particular*) I've been waiting here a
very long time indeed. (*reflecting*) At least, I think I have.

   *Nell, a young woman of about the same age, enters.
She wears simple plain peasant-type, somewhat 'fairy
tale' clothes. She carries a bundle containing her
costumes and props as do all the StoryPlayers.*

Nell (*seeing Fred*) Oh, hallo.

Fred Hallo.

Nell Why, it's – Isn't it –? Yes. Aren't you –?

Fred Fred.

Nell No, you're not. Surely you're . . .?

Fred Fred. My name's Fred.

Nell Well. Alright, then. I'm Nell.

Fred How do you do?

Nell Fred? (*She stares at him.*) Are you *sure* that's your
name?

Fred Don't start that again, please.

Nell Strange. It must have been another story, mustn't it?

Fred What?

Nell Another time. Yes. It was a happy time, I know that.

Fred (*suspecting she is slightly deranged*) Oh, yes? Good.

Nell So anyway what story are you in at the moment, Fred?

Fred Story? I'm not in a story.

Nell Oh, but you must be.

Fred What story?

Nell Whoever's telling it. The story by the person who made you up.

Fred Made me up? What are you talking about?

Nell Invented you. The reason you're here is because someone somewhere is telling a story about you. You knew that, surely?

Fred Someone's telling a story? About me?

Nell Yes. We're all a part of somebody's story.

Fred Really? That's your theory of life, is it?

Nell It's not my theory. How else did we get here? If you don't mind my saying so, you're not very well informed are you, Fred? You don't seem to know much.

Fred (*indignantly*) I know lots of things –

Nell It's not your fault, I'm not blaming you. Please don't get angry. You can't help it, can you? No, I blame the person who's put you in their story. They've just invented a very, very ignorant character, that's all. It's very thoughtless of them.

Fred I'm not ignorant. I know plenty of things, never you mind.

Nell What, for instance? You don't even look as if you know what you're doing here.

Fred I know what I'm doing here.

Nell What?

Fred I'm doing here – waiting – waiting patiently for these stories to start.

Nell Stories?

Fred (*indicating the sign*) These stories, there. Those.

Nell Oh, those stories. I see.

Fred Are they anything to do with you?

Nell Oh, yes.

Fred Well, when are they going to start? I've been waiting here for ages.

Nell How long? Exactly?

Fred (*puzzled*) I don't know. Exactly. Does it matter? Hours and hours. Days and days. I don't know. Years and years. For ever.

Nell For ever after. Fascinating. I'd love to know which one of them it is that's telling you. And why? It's a very weird story, indeed.

Fred Never mind about my story. More to the point, what about your story, then?

Nell My story? Well, my story is your story. It must be. Or yours is mine, I'm not quite sure. I'm not certain yet if I'm appearing in your story or you're appearing in my story. But the fact is we're both in the same story now.

Obviously. And the story is apparently that I should come on here ahead of the others in order to meet you alone. Presumably. Why?

Fred No idea.

Nell Why to meet you? There must have been a reason. We shall see, won't we? This must have an ending or they couldn't have started it. How exciting . . . Which one of them could possibly have told it like this? It must have been one of them . . .

Fred One of who?

Nell Well, either . . .

Before she can answer, though, the other StoryPlayers enter. They are, in no particular order, Bethany, Talitha, Jenkin and Albert. Each is dressed, as Nell is, in the basic costume of the character each most often plays. It would seem thus that Talitha usually plays mothers and countrywomen; Jenkin, princes and noblemen; Bethany, witches and sundry villains; Albert, wood-cutters, shepherds and assorted mechanicals. Like Nell, they each carry their own particular bundle of props and costume bits and pieces.

Nell Ah! Here they are . . .

Bethany Here we are.

Jenkin Here we are.

Talitha Here we are.

Albert Are we? Thank heavens.

Nell Everyone, this is Fred.

Jenkin (*coolly*) Oh, yes?

Talitha Oh, how lovely. Another character.

Bethany (*looking Fred up and down appreciatively*)
Another character. Delicious.

Albert Not before time.

Fred Hallo . . .

Nell Fred, this is Bethany . . .

Bethany Hallo. He seems familiar, doesn't he?

Talitha Yes, he does rather. I'm Talitha, hallo.

Fred (*a bit overwhelmed*) Hallo.

Talitha But I can't think where we could have met him, Bethany, can you?

Bethany No. But he's not someone you'd forget, is he, Talitha?

Talitha Not at all.

Bethany (*to Nell*) What did you say his name was, Nell?

Nell Fred.

Bethany Fred?

Talitha Fred?

Bethany No.

Talitha No.

Albert I knew a Fred once.

Nell Did you?

Albert (*indicating Fred*) But it wasn't this one.

Nell No?

Albert No, this particular Fred died when he was fifty-seven. Eaten by a giant.

Talitha Sad.

Jenkin Personally, I have never known anyone called Fred, alive or dead. But you are familiar . . . (*He walks away and starts to unpack his bundle in a distant corner.*)

Albert (*offering Fred his hand*) I'm Albert.

Fred How do you do?

Albert I'm usually a Woodcutter. Sometimes a Shepherd. Though I also do Little Tailors and I have a good line in loyal four-legged friends.

Fred Really.

Albert I'm flexible. Him over there. That's Jenkin. He does the nobs. Posh folk. Princes and noblemen and Emperors and that.

Fred Oh.

Albert That's why he's like he is. He's done them so often he thinks he's a royal himself.

Fred Good. Well, are we –? Are you all going to tell us a story then. Now you're here?

They all look at him blankly.

Please?

Albert Oh, no.

Bethany No.

Nell No.

Talitha No.

Jenkin Certainly not.

Bethany We're not the Story *Tellers* . . .

Nell We're Story *Players*.

Bethany Quite different.

Talitha Quite, quite different.

Albert Quite, quite, quite different.

Jenkin Utterly different.

Fred Oh. I'm sorry.

Nell You mustn't blame Fred. He doesn't know much. He's terribly, terribly ignorant, actually. It's not his fault. He just doesn't seem to have been given any brains.

Fred (*indignant*) I've got plenty of brains. Don't you worry. Alright then, who is telling these stories, if you're not?

Talitha They are, of course.

Bethany Who else?

Fred Who?

Nell Either Great Aunt Repetitus . . .

Albert If you like hearing things twice . . .

Talitha Or Uncle Erraticus . . .

Albert When he can remember to get it right . . .

Bethany Or Uncle Oblivious . . .

Albert If he can remember anything at all.

Talitha He forgot on the way here.

Bethany That's why we're late.

Nell (*to Fred*) Don't worry they'll be along shortly.

Talitha They're quite elderly.

Bethany *Extremely* elderly.

Jenkin They're all half dead. Well, I'm ready. I don't know about the rest of you.

Talitha Well, now you're going to have to wait, Jenkin, aren't you?

Bethany Because the StoryTellers aren't here, are they?

Jenkin Typical.

Albert We don't even know what story they're going to tell yet, anyway.

Jenkin I can guess what I'll be doing. Something Royal. Bound to be.

Bethany Why don't you make one up yourself, Jenkin?

Talitha Yes, off you go, Jenkin.

Nell Come on, Jenkin . . .

Albert Go for it, Jenkin.

Jenkin If you think I'm doing anything just so you lot can snigger . . . I can wait. Anyway, we haven't even got . . . Where is he?

Bethany (*alarmed*) Oh, no . . .

Albert (*equally so*) Oh!

Nell (*alarmed*) Oh, no . . .

Jenkin (*equally so*) Oh!

Fred What's the matter?

Talitha (*agitatedly*) Oh, oh, oh . . .!

Nell (*to Jenkin*) What have you done with him?

Fred Done with who?

Talitha (*in panic*) Well, it wasn't me, you can't blame me this time.

Bethany (*likewise*) Well, it certainly wasn't me.

Fred What's the problem? Who's gone missing?

Nell Kevin on Keyboards, of course.

Jenkin They'll be livid. Remember how angry they were last time we lost him.

Albert What are we going to do? What do we do now? They'll be here in a minute. What'll they say?

Nell Now, don't panic. Listen everyone. He can't be far away. We just have to look for him that's all. Everyone spread out and look for him.

Albert Spread out!

Talitha Spread out!

Bethany Spread out!

Jenkin Spread out!

They all spread out.

Fred (*still mystified*) I'm still not quite certain who we're looking for?

Nell Kevin on Keyboards. Who do you think? Honestly! Don't you know *anything*?

Albert Kevin on Keyboards! Come on call him, you lot.

Bethany Kevin on Keyboards!

Nell Kevin on Keyboards!

Talitha Kevin on Keyboards!

Jenkin Kevin on Keyboards!

Fred Kevin on Keyboards! (*to Nell*) What does he look like?

Nell Well, obviously he looks exactly like . . .

Bethany Shh!

Talitha Listen!

Albert Shhh!

Jenkin Shh! Everyone.

A distant squeaking noise, approaching.

Nell That's him. (*calling*) Kevin on Keyboards!

All (*shouting*) Kevin on Keyboards!

The roar of an engine, the squeal of tyres and Kevin on Keyboards arrives. He (or it) is a strange assemblage of wires and machinery mounted on an apparently self-propelled trolley. This carries a keyboard with accompanying hardware which controls – or maybe is even controlled by – a battered life-size mechanical figure. From Kevin emanate all the noises and musical sounds that we hear from now on. Overall he looks as if he's seen better days. He screeches to a halt at the edge of the stage.

Fred (*recovering from the sight*) What is it?

Nell Kevin on Keyboards.

Albert This is Kevin. This is his keyboard.

Fred Is he a story teller?

Bethany Not really, no.

Talitha But he does help tell the stories, don't you, Kevin?

Kevin presses a note and a voice from somewhere says
'YOU BET I DO, HONEYCHILD.'

Nell Kevin, this is Fred.

Fred Hallo, Kevin, how do you do?

Kevin presses a key and plays a chorus of 'hallo's'.

Bethany That's just his way of saying hallo.

Talitha I think he likes you.

Fred (*to Kevin*) You know, he seems familiar. I've met him before.

Nell Have you? That's interesting. Where?

Fred I can't think where.

Nell Try and think, Fred. It could be important.

Albert (*to Fred*) Were you ever a woodcutter? Maybe that's where we've met?

Fred No. I don't think so.

Albert A miller? A blacksmith? A magic shoemaker?

Fred No. I'm sure I'd have remembered.

Nell He doesn't remember anything, Albert. Who is he? Why do we all know him?

Talitha Someone should have given him some thoughts, surely?

Bethany And memories . . .

Talitha And ideas.

Bethany Careless. It wouldn't have taken long, would it?

Albert As the Swineherd once said to me . . . Ideas cost nothing.

Nell (*touching Fred lightly on the cheek*) You poor thing. We'll find out about you. Don't worry.

Fred (*frowning, taking her hand*) Nell . . .?

Nell Yes? What is it, Fred?

Fred Nell . . . Oh, Nell . . . (*He looks round the group.*) Bethany . . .?

Bethany Yes . . .

Fred Talitha?

Talitha Yes.

Bethany He's remembering . . .

Nell Sssh!

Fred Albert . . .?

Albert That's me.

Fred Jenkin . . .?

Jenkin Yes.

Nell Who are you? Who are you *really*, Fred

Fred I'm . . . I'm . . . I'm . . . (*He stops.*)

Bethany It's no good, he can't remember . . .

Talitha Maybe there's nothing to remember . . .

Albert Maybe he wanted to forget . . .

Jenkin He's probably nobody anyway . . .

Nell He must be somebody. Everybody's somebody. If only we . . .

    Kevin plays a fanfare.

Albert Here they come!

Bethany Here they come!

Talitha Here they come!

Jenkin Here they come!

Nell They're coming!

> *They all stand back respectfully. Fred follows suit. Almost immediately three incredibly old people arrive. They appear to be supporting each other. They stop in the doorway, exhausted.*
>
> *They are Great Aunt Repetitus who, predictably, tends to repeat herself and tell circular tales. Supporting her (or maybe supported by her) on either side: Uncle Oblivious who falls asleep a lot and forgets where he is in his stories and Uncle Erraticus who stays wide-awake but gets it all wrong. They all stare round them looking rather startled for a second. The Players stand motionless, waiting.*

Fred (*in a normal voice*) Are they the ones who'll be telling –?

Players (*sharply*) Sssssshhh!

Fred (*more quietly, to Nell*) Are these the ones who'll be telling the stories?

Nell (*whispering*) Yes, of course. They're telling this story now.

Fred (*whispering*) Are they?

Nell (*whispering*) Yes.

Fred (*whispering*) I can't hear them.

Bethany (*whispering*) In their heads. It's in their heads.

Talitha (*whispering*) All this is going on in their heads.

Albert (*whispering*) We mustn't disturb their concentration.

Fred (*whispering*) Mustn't we?

Nell (*whispering*) No.

Fred (*whispering*) Why not?

Jenkin (*whispering*) Because we'd all disappear, you fool.

Albert (*whispering*) We're only pigments of their imagination, you see.

Fred (*whispering*) I'm not a pigment.

Bethany (*whispering*) Figments not pigments.

Fred (*whispering*) I'm not a figment, either.

> *The elderly trio suddenly animate again, having rested motionless.*

Great Aunt Repetitus Here we are, then.

Uncle Erraticus Here we are.

Uncle Oblivious Here we are.

Great Aunt Repetitus Time for stories!

Uncle Erraticus Stories!

Uncle Oblivious Stories!

> *A fanfare from Kevin on Keyboards. The three Storytellers hobble to their positions outside the acting area where they seat themselves. The Players gather at the edge of the stage, and wait expectantly. Fred stands with them.*

Albert (*as they do this*) Here we go then.

Fred Great!

Talitha I hope it's one with a pretty princess . . .

Bethany (*sourly*) One that falls asleep for a hundred years if I've anything to do with it . . .

Albert Oh, now you two, don't squabble.

Great Aunt Repetitus And the first story will be told by . . . (*She pauses dramatically.*)

Nell Wait for it!

Great Aunt Repetitus Uncle Erraticus!

A groan from the Players.

Jenkin Oh no, really.

Bethany Oh!

Talitha Oh!

Nell Oh, dear!

Albert (*cheerily*) Never mind. We'll muddle through. We usually do, don't we?

Jenkin Muddle's the word.

Fred Is there a problem?

Nell Uncle Erraticus always gets everything wrong . . .

Fred How do you –?

But before he can ask another question, Kevin on Keyboards plays another fanfare.

Uncle Erraticus This is story of Grethel and Hansel . . .

Nell See what I mean?

Talitha (*disappointed*) Oh . . .

Jenkin Oh, Lord . . . There's nobody royal in this at all.

Bethany There's a great witch . . .

Albert Great story! Great story!

The Players scramble to gather up their props and bits of costume. Albert puts on a hat and holds a wood-cutter's axe. Talitha puts on an apron. Bethany goes and lurks in one corner of the stage and dons her witch's attire. Jenkin and Nell sit on the floor and attempt to look like children.

Fred (*to Nell*) What shall I do?

Nell You'd better sit and watch. They'll call you if they need you, I expect.

Uncle Erraticus Once upon a time, on the edge of a large forest

Kevin plays a few bird noises.

. . . lived a very poor couple – and their two children, Grethel and Hansel . . .

The Players have adopted a family group.

Nell (*softly*) So far so good.

Uncle Erraticus The father was a plumber . . .

Albert A what?

Uncle Erraticus And every day he'd go off to work . . .

Albert Excuse me! I say, excuse me

Uncle Erraticus (*irritably*) What? What is it?

Albert Excuse me, it's just that he's usually a wood-cutter . . .

Uncle Erraticus Who is?

Albert The father – he's generally a woodcutter . . . at least that's –

Uncle Erraticus Well, he's not. He's a plumber.

Great Aunt Repetitus Don't argue, that person . . .

Albert Right. I'm sorry. I'm ever so sorry. Just a second. Plumber. That's a very good idea. (*Albert dives into his bundle and swaps his axe and brings out his plumber's tool bag. He also changes his woodcutter's hat for a plumber's cap.*) Right. Ever so sorry. Carry on.

Uncle Erraticus Are you ready, then?

Albert Yes, yes, sorry.

Uncle Erraticus I've had trouble with you before, haven't I? Now, where was I?

Great Aunt Repetitus . . . lived a very poor couple

Uncle Erraticus Oh, yes . . . and their two children, Grethel and Hansel. The father was a plumber . . .

Uncle Oblivious has fallen asleep and starts snoring.

Great Aunt Repetitus (*sharply*) Stop!

The Players freeze as they always do whenever one of the StoryTellers says this.

Oblivious!

Uncle Oblivious (*wakening*) Uh-huh!

Great Aunt Repetitus Oblivious, you mustn't keep falling asleep like that . . .

Uncle Oblivious I'm very sorry. I'd no idea I had . . .

Great Aunt Repetitus Erraticus is telling a story . . .

Uncle Oblivious Oh, Lord, is he really . . .?

Uncle Erraticus May I be allowed to continue?

Great Aunt Repetitus Yes . . .

Uncle Erraticus Have I everyone's permission to continue . . .?

Uncle Oblivious Yes, get on with it . . .

Uncle Erraticus Thank you . . . On the edge of this forest lived a very poor couple – and their two children, Grethel and Hansel. The father was a plumber . . . And every day he'd go off to work deep in the forest to cut down plum trees.

Albert Oh, flipping heck. (*He goes back to his bundle and swaps the plumber's bag for the axe again. He retains his cap.*)

Uncle Erraticus (*furious at this further interruption*) What are you doing, now?

Albert Just a minute, I'm doing my best. Just make up your mind that's all.

Uncle Erraticus Listen, I've had enough of you . . .

Albert Look, it's not my fault, is it. First I'm a wood-cutter, then I'm a plumber, then I'm a fruit surgeon. I mean, it's not my fault if you keep changing your mind . . .

Uncle Erraticus (*shouting him down*) Not only was the plum tree cutter very poor indeed, but he'd lost his voice as well . . .

Albert mouths on silently, then stops as he realises.

And he lived quietly with his wife, who was the children's stepmother – and was secretly very wicked . . .

Talitha smirks.

. . . but he had two pretty little children to make up for it.

Nell and Jenkin do their best to oblige.

But as time went by, they became poorer and poorer and the food grew less and less. And the stepmother said to the husband . . .

Talitha Husband, how can we possibly feed our poor children when we have nothing left for ourselves?

Uncle Erraticus And the husband said –

Albert opens and shuts his mouth.

– nothing at all. And the wicked stepmother said:

Talitha I'll tell you what, I've got one hell of an idea. Tomorrow morning take the children out early into the woods and leave them in the thickest part of the forest. They're so stupid they'll never find their way back so we shall be rid of them. More food for us.

Uncle Erraticus And their father, who was appalled by this, said:

Albert opens his mouth.

– nothing very much. But little did the couple know that upstairs their little boy who was called Grethel –

Jenkin Grethel . . .?

Uncle Erraticus – Grethel had his ear to the floorboards and could hear every word that his parents said. He told his sister Hansel, who wept bitterly.

Nell weeps bitterly.

Jenkin (*in an undertone*) I thought I was Hansel . . .

Nell (*similarly*) Don't argue, keep going . . .

Jenkin I'm not strolling around with a name like Grethel . . .

Uncle Erraticus What's happening there?

Nell (*swiftly*) Nothing.

Jenkin (*equally so*) Nothing.

Uncle Erraticus And Grethel comforted his sister
Hansel . . .

Fred Excuse me. I think you've got them the wrong
way round . . .

Uncle Erraticus (*sharply*) What?

Great Aunt Repetitus Stop!

The Players freeze.

Fred It's just their names, I think you've . . .

Uncle Erraticus (*very sharply*) WHAT?

Fred Sorry. Carry on.

Uncle Erraticus And Grethel had a bright idea and he
went out into the moonlit garden –

Kevin produces the sound of an owl.

– and he gathered up from the ground a handful of
bright, shiny saucepan lids . . .

Jenkin (*who is holding a handful of white pebbles*)
Saucepan lids. I should have guessed . . . Hang on . . .

Uncle Erraticus What are you doing now?

Jenkin (*rummaging in his bag*) Just a second.

Uncle Erraticus Everyone's being extremely difficult
today . . .

Jenkin now holds a pile of saucepan lids.

Jenkin Sorry to keep you. Here we are.

Uncle Erraticus (*glaring at Jenkin*) Unfortunately as Grethel was gathering them he banged his leg rather hard . . .

> *Kevin makes a leg banging noise. Jenkin yells and drops the lids with clatter.*

And poor Grethel limped for weeks afterwards. Indeed we shall find out later in the story whether his leg ever got better at all . . .

> *Jenkin gathers up the lids and limps back to his place, scowling.*

Fred Excuse me . . .

Uncle Erraticus (*sharply*) What?

Great Aunt Repetitus Stop!

> *The Players freeze.*

Fred I don't think they were saucepan lids –

Uncle Erraticus (*sharper still*) What?

Fred They were stones. Hansel – I mean – Grethel – he picked up small white stones . . .

Uncle Erraticus Who's telling this story –?

Fred I –

Uncle Erraticus Me or you?

Fred You.

Uncle Erraticus Then shut up!

Fred Right.

Uncle Oblivious Who is that chap?

Great Aunt Repetitus No idea. He seems familiar somehow . . .

Nell (*to Fred in a whisper*) I shouldn't argue. It's dangerous to argue. They can do terrible things . . .

Jenkin (*rubbing his leg*) They certainly can . . .

Uncle Erraticus And morning came . . .

Kevin plays the dawn chorus.

And the wicked stepmother gave each of the children some bread.

Talitha Much against her better judgement . . .

Uncle Erraticus And said goodbye to them for the last time. And the father with heavy heart led the two children deep into the forest. But little did he know that even as they went, every few yards Grethel would cleverly contrive to drop a saucepan lid –

Jenkin does so with a clatter.

Jenkin This isn't half as good with saucepan lids . . .

Uncle Erraticus (*viciously*) Even though the brave little chap's leg still hurt him a good deal . . .

Jenkin (*with renewed limping*) Ow!

Uncle Erraticus When they reached the middle of the forest, Grethel and Hansel gathered up some wood and their father lit them a fire –

Kevin makes a fire crackling noise.

– and made them sit there whilst he went off further into the wood, pretending to look for plum trees. But secretly, he crept home.

Albert returns to Talitha, leaving Jenkin and Nell sitting on the ground.

And soon it got dark –

Kevin's owl noise again.

And the fire died down –

Kevin's fire noise stops abruptly.

And the two children huddled together waiting for the moon to rise – which it soon did –

Kevin makes a moon rising noise.

And when this happened, Grethel took his sister's hand and following the trail of saucepan lids that were gleaming so brightly in the moonlight – they made their way home.

Nell and Jenkin gather up the lids as they retrace their steps.

And their father, who had never thought to see the children again, was overjoyed to see them.

Albert opens and shuts his mouth.

Even though he couldn't say it in so many words. Whilst their stepmother was secretly very angry that they'd found their way home.

Talitha (*sourly*) Oh goody, it's you two.

Uncle Oblivious A few days later they were again so short of food and the wicked stepmother said to the plumber:

Talitha We've hardly any food left at all. You must take those kids back into the woods. And this time lose them properly.

Albert opens and shuts his mouth.

Uncle Erraticus And their father, who was an extremely weak character, said nothing though he was very unhappy about all this. And again Grethel was listening at the floorboards upstairs and heard every word their parents said. And he told Hansel who wept bitterly.

Nell weeps bitterly.

But Grethel said to her:

Jenkin Fear not, little sister. We can pull the old saucepan lid trick again . . .

Uncle Erraticus And he went to creep out into the garden but this time their stepmother had been too clever and had locked the door so he couldn't get out.

Kevin makes the sound of a rattling lock as Jenkin tries the door. Talitha laughs.

Jenkin (*as he does so, to himself*) Oh, help.

Uncle Erraticus And when the dawn came –

Kevin repeats the dawn chorus again.

– the stepmother gave the children each a piece of bread . . .

Talitha gives them each a tiny piece of bread.

Talitha Very much against her better judgement . . .

Uncle Erraticus . . . and their father with heavy heart led the children back deeper still into the forest. And this time Grethel, having no saucepan lids, crumbled his piece of bread and left behind a trail of breadcrumbs so that he and Hansel might later find their way home. And when they reached the very thickest part of the wood, Grethel and Hansel again gathered sticks and their father lit them a fire –

Kevin repeats the fire crackling sound.

And again he made them sit there whilst he went further into the forest to search for plum trees.

Albert leaves Nell and Jenkin as before.

And soon it grew dark

Kevin makes his own noise.

– and their fire died down –

Kevin stops the crackling sound.

– and the two children waited for the moon to rise so that they could see the trail of bread crumbs and find their way home. And soon the moon rose –

Kevin's moon rising noise.

But when the children went to search for the bread crumbs, they found that the birds had eaten them all. They were well and truly lost. Hansel wept bitterly . . .

Nell weeps bitterly.

Jenkin Hallo, she's off again . . .

Uncle Erraticus And Grethel – despite the fact that his poor little leg still hurt like mad –

Jenkin Ow! Sorry.

Uncle Erraticus Comforted her.

Jenkin (*doing so*) There, there, Hansel old thing.

Uncle Erraticus And they curled up under a pile of leaves and waited till the dawn came . . .

Kevin brings up the dawn chorus.

And when they awoke they started to walk again but they soon realised they were hopelessly lost. And then suddenly they came to a clearing and there stood a little cottage all on its own, looking so cosy and inviting. And the children drew closer and saw that the cottage was made not from bricks or stones but from delicious things to eat. And the hungry children rushed forward . . .

Jenkin Come on, little sister –

Uncle Erraticus Cried Grethel –

Jenkin You tuck in to the roof. I'll start on the walls.

Nell Yum-yum . . .

Uncle Erraticus And indeed the house was delicious. The roof was made of snakes and the walls were made of fingers –

Nell (*in mid mouthful*) Yerrk!

Jenkin (*likewise*) Uugg!

Uncle Erraticus What's the matter now?

Fred Excuse me . . . I say . . .

Uncle Erraticus What?

Great Aunt Repetitus Stop!

The Players freeze.

Fred I'm sorry to interrupt again – but I think the roof was made of cakes – not snakes . . .

Uncle Erraticus What? What?

Fred And the walls were ginger not fingers . . .

Uncle Erraticus Oh, it's you again, is it?

Fred Sorry.

Uncle Erraticus I won't tell you again.

Uncle Oblivious Who is that chap? Do we know him?

Great Aunt Repetitus I've no idea at all.

Uncle Erraticus And as they were both nibbling they heard a gentle voice from within calling:

Bethany
    Nibbling, nibbling like a mouse,
    Who's nibbling at my little house?

Uncle Erraticus And suddenly the door opened and a kindly old woman appeared and startled them –

Nell Oh!

Jenkin Ah!

Bethany Don't be frightened, children. Come inside. I mean you no harm.

Uncle Erraticus And she led them inside and gave them a huge meal and later on, when it was dark –

Kevin's owl sound again.

– she took them both upstairs to two little white beds. And they slept and slept. And as they slept the kindly old woman crept upstairs to look at them and laughed to herself. For she was really not a kindly old woman at all but a wicked witch. And when children strayed into her part of the wood she lured them into her cottage and then fattened them up to eat. For she liked eating children best of all . . .

Bethany cackles.

And she seized Grethel and dragged him downstairs and locked him in a cupboard with bars on the door. And then she woke Hansel . . .

Bethany Come on, you lazy slut, fetch some water and cook something nice for your brother. I'm fattening him up to eat.

Uncle Erraticus Hansel began to cry bitterly . . .

Nell cries bitterly.

Bethany And you can cut that out for starters.

Uncle Erraticus So whilst Hansel was fed on bones and leftovers, Grethel was fed all the best food in the house. And every day, whilst little Hansel hurried about, the witch would say:

Bethany Grethel, put your finger out for me to feel how fat you are.

Uncle Erraticus And Hansel instead of sticking out his finger would stick out a phone instead –

Jenkin (*who is already holding out a chicken bone*) A what?

Uncle Erraticus – a phone instead –

Jenkin Yes, that's what I thought you said. Just a minute. (*He goes to his bag and finds an old fashioned candlestick phone.*)

Fred Excuse me –

Great Aunt Repetitus Stop!

   The Players freeze. Uncle Erraticus looks at Fred.
Nothing.

Uncle Erraticus And Hansel instead of sticking out his finger would stick out a telephone instead –

   Kevin gives a quick phone ring.

Jenkin (*offering the phone*) I think it's for you

Uncle Erraticus (*glaring*) And even as Grethel was doing this, the poor little fellow banged his other leg on the bars.

Jenkin Ow!

Uncle Erraticus And the witch, whose eyes were dim, could not see that it wasn't his finger and was amazed that Grethel would not get fat . . .

Fred I'm not surprised if she's feeding him telephones . . .

Uncle Erraticus And how little Hansel wept . . .

Nell weeps.

Night and day

Kevin gives a very swift owl followed by a dawn chorus.

Day and night

Kevin repeats the same in reverse.

Until one day the wicked old witch said to Hansel:

Bethany Shut up! Alright, child, today is baking day. I can't put up with that din a moment longer. I've already heated the oven. Creep inside and tell me if it's warm enough.

Uncle Erraticus She intended of course, as soon as Hansel was inside, to shut the oven door and roast her. But Hansel pretended not to understand what the witch meant and said:

Nell I don't know how to get in. How do I get in?

Bethany You stupid goose!

Uncle Erraticus Said the witch.

Bethany It's perfectly simple. You get in like this. See?

Uncle Erraticus And as soon as the witch was half way into the oven, Hansel gave her a mighty push –

Bethany cries out.

Slammed the oven door.

Sound from Kevin.

And switched it up to gas Mark 7. Then Hansel ran and released her brother, crying:

Nell Grethel, we are saved, saved. The old witch is dead.

Uncle Erraticus And Grethel said:

Jenkin Good!

Uncle Erraticus And they found that the witch's house was filled with jewels and precious stones that she had stolen during her wicked life. And they loaded themselves up with these. And Grethel saw it was time to go home and said to his sister:

Jenkin It's time to go home.

Uncle Erraticus And they picked their way back through the enchanted wood. And because it was no longer enchanted it was much easier to find the path. Until that is they came to a stream which looked too deep to cross.

Jenkin Oh!

Nell Oh!

Jenkin Looks too deep to cross.

Uncle Erraticus But fortunately there was a chicken swimming past –

Kevin makes a splash/chicken noise.

Fred It was a duck . . .

Uncle Erraticus What?

Great Aunt Repetitus Stop!

The Players freeze.

Fred It was a duck not a chicken . . .

Uncle Erraticus Now listen. I don't know who you are but I've had enough from you. . . .

Fred Sorry.

Uncle Oblivious Who is that chap?

Great Aunt Repetitus I keep telling you, I've no idea. And yet . . .

Uncle Oblivious Any more arguments?

Nell No . . .

Jenkin No, no. Looks exactly like a chicken to me . . .

Nell Oh, look –

Uncle Erraticus Cried Hansel –

Nell Maybe that chicken will give us a ride on its back.

Uncle Erraticus And the chicken said –

Chicken noise from Kevin.

And the children cried:

Nell and Jenkin (*together*) Oh, thank you, thank you, chicken!

Uncle Erraticus And they clambered, each in turn, on the bird's back and she swam with them to the other side of the stream.

Nell and Jenkin both do this with appropriate noises from Kevin.

And once safely across they were able to see their own little cottage and they both scampered home and through the gate. And there to welcome them, who else but:

Albert stands beaming at them, arms extended.
Talitha stands beside them looking appalled.

– their dear father who had wept bitterly from the day he had left them. As for their wicked stepmother, as soon as she saw them both, she choked on the bread she was eating and dropped dead on the spot . . .

Talitha gurgles and falls on the floor.

– and good riddance to bad rubbish. So the children went inside with their father and showed him all the jewels and precious stones they had brought back with them. And the old plumber cried:

Albert Kids, we're rich . . .

Uncle Erraticus And although money isn't everything, it's a lot better than nothing. And although it didn't make them happy all by itself, it certainly helped. It certainly helped Grethel and Hansel and their father, the plumber, to live happily ever after.

A final chord from Kevin. Fred applauds.

Great Aunt Repetitus And now – a story from Uncle Oblivious . . .

Another chord from Kevin. They all look towards Uncle Oblivious who seems unaware of them, lost in his own thoughts.

Oblivious . . .

Uncle Oblivious Mmmm?

Great Aunt Repetitus It's your turn . . .

Uncle Oblivious My turn for what?

Great Aunt Repetitus Your turn to tell a story

Uncle Oblivious Oh, yes. Right. Here we go.

Kevin repeats his chord.

Yes . . .

Nell (*softly, to Fred*) This could take some time.

Jenkin (*softly*) This could take all night . . .

Fred (*softly*) Why?

Nell (*softly*) He sometimes can't remember . . .

Bethany (*softly*) He can never remember a thing . . .

Talitha (*softly*) He's hopeless . . .

Uncle Oblivious Here we go then . . .

Kevin plays his chord.

This one's called the . . . oh, dammit . . . er – whatjama-callit . . . thingy . . . the thing thingy . . . what's it called now?

Uncle Erraticus Oh, get on with it, man . . .

Uncle Oblivious I'm going to . . . just a tick. Oh, what are they called? Hopping things . . .?

Uncle Erraticus Kangaroos?

Uncle Oblivious Certainly not. Kangaroos? What a stupid suggestion.

Great Aunt Repetitus Oh, do get on with it, Oblivious . . .

Uncle Oblivious I'm trying to. People keep interrupting me . . . er . . . Prince. Prince. That's the word.

Great Aunt Repetitus Prince? The Prince who Hopped?

Uncle Oblivious No, no . . .

Uncle Erraticus The Hopping Prince?

Uncle Oblivious No, no, no. The something Prince. The something-that-hops Prince.

Great Aunt Repetitus Grasshopper?

Uncle Oblivious The Grasshopper Prince? No, no, no . . . What else hops?

Uncle Erraticus A three-legged dog?

Uncle Oblivious The Three-Legged Dog Prince? No, no, no . . .

Fred Frog.

Uncle Oblivious What? No, I've just said not dog. Didn't you hear me?

Fred No, Frog.

Uncle Oblivious Frog?

Fred Prince. The Frog Prince.

Uncle Oblivious The Frog Prince. Exactly. What about it?

Fred Well, was that the story you wanted to tell?

Uncle Oblivious Well, of course it was if you'll only let me get on with it. (*to the others*) Who is he?

Uncle Erraticus No idea.

Great Aunt Repetitus (*looking keenly at Fred*) I've seen you before, haven't it?

Fred No, I don't think so . . .

Uncle Oblivious The Frog Prince. In olden times when wishes actually meant something, unlike today when you can wish for things till the cows come home and you might just as well whistle for all the good it'll do you . . . there lived a king –

Jenkin steps forward. He has donned a crown.

Jenkin Hallo, there. This is a better part.

Uncle Oblivious And this particular king had an especially fine line in daughters.

Talitha and Bethany step forward. They have also donned crowns.

Jenkin Hallo, kids.

Talitha and Bethany (*in chorus*) Hallo, Daddy.

Uncle Oblivious But it has to be said that it was the youngest of them that was the real cracker –

Nell steps forward.

Jenkin Wothcha, nipper.

Nell Hi, Daddy.

Uncle Oblivious Now, near the King's Palace there was a large forest . . .

Kevin produces more birdsong.

There always is. And in this forest, under an old lime tree, was a deep well . . .

Kevin makes a water-plopping sound.

Now, when it was a very hot day, this youngest Princess used to go and sit by this cool well. And when she got cheesed off with doing that she used to play with this golden ball she'd had given to her. Chucking it in the air and generally giving it a few brisk overs of right arm spin.

Nell has produced the golden ball and is leaping about with it.

Now, on this particular afternoon, she was prancing about as usual – the way girls do when they think no one's watching them – and, of course, the inevitable happened, she dropped one slightly short of a length and

before you could say Ray Illingworth the ball had gone
and dropped straight down the – oh . . . (*He breaks off
abruptly. The action freezes. A pause.*)

Fred (*to Talitha, in a whisper*) What's happening?

Talitha (*whispering*) He's forgotten the next word. We
can't go on till he remembers it.

Fred How long's he going to be?

Bethany No idea. Hours, sometimes. He usually falls
asleep.

Fred He can't fall asleep now. I want my dinner. (*loudly*)
Down the well.

Uncle Oblivious Eh?

Great Aunt Repetitus Stop!

Fred Well.

Uncle Oblivious Well, what?

Fred Down the well. The ball. Down the well. Fell.

Uncle Oblivious Down the well, yes. Who's telling this
story? Who is he?

Great Aunt Repetitus We've definitely seen him before,
you know . . .

Uncle Erraticus Yes, I think we have seen him before . . .

Uncle Oblivious If I may continue. And before you
could say Ray Illingworth the ball had gone and dropped
straight down the well.

A splash from Kevin.

Nell Oh, botheration!

Uncle Oblivious Cried the Princess. And she began to
weep bitterly.

Nell weeps bitterly.

And after a bit, out of the well pops this frog.

Albert emerges in frog headgear.

Albert Hallo. What's all this ghastly racket about?

Uncle Oblivious Asked the frog.

Nell I've lost my golden ball down the well –

Uncle Oblivious Wept the Princess.

Albert Well, you ought to learn to pitch 'em up, then.

Uncle Oblivious Cried the frog. Who, it has to be said, could turn his arm over himself, if asked to do so . . .

Albert Line and length, girl. Line and length. Did your mother teach you nothing? Tell you what. If I dive in and fetch it for you, what'll you give me?

Nell Oh, anything – practically anything.

Uncle Oblivious Wept the Princess.

Nell My pearls and diamonds. Even the golden – golden –

Uncle Oblivious – golden . . . thingy –

Nell – golden . . . thingy – on my head.

Uncle Oblivious And the frog said:

Albert I care not for your pearls or your diamonds. Or for the golden thingy on your head. But if you'll be fond of me, let me be your best friend, sit by you at table, eat out of your plate, drink out of your cup and doss down beside you in your little milk-white bed, if you promise me this, I'll fetch your ball for you.

Uncle Oblivious And the princess replied:

Nell Oh, yes. Anything, anything you like, if you'll only rescue my ball.

Uncle Oblivious But secretly she thought:

Nell Fat chance, froggy face.

Uncle Oblivious And the frog, as soon as he had her promise, dived beneath the water and returned with her ball.

Nell Thanks! (*She takes the ball and moves off.*)

Albert Wait, wait! What about me? Take me with you.

Nell Where?

Albert Home. With you. You promised.

Nell You're joking. I'm not going home with a frog. What would Daddy say? He'd never forgive me.

Uncle Oblivious And she tossed her pretty head and off she ran –

Nell does this.

Leaving one very disgruntled frog.

Albert Well, really. Some people

Uncle Oblivious Now, that same evening, the princess was sitting having dinner with her father, the king –

Kevin plays some Royal Dinner Music. Nell and Jenkin sit at a table.

– when there was this knock at the door.

Jenkin Who on earth can that be? It's quarter past seven.

Uncle Oblivious Said the king.

Talitha (*now a maid*) Excuse me, Your Majesty, Sir, Your Royal Highness, Madam, but there's a frog at the door to see you, Madam, Your Royal Highness.

Nell Oh, no.

Jenkin Who is it? A frog did you say, Potter?

Talitha Yes, Your Royal Majesty.

Jenkin Well, tell him to go away. The princess is having her pilchards . . .

Nell Yes, tell him to go away, Petherbridge.

Talitha He's very insistent, Your Royal Highness, Madam. He's hopping up and down something terrible.

Jenkin Why should he be doing this, daughter? Any idea? Do you owe him money?

Nell No, no. I made him this silly promise. It was nothing.

Jenkin What promise?

Uncle Oblivious And the princess told her father all about the promise she had made to the frog.

Jenkin Well, in that case we'd better haul him in then.

Uncle Oblivious Said the king.

Nell Oh, daddy, no . . .

Jenkin A promise is a promise, isn't it? Eh? Pour him in, Peters . . .

Talitha Yes sir, Your Majesty, Sir.

Nell Oh, Daddy . . .

Jenkin No, fair's fair . . .

Nell What are we going to have to talk about?

Talitha The frog, Madam.

Albert 'Evening.

Jenkin Fetch the frog a whatsit, Perkins.

Albert Much obliged.

Jenkin And put the whatsit – chair – that's the word – next to Her Royal Highness, Povey.

Talitha Yes, Your Highness Majesty, Sir.

Nell Oh, Daddy, no, no, no!

Talitha Pardon me, Your Highness Royal, Madam.

Albert Thanks very much. Actually, I think I'll be better off on the table, if it's all the same. Easier to share your plate from here. (*He climbs on the table.*)

Nell What are you doing? Get your feet out of my pilchards.

Albert Pilchards. Oh, grand.

Uncle Oblivious Said the frog.

Albert I wonder, would you mind pushing your golden plate a bit closer. So's we can share them.

Nell Certainly not.

Jenkin Do as he says, girl. A promise is a promise.

Uncle Oblivious And so the princess finished up sharing her dinner with the frog. Though it has to be said she didn't eat much of it herself. Whereas the frog really tucked in. Not only polished off her pilchards but drank most of her Tizer.

Albert Well, that was champion. Thanks very much. (*belches*) Well, I don't know about you, lass, but I think I could do with a lie down and a spot of kip. Coming up, are you?

Nell Certainly not!

Jenkin Do as he tells you, girl.

Nell Daddy, no, no, no, no, no . . .

Jenkin A promise is a promise.

Nell But I'm not getting into bed with a frog. I couldn't.

Jenkin Well, you should have thought about that before you made these promises . . .

Nell But I'd lost my ball . . .

Jenkin Well, you shouldn't have done, should you? If you'd learnt to pitch it up like I taught you –

Albert Wrong line. She was bowling a wrong line, too.

Jenkin Well, there's something basically wrong with her run up, there always has been. She's running wide of the crease, you see. If she only ran closer to the stumps . . .

Albert She'd have a better line . . .

Jenkin She would. Now her older sister, my middle one, Enid, she's a promising little quickie –

Albert Is she? Is she, now?

Jenkin Just short of a length, bangs them in. Easy run up, nice action, fast medium . . .

Talitha Great ground fielder, too . . .

Nell Alright, alright! Let's go to bed, then. If you're going to talk cricket all night . . .

Albert Thanks very much. Going to give us a carry?

Nell No, I'm damn well not. You can hop.

Jenkin Porterhouse, carry the frog upstairs.

Talitha Yes Sir, Your Royal Majestic Highness, Sir . . .

Jenkin Goodnight, daughter . . .

Nell (*kissing him*) Goodnight, Daddy. (*to Albert*) Come on. I hope she drops you downstairs.

Uncle Oblivious And so very reluctantly the princess went upstairs to her pretty little milk-white bed – followed by the maid with the frog. And the Princess sat in front of her mirror and brushed her long flowing hair with her hatstand . . .

Nell Hatstand? (*She shrugs.*) Put him down over there, Pattison. He can sleep over there. In the corner.

Albert In the corner? What about the bed?

Nell Certainly not. That is my bed. You're not sleeping in that. Not between my pretty little milk-white sheets, you're not.

Albert I'm not sleeping in the corner. Why don't you sleep in the corner?

Nell Because. That is my bed, frog!

Albert You promised I could have the bed.

Nell Well, you can't. Now stay over there or I'll throw my hatstand at you. You may go, Pullborough.

Talitha withdraws.

Uncle Oblivious And without another word the princess climbed into bed, whilst the frog sat in the corner watching her. And after a little time, she fell asleep. And the full whatsisname rose in the sky –

Kevin makes an owl noise.

And the frog crept over and sat on the side of her bed.

Albert Hallo, then.

Nell (*waking*) Wah!

Albert It's alright. It's only me. And I've hidden your hatstand, so don't try it.

Nell I shall scream, I warn you.

Albert Oh, come on. Give us a kiss.

Nell Certainly not.

Albert Come on.

Nell I could catch all sort of – frog things.

Albert You promised.

Nell Didn't.

Albert Did. I'll tell your Dad. (*Pause.*) A promise is a promise, remember.

Nell You bully! You great – bullying – bullfrog . . .!

Uncle Oblivious And very, very, very reluctantly indeed she leant forward and – kissed the frog . . .

Nell (*as she does so*) Yeurrk!

Uncle Oblivious But even as they touched . . .

 Dramatic chord from Kevin.

There was a puff of wool, a great rushing of thing and a flash of thunder which hurled them both apart – and lo and behold when the Princess opened her eyes the frog had been transformed into a – a handsome . . . oh, dammit what's the word – oh – what's the matter with me these days? – er . . . an incredibly handsome . . .

Fred (*standing up*) Prince.

Uncle Oblivious Prince. Exactly. Well done, that man. And the princess, as soon as she saw the young prince, fell immediately in love with him . . .

Nell (*falling immediately in love*) Oh!

Fred Thank you. I am Prince Florizel and you have saved me from a witch's curse. Only you could do this.

Nell Oh.

Uncle Oblivious (*a bit startled*) Just a minute, who are you?

Fred I am yours forever.

Nell And I am yours . . .

> *Nell and Fred stand gazing into each other's eyes adoringly.*

Uncle Oblivious And they both lived happ – Who is that chap? He wasn't supposed to be in this story . . .

Great Aunt Repetitus Stop! Oh, now I know who that is . . .

Uncle Erraticus So do I, now

Great Aunt Repetitus It's him . . .

Uncle Erraticus It's him . . .

Uncle Oblivious Good Lord. *Him* . . .

Talitha Who is he?

Great Aunt Repetitus (*sharply*) Mind your own business.

Uncle Oblivious What are we going to do?

Great Aunt Repetitus It's a bit late to ask that now, isn't it?

Uncle Oblivious But he can't stay, can he? He's dangerous.

Uncle Erraticus It's your fault, Oblivious, for putting him in your stupid story . . .

Uncle Oblivious It wasn't my fault. I forgot.

Uncle Erraticus Forgot? He'll be in all the stories now, don't you see? We'll never get him out again, you idiot . . .

Uncle Oblivious Don't call me an idiot, how was I to know

Uncle Erraticus Idiot! Idiot! You'll forget your head . . .

Great Aunt Repetitus Stop that at once! Stop it! STOP IT! (*Silence.*) That's better. What behaviour. Men of your age.

Uncle Oblivious But what are we going to do, Great Aunt?

Great Aunt Repetitus It's very simple, Oblivious. We don't panic. That's the first thing. All we need do – is –

She looks up and is aware that the Players are all listening.

Just a moment. (*narrating*) And all around the palace both inside and out a strange sleep descended on everyone, man, woman and child . . .

All the Players fall asleep where they stand.

That's better. Now they can't hear us. It's very simple. All we need do – all I need to do – is to tell a story with the boy in it – in which he'll – disappear . . .

Uncle Oblivious Disappear?

Great Aunt Repetitus For ever.

Uncle Erraticus Can you make that happen?

Great Aunt Repetitus Of course I can. I promise you – by the time I've finished my story – he'll never be seen again. Ever.

Uncle Oblivious It hope it works. If he starts his . . .

Great Aunt Repetitus It'll work . . .

Uncle Oblivious If he starts his . . .

Great Aunt Repetitus (*sharp*) I said it'll work. That's enough. Leave it to me. (*narrating*) And the following morning –

Kevin plays some birdsong.

– thank you, Kevin – they all awoke from a deep refreshing sleep . . . remembering nothing of what they had heard before they slept . . .

The StoryPlayers all awake.

Nell Fred . . .

Fred Hallo, I . . .

Nell What are you doing there?

Jenkin Yes, what exactly are you doing there? Get off at once.

Talitha Off . . .

Bethany Get off!

Nell You're not supposed to be here, Fred, if you're not in the story . . .

Fred Sorry.

Great Aunt Repetitus Oh, but he is, child. He is in the story, you see.

Nell Fred? Fred is in the story?

Great Aunt Repetitus That's not his name, either. He's a StoryPlayer like you and his real name is Flavius.

Nell Flavius? Flavius!

The other Players look at her sharply.

Great Aunt Repetitus Come here, child. What do you know about Flavius?

Nell Nothing, Great Aunt.

Uncle Erraticus Have you ever heard that name before?

Nell No.

Uncle Oblivious You don't remember it from anywhere?

Nell No. I've – never heard it

Great Aunt Repetitus Are you sure?

Nell Yes, Great Aunt.

Great Aunt Repetitus Have any of you ever heard the name Flavius before?

All the Players hastily deny it.

(*looking at them suspiciously*) No. I hope not. We'll pause there for a little while before the next story which will be mine. And since Flavius is our newest recruit, it's a story that will concern him a good deal. I look forward to that. Come.

She rises and reaches out her hands. Erraticus and Oblivious move to her. Together they move out.

(*as this happens*) In the meantime, all of you, I should rest. It's going to be a very busy story for you all. Plenty of excitement, I can promise you that. (*She laughs to herself.*)

The three go off, laughing. The others look at Fred.

Nell I can't believe it. You're really –?

Bethany Shhh!

Talitha Don't even say the name.

Bethany Don't speak it.

Jenkin We're not supposed to remember it.

Albert It's alright to say it now. They've just told us it, haven't they? They thought we'd forgotten.

Fred What is this about?

Nell He still doesn't remember.

Bethany There is a secret legend amongst all Story-Players that at one time the Players told their own stories, freely, as they wanted to tell them.

Talitha But a few of them, a powerful few, banded together and in time became the Storytellers . . .

Albert Like those three. And from then on, only they, the Tellers, could tell the stories.

Jenkin They controlled the Players who lost all their power . . .

Fred I see. Then who's –?

Nell There was apparently one player . . . who defied them. He continued to tell his own stories . . .

Bethany His name was Flavius.

Jenkin That's your name.

Fred Me? But I'm not a Player, I'm –

Talitha He still can't remember a thing . . .

Albert The Storytellers got very angry, you see. So they put this feller into a story . . .

Jenkin A story where he was made to vanish . . .

Fred Vanish? Where?

Jenkin Nobody knows. To ever after somewhere, I suppose. Nobody even remembers the story or who told it.

Bethany The point is, none of us were ever meant to remember him. The story ended with us forgetting him. But we never did.

Albert Really.

Talitha Any of us.

Jenkin Quite . . .

Nell Ever. Ever.

A pause. Fred looks at them.

Fred Well, if I am this – this Flavius bloke . . . what am I supposed to do . . .

Nell Heaven knows how, but you've been given another chance to save us, Flavius.

Talitha Rescue us . . .

Jenkin Lead us out of their stories . . .

Bethany So we can tell our own . . .

Nell Help us . . .

Talitha Please . . .

Bethany Please . . .

Fred (*nervously*) Well. How should I go about it, do you think?

Albert They're planning to put you in a story. It'll be a test of strength. If you are Flavius – then you might just be strong enough to fight them . . .

Fred (*flustered*) Yes, OK. If you think so. I could have a go, I suppose.

Bethany Wonderful.

Talitha Marvellous.

Albert Great.

Jenkin Good man.

Nell Thank you, Flavius.

Fred No harm in that, is there? Can't be dangerous? Can it?

Jenkin Oh, yes, it can be very dangerous, Flavius.

Nell They'll try and make you disappear, Flavius.

Fred Where . . . whereabouts . . .

Albert Oh. Ever after. Who knows?

Fred Like in happily ever after, you mean?

Albert Not necessarily. See you later, Flavius. Beware, that's all.

 Albert starts to leave.

Jenkin Beware! (*He follows Albert.*)

Bethany Beware! (*She follows Jenkin.*)

Talitha Beware! (*She follows Bethany.*)

Nell (*kissing him lightly*) Beware, Flavius! (*She follows Talitha.*)

 The Players have all gone. Fred stands a little nervously.

Fred Well – I'll come back soon, I suppose. I suppose so. (*to Kevin*) What do you think I should do?

*Kevin touches his keyboard. A deep hollow voice
booms 'BEWARE!' followed by a sinister hollow
laugh. Fred rushes off. Kevin also trundles away, still
laughing.*
    End of Part One.

Part Two

The same somewhere or other. Fred waits by the sign that says, 'STORIES TOLD HERE TODAY AT 10.30 A.M.' (or whenever) as before.

Fred (*to no one in particular*) I've been waiting here a very long time indeed. (*reflecting*) At least, I think I have.

Nell enters rather furtively.

Nell Flavius . . .

Fred Oh, there you are. I wondered where you'd all got to.

Nell Sorry. I think the StoryTellers managed to split us all up somehow.

Fred How? How did they do that?

Nell That's the way they told it. Whatever they tell happens. You find yourself doing things whether you like them or not.

Fred Maybe you do. I don't. I make up my own mind.

Nell Be careful. That's what they'd like you to believe. You may only think you are –

Fred Really?

Nell You need to be on your guard, all the time.

Fred Me?

Nell Especially you. Being who you are.

Fred What have they got against this bloke, whatsis-name, Flavius . . .?

Nell Shh! Because while you're alive – you're a danger to them, don't you see? You're the only StoryPlayer who ever, *ever* managed to stand up to the StoryTellers. Who nearly succeeded in taking their power away from them and returning it to the Players where it belongs. You so nearly managed it . . .

Fred Did I? But I didn't, did I? And what makes you all think I'm him, anyway? He's dead, isn't he? And I'm alive. His name is Flavius; my name is Fred.

Nell Flavius was – you were never dead, you were . . .

Fred What?

Nell You were – ever after –

Fred Ever after?

Nell That's the only way to say it. Out of the stories. Where all the characters go when they've finished with them.

Fred Ever after?

Nell Right.

Fred Happily ever after?

Nell Some of them, yes.

Fred *Unhappily* ever after?

Nell Some of them, yes.

Fred I can guess where I was.

Nell You still can't remember?

Fred Not a thing. Anyway, what am I doing back here? Why aren't I still living unhappily ever after?

Nell I don't know. It could be a number of things.

199

Fred Like? Like? You have to tell me. If they're going to try and send me back, I need to know what I'm into here. What brought me back again?

Nell Well – it could have been Uncle Erraticus. He does get things wrong quite a lot. He may have brought you back by mistake. Or – possibly it was Uncle Oblivious . . . He could have forgotten you ever existed and somehow reinvented you . . .

Fred Or Great Aunt Whatsername? Could she have had anything to do with it?

Nell Great Aunt Repetitus? It's unlikely. She never usually makes mistakes. She's too clever. Far and away the most dangerous. Whatever you do, be careful of her. She'll be telling the story today.

Fred I'll be careful of all of them. Hey –

Nell What?

Fred If they write everything . . .?

Nell Practically everything . . .

Fred How do we know they haven't written this bit?

Nell We don't know for sure.

Fred So the chances are the conversation we've just been having they might have invented anyway. In which case there'd be no point in having the conversation. In which case – oh, this is all too complicated for me . . .

Nell I've told you – they don't invent everything . . .

Fred Well, how do we know what they don't –

Nell kisses him.

(*startled*) Wha –?

Nell (*smiling*) Nobody else invented that, I promise you. (*She stops and listens.*) Someone's coming. Oh, it's the others . . .

> *Bethany, Talitha, Albert and Jenkin come on. They carry their bundles of props and costumes, as previously.*

Nell Ah! Here they are . . .

Bethany Here we are.

Jenkin Here we are.

Talitha Here we are.

Albert Are we? Thank heavens.

Bethany (*looking at Fred*) Is he ready?

Nell He's ready.

Fred I'm ready.

Talitha Good luck – Flavius.

Fred I'm ready for anything.

Jenkin Frightened of nothing, eh?

Fred Frightened of nothing –

Albert And no one –

Fred And no one –

Nell Here's to Flavius!

All (*except Fred, in a whisper*) Flavius!

> *Fred stands impressively. The roar of a car engine and the scream of brakes. Fred jumps a mile. Kevin on Keyboards comes on as before, keyboard screaming to a halt.*

Bethany Good afternoon, Kevin on Keyboards.

*Kevin presses a note. A hollow voice booms
'BEWARE!' as before, followed by sinister laughter.*

Fred Yes. Very funny.

Albert The others must be on their way. Listen, Flavius –
er – I don't know how to put this but – once the story
starts – once things get under way – you may be on your
own, mate. You understand?

Fred How do you mean?

Jenkin He means that once we get into the story, most
of us most of the time won't be responsible for our own
actions. Do you see?

Bethany We'll do what we can to help . . .

Talitha Everything we can . . .

Jenkin But trust none of us. Especially her.

Albert Especially her.

Bethany Especially me.

Albert (*talking to Fred like a boxing second*) You're on
your own. Keep moving, that's the secret. Don't let them
settle. They'll try and set up a pattern, you see . . .

Fred A pattern, yes . . .

Jenkin You've got to break the pattern. Break it, you
see?

Fred (*trying to take all this in*) Break it, yes.

Albert They'll try and lull you into a false sense of
security, you see?

Fred Security, yes.

Jenkin If you let them do that, you're done for . . .

Albert So keep your guard up . . .

Jenkin Don't let them get you into a corner . . .

Bethany Look out!

They scatter to the corners of the stage. Fred stays with Nell for a second longer.

Fred Nell, can't I even trust you?

Nell I hope you can, Flavius. I'll try. But I can't guarantee it. None of us can. But just remember the one other reason that could have brought you back. The strongest reason of all of them.

Fred What's that?

Nell Love, Flavius. Love.

Kevin plays a fanfare. The three Storytellers enter, as before. Great Aunt Repetitus supported on either side (or perhaps supporting) Uncle Erraticus and Uncle Oblivious.

Great Aunt Repetitus Story time, then.

Uncle Erraticus Story time.

Uncle Oblivious Story time.

Great Aunt Repetitus And my turn, I think . . .

The Storytellers shuffle to their respective places off the acting area. The StoryPlayers whisper hurriedly behind their backs.

Albert (*sotto, to Fred*) It's going to be one of her own stories, by the look of it . . .

Bethany Be extra careful . . .

Fred Anything special I should look out for?

Jenkin Everything.

Talitha Remember her name – Great Aunt Repetitus. That means her stories tend to go round in circles . . .

Nell Sometimes they do.

Bethany But not always . . .

Fred (*bewildered*) Is that good?

Albert It can be . . .

Jenkin But not always . . .

Fred (*sarcastically*) Oh, thanks. That's a lot of help.

The Storytellers have reached their respective positions.

Great Aunt Repetitus Pay attention. This is a story of The Enchanted Farmer's Sons.

Albert (*whispering*) I don't know that one . . .

Bethany No . . .

Great Aunt Repetitus (*sharply*) Then you'd better listen then, hadn't you, Albert?

Albert (*nervously*) Oh, yes . . .

Great Aunt Repetitus You know what happens to people who don't listen, don't you, Albert?

Albert Oh, yes.

Great Aunt Repetitus Something awful happens to them in Chapter Two, doesn't it, Albert?

Albert Yes, yes. I'm listening.

Great Aunt Repetitus Good. Then I shall begin. There was once a rich farmer . . .

Albert dives at once into his bag for the appropriate headgear etc.

. . . who owned a great deal of land. And the land was so rich that his crops flourished and his cattle grew big and fat . . .

Albert has put on his woodcutter's hat and is holding an axe.

(*impatiently*) I said a farmer, Albert, a farmer not a woodcutter.

Albert (*nervously*) Sorry. Just a second. (*He dives back in his bag again for a fresh disguise.*)

Great Aunt Repetitus You're not even going to last through Chapter One at this rate, are you, Albert? The farmer's rich land was bounded on one side by a wide river and on the other by a thick wood. And in this wood, so people said, lived a wicked witch – but nobody had ever seen her – and she never bothered anyone, not at all.

Albert has now equipped himself with appropriate farmer's gear.

Now with the farmer – that's better, Albert – lived the farmer's wife . . .

Talitha immediately stands next to Albert, donning an apron.

A cheerful, good-natured woman who worked hard alongside her husband and bore him two fine twin sons, Jethro . . .

Jenkin steps forward to join the group.

. . . and Jonas . . .

Fred steps forward to join the group.

And because they were rich and food was plentiful and their parents happy and easy-going, the two boys grew up big and strong and were a credit to their parents. They worked alongside their father in the fields and because all of them worked so hard the farm prospered and their happiness increased day by day.

Jolly scenes at the farm from the four concerned.

They were all quite content in each other's company. Which was fortunate since their nearest neighbour, another farmer, lived several miles away, further along the river valley. Though sometimes his daughter Molly would pass by on her way to market. Whenever she did, she would always smile and wave to them.

Nell passes by, smiling and waving.

Nell 'Morning, all.

Others (*equally*) 'Morning, Molly.

Great Aunt Repetitus And so it continued, year after year, until the sons had grown to manhood and the farmer and his wife were no longer quite as young as they had been. And then one year, on the boys' seventeenth birthday, the family were celebrating as usual when there was a terrible storm . . .

Kevin supplies the thunder and rain.

And the storm wasn't just an ordinary storm but continued for days on end. And the fields became flooded and the crops were ruined and finally the river burst its banks and many of their cattle were swept away . . .

Cattle noises above the storm from Kevin.

. . . despite every attempt to save them. And the waters continued to rise and soon even their home was flooded and for several days the family had to sit on their roof,

hoping the river would get no higher or they would all
be drowned without a doubt. And when finally the
storm stopped . . . and the river went down . . .

Gurgling noise and then F/X cease.

. . . and the poor family finally came down off the roof,
they found they'd lost everything. They were no longer
rich at all but quite poor. And they sat and stared at the
damage and destruction and felt very sad indeed.

The family sit, gloomily.

Just then, a stranger came riding by, a dark eyed woman
on a jet black stallion . . .

Stallion noises as Bethany rides up.

Bethany Whooaa, there, Cyanide!

Great Aunt Repetitus She was elegant and beautiful and
looked, at the very least, like a royal princess or even a
queen. But she was neither of these. She was, in fact, the
wicked witch from the thick, dark wood. All these many
years she had lived alone weaving her spells and mixing
her potions but lately she had begun to feel lonely.
For she realised that even witches grew old, though they
live much longer than we do – she was now 450 – and
that she wanted companionship. For though she had
married – several times – she had grown tired of all her
husbands over the years and had got rid of them all –
either by poisoning them or eating them. Moreover, none
of them had lived long enough to give her the child she
so wanted. And lately over the last few days she had
found herself weeping bitterly – indeed it was her tears
that had caused the rain to fall and the river to rise.
But now she had stopped crying, she had decided to
seek out a new husband. Someone young and strong
and handsome. And as she rode past the farm she espied

Jethro and Jonas. And although she could not immediately choose between them she knew her search was
over. She wanted one of them for her own. And she
determined somehow she would have him, by fair means
or foul.

> *Bethany hisses to herself. Her horse whinnies,*
> *courtesy of Kevin.*

But the witch was cunning and she decided first to try
and trick them.

Bethany (*cheerily*) Hallo, there

Albert 'Afternoon.

Talitha 'Afternoon.

Jenkin 'Noon.

Fred 'Noon.

Bethany Golly! What a mess! Poor old you!

Albert Aye.

Talitha Aye.

Jenkin Aye.

Fred Aye.

Bethany Lot of clearing up for you to do.

Albert Happen there will be.

Talitha Aye.

Jenkin Aye.

Fred Happen.

Bethany Anything I can do to help?

> *They all look at her.*

If I can help in any way at all . . .?

Albert (*grunts negatively*)

Talitha (*grunts negatively*)

Jenkin (*grunts negatively*)

Fred (*grunts negatively*)

Bethany (*doubtfully*) Yes. Look – er – I'm – I do know
a bit of magic . . .

Albert Magic?

Bethany Just a teeny-weeny bit . . .

Talitha (*doubtfully*) Well . . .

Bethany I mean, it's white magic – it's perfectly harm-
less, I promise you . . .

Albert (*suspiciously*) Oh, aye?

Bethany Oh, yes. I do assure you of that. I would never –
no – not at all. It's just – well, you've got the most
frightful job on your hands otherwise, haven't you?
I mean just clearing the place up. It could take years.

Talitha (*unhappily*) Aye. Reckon it could . . .

Bethany I mean, even with your two fine strapping boys
to help you. What are their names, may I ask?

Talitha This one's Jethro

Jenkin How dy' do?

Talitha And this is Jonas.

Fred How'do.

Talitha Jonas is half a minute younger than Jethro.

Bethany You must be very proud of them both.

Talitha Oh, we are.

Bethany (*smiling at Talitha*) I really must congratulate you. Glorious boys. They're a credit to you.

Talitha Thank you very much.

Bethany Well, I must be getting along . . .

Talitha Just a moment . . . 'Scuse me . . .

Bethany Yes?

Talitha What's – What about this magic, then?

Albert Now, Mother . . .

Talitha I'm only asking . . .

Albert You don't want to be doing with all that

Talitha I'm only asking her, that's all. I'm only asking. No harm in asking.

Albert Well . . .

Talitha What about it, then?

Bethany Oh. Well, it's quite simple. All you'll need to do is to cut the heart and liver from one of your dead cattle . . .

Talitha Heart and liver, yes . . .

Bethany Then mince it well and then crush it with some fresh elderberries – or if you can't get elderberries, juniper berries will do the trick just as well –

Talitha Juniper berries, yes . . .

Bethany Leave that to marinate in a small earthenware pot or basin . . .

Talitha Pot or basin, yes . . .

Bethany Then in a couple of hours, all you do is add the ears from a dead vole and four tablespoonsful of common or garden black treacle. Yes?

Talitha Vole . . . black treacle, right.

Bethany Then bury that, in the bowl, at midnight, under a holly bush. Female bush, remember. With berries. Not male. Very important, that. OK? Got that?

Talitha Yes. Got that.

Albert Sounds a load of mumbo to me.

Bethany Yes, doesn't it just? But mock ye not. More often that not, you'd be amazed, it actually works. Give it a try.

Talitha I will. Thank you.

Bethany Cheerio, then. I may pop back – Easy, Cyanide, boy! – see how you got on! Byee!

Kevin provides a whinny and the sound of hooves as Bethany gallops away. The others stare after her.

Albert Bye.

Talitha Bye.

Jenkin Bye.

Fred Bye. (*A pause.*)

Talitha Nice woman. I think I might give all that a try . . .

Albert Oh no, you won't.

Talitha Why not? Where's the harm?

Albert Because it's magic. That's where's the harm.

Talitha White magic. You heard her. White magic.

Albert White magic. Black magic. Magic's magic and no good came of anyone who touched it. You start on any of that, I'll lock you in the pig pen, alright?

Talitha (*sulkily*) Alright.

Great Aunt Repetitus And so, despite the mother's protests, the family set about cleaning up by hand. But once they'd cleaned they realised they'd then have to plough and replant and restock the farm. And that would all take years and years and years. But nobody dared mention the magic. Because nobody particularly wanted to spend the night in the pig pen. And when it grew dark . . .

Owl noise from Kevin.

. . . because they were all so tired they went to bed early. But the mother lay awake and as soon as the others were asleep, she crept downstairs and set about finding the ingredients for the witch's magic spell. Luckily they had a juniper bush and she found a drowned vole just round the back of the house – and she buried the bowl under a nearby holly tree. Then, having followed the witch's instructions to the letter, she crept back to bed. And the following morning, at dawn . . .

Cock crow from Kevin.

. . . they all arose and looked out of the window:

Albert Well!

Talitha Oh!

Jenkin Cor!

Fred Lummy!

Great Aunt Repetitus The place was transformed. Where once there'd been mud and dead animals, contented cattle were grazing on rich green grass . . .

Cow noises from Kevin.

Chickens were foraging . . .

Add chicken noises from Kevin.

Lambs were leaping . . .

Add sheep noises from Kevin.

Pigs were rooting

Add pig noises from Kevin.

And the whole farmyard was a hive of activity.

Kevin adds full barnyard cacophony for a second or so. Then fades under.

Albert This any of your doing, Mother?

Talitha Me? Now would I?

Albert You! You ought to be in that pig pen, you ought, woman.

He stares at her for a moment. Then he smiles. She smiles at him. The two boys smile, too.

Albert (*with a great whoop*) Yeehaw!

Talitha Yayho!

Jenkin Yahoo!

Fred Yessirreee!

They do a swift barn dance. They collapse happily. Nell has entered.

Great Aunt Repetitus . . . and young Molly, passing on her way to market, stared at them all in amazement . . .

Nell 'Morning.

Others 'Morning, Molly.

Nell (*more intimately*) 'Morning, Jethro.

Jenkin How d'you do?

Nell (*more warmly still*) 'Morning, Jonas.

Fred (*awkwardly*) 'Llo, then.

Nell (*softly and urgently*) Be careful, Flavius.

Fred What?

Nell Careful . . .

Fred Why, what's –?

> *Before she can say more, Great Aunt Repetitus looks at them suspiciously. Nell hastily draws back.*

Great Aunt Repetitus (*firmly continuing*) And young Molly continued on happily to market.

> *Nell moves away, reluctantly.*

Jenkin (*to Fred*) She's after you.

Fred What?

Jenkin That Molly. She fancies you an' all.

Fred (*scornfully*) Nar. (*staring after her*) Reckon so?

Jenkin Reckon.

Great Aunt Repetitus And so life on the farm was back to normal. Or nearly back to normal. For as the farmer so wisely pointed out, once you have dabbled in magic of any kind, life can never really be back to normal again. And as we shall see, this family now found themselves in debt to a witch. A few days later she returned.

> *A whinny and sound of horse's hooves as before. Bethany gallops into view.*

Bethany (*cheerfully*) Whooaaa, Cyanide! Hallo, there!

Albert (*equally cheerful*) Afternoon!

Talitha Afternoon!

Jenkin Afternoon!

Fred Afternoon!

Bethany I see it worked. The recipe. It worked.

Albert Oh, aye, we reckoned to give it a try. The wife here was against it but . . .

Bethany Splendid!

Talitha Thank you very much. Say thank you to the lady, boys.

Jenkin Ta!

Fred Ta!

Bethany Magnificent boys! Bigger than ever. Well, see you around sometime, I expect. Yup, Cyanide! Byeee!

Bethany gallops away as before. The others stare after her.

Albert Bye.

Talitha Bye.

Jenkin Bye.

Fred Bye.(*Pause.*)

Talitha Nice woman.

Albert Very pleasant.

Jenkin She's a looker an' all!

Fred (*smirking*) Aye.

Talitha That's enough of that, you two! None of that smuttin' around here, right? Or your dad'll put you both in the pig pen. Right, Dad?

Albert Right. Back to work, then.

Jenkin (*as they go about their tasks, to Fred*) I wouldn't mind getting with her in a pig pen.

Fred sniggers.

Great Aunt Repetitus And, for a few months, life continued happily as before on the farm. Winter ended, spring came and went and then came summer and day after day of glorious sunshine. At first the family welcomed the sun. But the days got hotter still and the wide river began to shrink in its bed until finally it dried up to a trickle of mud. And suddenly as the animals started to grow thirsty and die, the sun was no longer a friend but a foe that had brought the farmer's most feared enemy of all – drought. Little did the family know that all this was caused not by the sun but by the increasing heat of the witch's lust. It was so hot, even at night – especially at night – that no living creature wanted to move.

The family sit on the ground, panting in the heat.

Albert (*speaking with difficulty*) How much water we got left?

Talitha Just till tomorrow. Then we're dry, that's it.

Jenkin What we going to do? We can't not drink. What we going to do then?

Fred We got to drink, haven't we? What we going to do?

Talitha Dad?

Albert I don't know. I don't know.

The sound of galloping hooves and the whinny of a horse. Bethany rides into view.

Bethany Hallo there! Isn't it glorious? Another scorching day. Whoaa there, Cyanide! Easy, boy. What weather!

How long can it last? That's what we'd all like to know, eh?

Albert (*grimly*) We would.

Talitha Aye.

Jenkin Right.

Fred Ar.

Bethany Oh dear. Problems?

Albert (*indicating*) Problems? Look at it.

Bethany Oh, yes. Oh, dear. Why are all your cattle lying down? Are they having a nap?

Albert They're dead, aren't they?

Bethany Dead?

Talitha Drought.

Bethany Oh, dear. One just doesn't realise. Living alone. Of course, I have a private well so I'm laughing. Oh dear. Look, I don't know if I can help at all but – I do know a recipe that might – I repeat might – just work . . .

Talitha Recipe?

Albert More magic?

Bethany *Sort* of magic, yes. Very, very, very mild though.

Albert (*doubtfully*) Well . . .

Talitha What is it?

Bethany Well – you all have to do this together – if it's going to work . . . Alright?

Albert Maybe. Yes.

Bethany It won't work otherwise. It sounds a bit silly but – Have you any nails or sharp tin tacks in the house. . .?

Albert Yes, we got a few of them.

Bethany Good. Now, you sprinkle some of them about an inch deep into four large bowls, alright?

Talitha Four large bowls, right.

Bethany Then, at the time you'd normally go to bed, you each stand barefoot in one of the bowls, OK?

Talitha Barefoot?

Albert On the tin tacks?

Bethany Yes. With a pillow case over your head.

Talitha . . . pillow case . . .

Bethany And then – here's the tricky bit – you must all say together:

A rabbit cannot whistle Strauss,
Picasso couldn't paint a mouse,
But may it rain upon this house.

Have you all got that? All together:

All (*except Bethany*)
A rabbit cannot whistle Strauss,
Picasso couldn't paint a mouse,
But may it rain upon this house.

Bethany Splendid.

Albert How many times do we have to say that?

Bethany Just until the cock crows.

Jenkin All night?

Fred Flippin' heck!

Talitha Now, now! Language!

Bethany Sorry. It doesn't sound like a load of fun – but if all else fails – you might like to try it. Mouth watering boys! Must dash now, sorry. Byee!

Bethany gallops away with noises, as before. The others stare after her.

Albert Bye.

Talitha Bye.

Jenkin Bye.

Fred Bye.

Pause.

Talitha Well, I'm afraid I'm not doing that. Standing in a bowl of tintacks all night with a bag on my head, chanting. Not for no one, I'm sorry.

Jenkin Nor me.

Fred Nor me.

They look at Albert.

Talitha Dad?

Albert (*less certainly*) Oh, no. Nor me.

Great Aunt Repetitus And so that night, they all decided to ignore the witch's advice, since none of them fancied standing in a bowl all night with a bag on their head chanting. So they lay in bed and tried to sleep. But the father, as soon as he thought all the others were asleep, crept downstairs on his own with his pillowcase. After all there was no harm in trying. And maybe the magic would work with just him on his own.

Albert Happen it might.

Great Aunt Repetitus He took off his shoes and socks and, having filled a kitchen bowl with tin tacks, stood in it barefoot.

Albert has produced a bowl from his bag and a pillow case. He stands in the bowl.

Albert Oooh! Aaaa! Eeee! (*Having pulled the pillow case over his head he starts to mutter under the next the witch's incantation.*)

A rabbit cannot whistle Strauss,
Picasso couldn't paint a mouse,
But may it rain upon this house, etc.

Great Aunt Repetitus And soon the mother had also crept downstairs with her pillowcase . . .

Talitha creeps down and repeats Albert's business.

Talitha (*as she stands in the bowl*) Ooo! Aaa! Eee! (*She puts the pillow case over her head.*)

A rabbit cannot whistle Strauss,
Picasso couldn't paint a mouse,
But may it rain upon this house, etc.

Jenkin and Fred in turn do the same until they are all standing in bowls with pillow cases on their heads and chanting.

Great Aunt Repetitus And so they continued all night. Of course, if they had only known, what they were doing wasn't magic at all. No real witch would ever give away her spells to ordinary mortals. And even as they stood there chanting all through the night, the witch watched them from her castle deep in the wood and laughed and laughed . . .

Bethany cackles.

But she also did a little real magic of her own so that in the morning, as soon as the cock crew . . .

A cockcrow from Kevin followed by a clap of thunder and rain. The family stop chanting.

Albert (*removing his pillowcase*) Rain! (*seeing the others*) Oh!

Talitha (*doing likewise*) Rain! (*seeing the boys*) Oh!

Jenkin (*doing likewise*) Rain! (*seeing Fred*) Oh!

Fred (*doing likewise*) Rain! It worked!

Albert (*with a great whoop*) Yeehaw!

Talitha Yayho!

Jenkin Yahoo!

Fred Yessirreee!

They do a swift barn dance. They collapse happily. Nell has entered.

Great Aunt Repetitus . . . and young Molly who was passing on her way to market stared at them all in amazement . . .

Nell 'Morning.

Others 'Morning, Molly.

Nell (*very warmly*) 'Morning, Jonas.

Fred (*awkwardly*) 'Llo, then.

Nell (*softly and urgently*) Be careful, Flavius.

Fred What?

Nell Careful . . .

Fred Why, what's –?

Again, before she can say more, Great Aunt Repetitus looks over suspiciously. Nell hastily draws back.

Great Aunt Repetitus (*firmly continuing*) And young Molly continued on happily to market.

Nell moves away, reluctantly.

Jenkin (*to Fred*) Whey-hey!

Fred Gerroff!

Great Aunt Repetitus And so life on the farm was back to normal. Or nearly back to normal. For as I have said before, once you have had dealings with witches, however slight, life can never really get back to normal again.

A whinny and sound of horse's hooves as before. Bethany gallops into view.

Bethany (*cheerfully*) Hallo, there! Whoaaa, Cyanide!

Albert (*equally cheerful*) Afternoon!

Talitha Afternoon!

Jenkin Afternoon!

Fred Afternoon!

Bethany I see it worked. My little tip. It worked.

Albert Oh, aye, the wife reckoned to give it a try. I was dead against it but . . .

Bethany Splendid.

Talitha Thank you very much. Say thank you to the lady, boys.

Jenkin Ta!

Fred Ta!

Bethany Pulse-racing boys! Well, see you around sometime, I expect. Byeee! (*She is about to depart.*)

Talitha Er – excuse me . . .

Bethany Steady, Cyanide. Hallo?

Talitha Would – would you care to have a spot of supper with us sometime? If you've a moment? Just to say thank you, like. We was wondering if you would, weren't we, Dad?

Albert Were we?

Talitha We were.

Bethany Oh, how sweet of you. I'd love to. When would suit?

Talitha Well, any time really. We aren't going anywhere.

Bethany Tomorrow night any good?

Talitha Oh, yes, tomorrow would be perfect.

Bethany Super! Look forward to it. Byee! Yup, Cyanide! (*Bethany gallops off, as before.*)

Albert Bye.

Talitha Bye.

Jenkin Bye.

Fred Bye.

A pause.

Albert What you want to go and do that for?

Talitha What?

Albert Ask her to supper.

Talitha Why not?

Albert She's a lady. She don't want to eat supper with us.

Talitha She's also a very nice woman and I like her. So there. She's also done us a good turn – two good turns and we ain't done her any, so we owe her. And she's coming and that's final, alright?

Talitha stamps indoors. The three men look at each other.

Albert Well then. You'd better comb your hair then, you two, hadn't you?

Great Aunt Repetitus Next day, they all worked hard to make the place neat and tidy. The boys helped their mother in the kitchen whilst she prepared the most splendid supper she could. When they had finished, they waited anxiously for their guest to arrive. Alas, if only they had known who their guest really was. For if there is one thing worse than accepting favours from witches, it is allowing them into your home to sit at your table.

The family are standing round the table.

Talitha Think it looks alright?

Albert Looks good to me, Mother. Eh, lads?

Jenkin Yes.

Fred Yes. Can we start, then?

Talitha No, you can't. You wait for your guest.

Jenkin Where is she, then? Gone half past.

The sound of the horse as Bethany appears. She clutches a bottle.

Albert This'll be her.

Bethany Whooaa there, Cyanide! Good boy! Hallo there.

Albert Evenin'.

Talitha Evenin'.

Jenkin Evenin'.

Fred Evenin'.

Bethany I hope it's alright, I brought a bottle of vino. That OK?

Albert Vino? I don't think we've tried it. What is it?

Bethany Wine.

Talitha Oh, wine!

Bethany Help! You're not teetotal by some ghastly chance?

Albert Oh, no, we're partial to a drop of wine.

Bethany Super! I hope the boys will be allowed some?

Talitha Just a drop. We don't encourage it.

Jenkin Oh, Mum.

Great Aunt Repetitus And so they all sat down to supper. And the witch had the farmer open her bottle of wine and then insisted that they all drink a toast.

Bethany Now listen, everyone. Before we eat. I want to drink one toast, OK?

Albert Right.

Bethany To us all. To new found friends.

All New found friends.

They all drink.

Great Aunt Repetitus The meal was a great success. The witch knew dozens of very funny stories – some of them a little bit risky, I'm afraid – but she kept them amused all through the meal. Maybe some of the merriment was due to the wine which seemed, it has to be said, rather strong. At last it was time for the witch to leave.

Bethany Well, thank you again. This has been terrific.

Albert No, no . . .

Talitha No, thank *you*.

Bethany You're just dear people, all of you. (*turning to the boys*) And as for you two, I want to wrap you both up and take you home with me, I really do. (*She laughs.*)

They all laugh.

Jenkin Wouldn't mind that myself . . .

Talitha Now, now . . . You wouldn't want them for long, I can tell you . . .

Bethany I don't know which is the more handsome, do you? Which would you say, Mother?

Talitha Neither of 'em. They're both as ugly as sin, if you ask me.

Bethany Hark at her! Hark at her! Pay no attention to her, boys, do you hear? (*She hugs them both in turn, rather lingeringly. Softly, as she does this*) And remember this, boys. Sin doesn't necessarily have to be ugly, either. Believe me, it can sometimes be very, very beautiful. Sleep tight, little heartwrenchers. (*She moves to her horse and remounts.*) Goodnight, all. Easy, Cyanide! 'Night then! 'Night! (*She gallops away, as before.*)

Albert 'Night.

Talitha 'Night.

Jenkin 'Night.

Fred 'Night. (*A pause.*)

Talitha A real nice woman.

Jenkin (*gazing after her with some desire*) Yes. Real nice . . .

Fred (*likewise*) Real, real nice . . .

Albert That wine was a bit of alright.

Great Aunt Repetitus But it wasn't really. For, as you may have guessed, the witch's wine was actually a magic potion with many powers. The mixture had no effect on the witch herself – she had made sure it wouldn't – but it did strange things to the family. Like all wine, only more so, it was half a love potion and half a poison. And so it was that their sleep was filled with weird dreams.

Dream music from Kevin.

For Jethro and Jonas, it seemed that the witch visited them both looking more beautiful and desirable than ever.

Bethany appears. She beckons Jenkin and Fred who arise dream-like from their beds and move to her.

(*as this happens*) For the witch couldn't yet decide which one she should choose to love her for ever. She wanted them both equally . . . (*She kisses them both in turn on their foreheads.*) But she knew that finally the choice would be hers alone. Whichever of them she wanted she need only kiss his forehead and he would be hers for ever after.

Bethany takes Jenkin and Fred's hands and whirls them round her as if trying to chose between them.

227

(*during this*) Meanwhile, their parents were having a much less enjoyable dream . . .

Albert and Talitha sit up and produce two large foam rubber mallets from their bags. Each starts to batter himself on the head for a bit. Kevin provides percussive accompaniment.

Albert and Talitha Ooo! Ow! Ooo! Ow! etc.

Great Aunt Repetitus Until at last all of them, for one reason or another, were quite exhausted.

They all return to their beds exhausted. Bethany withdraws.

Came the dawn . . .

Kevin gives a cock-crow.

Albert (*sitting up, groaning*) Ooo! My head . . .

Talitha (*likewise*) Aaaaaah!

They both stagger downstairs.

Albert I think I'm dying.

Talitha So am I . . .

Great Aunt Repetitus The brothers, on the other hand, seemed to have suffered no ill effects . . .

Jenkin (*sitting up with a smile*) Oh!

Fred (*likewise*) Ah!

Great Aunt Repetitus Unless you call being hopelessly in love an ill effect . . .

Jenkin (*to himself*) I love her . . .

Fred (*to himself*) I love her . . .

Jenkin (*to himself*) For ever

Fred (*to himself*) And ever . . .

They both get up and, passing their parents, go outside.

Albert 'Mornin, Jethro . . .

Talitha 'Morning, Jonas . . .

Great Aunt Repetitus But the boys had eyes now for one and only one . . .

Albert What's up with those two, then?

Talitha Search me. Want your breakfast? Bacon and eggs?

Albert (*feeling sick*) No, I don't.

Great Aunt Repetitus And the brothers stood in the field and dreamt of the woman they both loved – though as yet, neither knew that they both loved the same woman. But when Molly came by on her way to town . . .

Nell passes by.

Nell 'Morning. (*smiling at Fred*) Morning, Jonas.

Great Aunt Repetitus Neither noticed her at all . . .

Nell Jonas . . . Jonas . . . It's me. (*softer*) Flavius! Flavius! (*urgently*) Flavius . . .

Fred (*impatiently*) What? What is it . . .

Nell Flavius . . .

Fred Go away.

Nell Flavius, I . . .

Great Aunt Repetitus Stop!

The Players freeze.

What are you doing there, child?

Nell Nothing, Great Aunt.

Great Aunt Repetitus Yes, you are. You keep doing it, I've been watching you. You behave as you're told, alright?

Nell Yes, Great Aunt.

Great Aunt Repetitus (*studying her*) Yes. I think something nasty could well happen to you in the next chapter.

Nell Oh no, I . . .

Great Aunt Repetitus (*firmly continuing*) And young Molly continued unhappily to market. Unaware of the events that lay ahead.

Nell moves away reluctantly.

Jenkin What's up with you, then?

Fred What?

Jenkin Don't you say good morning to her any more then, your lover girl?

Fred She's not my lover girl.

Jenkin Course she is.

Fred Not any more. Somebody else now, isn't there?

Jenkin Who?

Fred Her. Who else. Her from last night. That's who. She's the one now.

Jenkin Oh no, she's not. She's mine that one.

Fred Yours?

Jenkin Mine.

Fred She's not, you know.

Jenkin She is, you know.

Fred Oh, yes?

Jenkin Yes.

Fred Over my dead body . . .

Jenkin If necessary.

Fred Right.

Jenkin Right.

They start to fight. Rolling on the ground. Albert and Talitha come out to discover them.

Albert What's happening here . . .?

Talitha What's going on?

Albert Jethro . . .

Talitha Jonas! Stop it both of you. They've never fought like this before. Never. What's happened to them, father?

Albert I don't know. I don't know. It's like the devil's in them.

Albert and Talitha try vainly to separate the two fighters.

Great Aunt Repetitus It was indeed the devil in them both. And – talk of the devil –

Bethany comes riding up. Effects as before from Kevin.

Bethany Whooaa! Whoa there, Cyanide! 'Morning. What's all the ballyhoo?

Talitha Oh, my lady, stop them. Please, please stop them . . . Before they kill each other.

Bethany (*firmly*) Jethro! Jonas! Stop! Please . . .

*The brothers stop immediately. They sit on the
ground, staring up at her in adoration.*

Jenkin Oh!

Fred Oh!

Bethany That's better. You bad, bad boys. Now what's
the trouble? Tell me the problem.

Jenkin I love you.

Talitha Jethro!

Fred So do I.

Talitha Jonas!

Jenkin Desperately!

Fred Passionately!

Albert Beg pardon, Miss. I'll lock them both in the pig
pen. That'll cool 'em.

Bethany No, no . . . Please, not on my account.

Talitha You daft pair. You can't love her. What are you
saying? She don't want you, does she?

Bethany (*swiftly*) Oh, but I do, I do, I do. (*recovering*)
I mean I might. I could. Given time. Perhaps. Possibly.
Who can tell with a woman's heart?

Jenkin You could love me?

Fred Or me?

Bethany Oh, yes. Quite possibly.

Jenkin Oh.

Fred Oh.

Albert Well . . .

Talitha Well, that's very nice of you, I'm sure . . .

Bethany But which one of you, that's the problem. . . .

Jenkin Better be me, hadn't it?

Fred Has to be me, hasn't it?

Jenkin Gerroff! (*He threatens Fred.*)

Fred Gerroff! (*He threatens Jenkin.*)

Bethany Now, now, boys. May I suggest something?
(*to Talitha*) May I borrow them from you for three
days?

Talitha Three days?

Bethany To stay with me whilst I decide? I promise you,
at the end of three days, one of them will be returned to
you. As good as new.

Albert Well, I suppose three days . . .

Talitha No longer . . .

Albert There's the harvest . . .

Talitha And the animals . . .

Bethany Three days is all I need. I promise.

Albert Right.

Talitha Right.

Bethany Happy, boys?

Jenkin 'Spose

Fred 'Spose

Bethany Then away we go. Yup there, Cyanide.

Great Aunt Repetitus And so the two brothers went
with the witch deep into the forest, walking each side of

her huge black stallion. As they reached the edge of the dark wood, they turned and waved to their parents – and despite their love for the witch, they both felt sudden sadness for they knew that only one of them would ever return again to the sunshine. The forest was darker than they could possibly have imagined. And although they were both grown men, they were rather glad to have company with them. The witch, on the other hand, seemed quite at home in the wood. As she rode along she sang softly to herself . . .

Bethany (*singing*)
As loud as you scream, as much as you shout.
Once you're in here, you will never get out,
Without any doubt, you will never get out,
Never get out, never get out . . .

Great Aunt Repetitus And the brothers joined in . . .

Jenkin and Fred (*singing with her*)
Never get out, never get out –

Great Aunt Repetitus Finally they arrived at the very darkest part of the forest and there before them huge and lowering and dripping with green slime – stood the witch's castle itself.

Chord from Kevin.

And before the brothers could say anything, the witch led them inside and straight to their room.

Kevin makes dripping water sound.

Bethany Here we are, boys, you don't mind sharing, do you? Make yourselves comfortable. Dinner's at eight.

Kevin plays a huge door slam. Bethany leaves them.

Fred (*nervously*) It's very dark, isn't it?

Jenkin (*likewise*) I can't find the light switch.

Fred It's a funny sort of bedroom. I can't find a bed.

Door handle rattling from Kevin as Jenkin tries the door.

Jenkin The door's locked. She's locked us in

Fred It's more like a dungeon . . .

Jenkin The roof's leaking.

Great Aunt Repetitus The brothers stood in the dark for hours – for they couldn't even find anywhere to sit down and the floor was very damp. Secretly they both wished they were back home in their snug, dry farmhouse – but it was too late now . . . Far too late.

Door opening sound from Kevin. Bethany reappears.

Bethany Come on, boys. Dinner time. (*She moves off again.*)

Great Aunt Repetitus And the brothers came blinking into the light and, after a little searching, found their way to the castle dining room.

Kevin plays some witch's dining room music.

Bethany Oh, there you are. Come in. Sit down. Shame you didn't bother to dress for dinner.

Jenkin We couldn't find the light . . .

Bethany The light?

Jenkin To see anything.

Bethany Light. You don't need light. Not here, I promise you. Once you've lived here for a little while you'll be able to see in the dark. Like everything and everyone that lives around here.

A trumpeting sound of some strange beast echoes along the corridors. The brothers jump in alarm. Nell enters in an apron carrying a serving dish. She appears to have been crying.

Ah, now. I think you know my new little maid, don't you? You both know Molly?

Fred Molly!

Bethany Yes, Jonas. You remember Molly, I'm sure. She's just joined the staff here. She was a little unhappy to start with, but she's settling in nicely now, aren't you, Molly?

Nell does not reply but continues serving.

(*sharply*) Aren't you, girl?

Nell (*jumping*) Yes, madam.

The background muzak takes a turn for the worse.

Bethany Oh, I adore this tune . . . (*She closes her eyes.*)

Nell (*whispering*) Flavius . . . Flavius . . .

Fred (*seeming not to understand*) Flavius . . .

Nell You're in terrible danger . . .

Fred (*still bemused*) What?

Nell Flavius!

Fred (*loudly*) What?

Bethany (*opening her eyes*) What?

Fred Nothing.

Bethany Get back to the kitchen, Molly.

Nell Yes, Madam.

Bethany And clean the floor in there, it's filthy.

Nell There's no mop, madam.

Bethany Then lick it, girl. Lick it. What do you think your tongue's for?

Nell Yes, madam. (*She moves away.*)

Bethany Eat up, boys. You must both be starving. I like my men big and strong. Eat up . . .

Jenkin (*unhappily*) I don't reckon I'm that hungry –

Bethany (*savagely*) Eat it!

Jenkin Right.

Fred Right.

The two men start eating.

Jenkin (*after a mouthful*) Ugghhh!

Fred (*likewise*) Ugggh!

Bethany Nice?

Jenkin What is it?

Bethany Secret recipe.

Jenkin Oh.

They both take another tentative mouthful.

Bethany But I will tell you it was only freshly killed.

Fred Grug!

Jenkin Grew!

Bethany You're not vegetarians, are you?

Jenkin No.

Fred No.

Bethany Only I don't like vegetarians. Do you know what I do to vegetarians?

Jenkin No?

Bethany I dig a hole and plant them. Headfirst.

Fred Ah.

Bethany (*smiling at them*) Do you know, I have actually come to a decision already. Which of you it is who's going to stay here with me. Isn't that exciting?

Jenkin (*dully*) Yes.

Bethany I'll tell you both after dinner, shall I?

Fred Yes.

Bethany Aren't you both dying to know who I've chosen? (*No reply. Sharply*) Aren't you?

Both Men Yes!

Great Aunt Repetitus Suddenly, despite the fact that the dinner tasted quite, quite disgusting, the brothers lingered over the food as long as possible, savouring every mouthful – for neither wanted the meal to end. But finally, even bad things come to an end.

Nell has returned.

Bethany Clear away, Molly. And then bring us some wine. We have a toast to make to the lucky winner.

Nell Yes, Madam. (*She looks despairingly at Fred.*)

During the next, Nell removes the plates and returns at once with the wine.

Bethany Up you get, boys, and stand over there.

Fred and Jenkin obey her.

(*surveying them*) Now, let me take one last look. (*She surveys them from all angles.*)

Jenkin (*to Fred*) I don't mind – if you'd rather stay – I don't mind leaving at all . . .

Fred No, no. Please. After you. I'm happy to go, if you'd rather . . .

Bethany (*ending her inspection*) Alright. Gorgeous. Now. We have the wine? Good. My choice of who shall stay with me ever after. My choice . . . My choice is . . .

Both men close their eyes. So does Nell.

Great Aunt Repetitus Stop!

The StoryPlayers freeze.

Uncle Erraticus Why are you stopping there?

Uncle Oblivious It was just getting to the exciting bit.

Great Aunt Repetitus I'm tired. It's been an exhausting story.

Uncle Erraticus Well, you can't stop there.

Great Aunt Repetitus Just for a moment, I need a rest.

Uncle Oblivious I want to know what happens . . .

Uncle Erraticus You're impossible, Repetitus, you really are . . .

Great Aunt Repetitus You finish it then, Erraticus.

Uncle Erraticus Me?

Great Aunt Repetitus If you want to. If you think you can be trusted to. There's only one more sentence. Mind you, you'll probably get that wrong, too, won't you?

Uncle Erraticus Of course I won't get it wrong, don't be so ridiculous . . .

Great Aunt Repetitus I'm not so sure. (*scornfully*) Grethel and Hansel!

Uncle Erraticus Alright, alright . . .

Great Aunt Repetitus Snakes . . .

Uncle Oblivious And fingers . . .

Great Aunt Repetitus And telephones . . .

Uncle Oblivious And saucepan lids . . .

Uncle Erraticus Alright, alright, alright! We'll see. We shall see who can't finish a story. Here we go. Where were we?

Great Aunt Repetitus The witch was about to chose.

Uncle Erraticus Yes.

Great Aunt Repetitus Which brother she would keep for hers.

Uncle Erraticus Yes, yes, yes . . .

Great Aunt Repetitus And we know which one she keeps, don't we, Erraticus?

Uncle Erraticus Yes, we do. Thank you. So to continue:

Bethany Alright. Gorgeous. Now. We have the wine? Good. My choice of who shall stay with me ever after? My choice . . . My choice is . . .

> *Both men close their eyes. So does Nell.*

Is you!

> *Bethany crosses and kisses Jenkin on the forehead. She starts to lead him away by the hand. Jenkin is in a daze. Fred opens his eyes and looks at Nell.*

Great Aunt Repetitus (*with a scream*) That's the wrong one. Erraticus, you fool, you've made her pick the wrong one . . .

Uncle Oblivious (*simultaneously*) You fool, you fool!

Uncle Erraticus (*simultaneously*) Alright! Alright! Alright! Alright!

Fred (*during this*) Nell!

Nell (*opening her eyes*) What? What's happened?

Fred Quickly . . . Come on!

Nell Where?

Fred Anywhere – away from here – come on . . .

Fred grabs Nell's hand and they start to run hither and thither to find their way out of the castle. Chase music from Kevin.

Great Aunt Repetitus What's going on?

Uncle Erraticus They're running away.

Uncle Oblivious What are they doing?

Great Aunt Repetitus This is all your stupid fault, Erraticus – how can you ruin a perfectly good story with one stupid sentence . . .

Uncle Erraticus It was not my fault – you just like to make things complicated. Why didn't you have a tree fall on him and have done with it . . .?

Uncle Oblivious Just a minute, I'll deal with it. Don't panic. I can deal with it! To continue. They ran up and down corridors for several minutes but they could find no way out.

Fred There's no way out.

Uncle Oblivious They were lost.

Nell We're lost.

Uncle Oblivious Finally, they ran through a small door and found themselves at a dead end. The door behind them slammed –

Slam from Kevin.

– shut! Jonas tried the handle –

Rattle from Kevin.

But the door had locked itself.

Nell We're trapped!

Fred Looks like it. I'm sorry, Nell.

Nell Oh, Flavius!

They cling to each other.

Uncle Oblivious Stop!

The Players freeze.

There you are. Perfectly simple, if you know what you're doing.

Great Aunt Repetitus Well done, Oblivious, congratulations.

Uncle Erraticus (*sulkily*) Amazing you got that far and managed to stay awake – and remembered both their names. Quite a record for you.

Uncle Oblivious At least I did it. Unlike some. (*to Erraticus*) Well, do you want another try at finishing it?

Uncle Erraticus No, no, no, no, no. You finish it. Cleversocks.

Great Aunt Repetitus Go on. Finish it, Oblivious. You finish it.

Uncle Oblivious If you insist. Thank you, Great Aunt.

Great Aunt Repetitus You know what to do?

Uncle Oblivious Yes.

Great Aunt Repetitus You fetch the witch . . .

Uncle Oblivious Yes, yes . . .

Great Aunt Repetitus To kiss the boy . . .

Uncle Oblivious (*impatiently*) Yes, yes, yes . . .

Uncle Erraticus What about the girl?

Great Aunt Repetitus Oh, she might as well kiss her as well. Let's get rid of both of them. They're both infernal nuisances . . .

Uncle Oblivious Do you mind? Am I telling this story, or aren't I?

Great Aunt Repetitus Go on then.

Uncle Oblivious Right. (*Slight pause.*) Where were we?

Uncle Erraticus Oh, dear heavens . . .

Great Aunt Repetitus We were here:

The characters reanimate.

Nell We're trapped.

Fred Looks like it. I'm sorry, Nell.

Nell Oh, Flavius.

Uncle Oblivious Oh, yes. And as they stood there, they heard the sound of the witch's footsteps coming slowly along the passage towards them.

Hollow footsteps from Kevin.

They both looked around but there was no escape.

Fred There's no escape.

Uncle Oblivious The footsteps stopped, the handle turned . . .

Doorhandle rattle from Kevin.

. . . the door slowly opened . . .

Door creak from Kevin.

. . . and there stood the witch.

Bethany has appeared.

Bethany Did you know, there was an old saying. It's a witch's privilege to change her mind. I've just changed mine. I've let your brother go, wasn't that kind of me? Instead, I now choose –

She points a finger at Fred. Fred closes his eyes.

You!

Nell (*softly*) No, you can't – you mustn't – you can't –

Bethany Can't? Can't? What's can't? Who can't? Why can't I? Who's to stop me?

Nell Me.

Bethany How? How?

Nell (*quietly*) Because – because I love him . . .

Bethany (*murmuring sweetly*) Too bad, child. Too bad.

Nell closes her eyes.

Uncle Oblivious And the witch stepped forward, took the boy by the hands and kissed . . . kissed him on the . . . oh, dammit what's the word . . . thingy . . . kissed him on the thingy . . .

Great Aunt Repetitus (*screaming with fury*) Oblivious!

Uncle Erraticus (*likewise*) Oblivious!

Great Aunt Repetitus You fool! How could you go wrong with that? It was all set up for you . . .

Uncle Erraticus (*simultaneously*) I knew it! I knew he'd make a mess of it. He always does . . .

Uncle Oblivious (*with them*) What's the word? What's the stupid word? Just one word, that's all it was . . .

> *During this Fred opens his eyes. Bethany stands frozen waiting for the sentence to be completed, half-way through a kiss that has never been planted.*

Fred Nell!

Nell (*opening her eyes*) Flavius – What's –?

Fred Come on – quickly . . .

Nell I think I've remembered a way out –

Fred Where?

Nell Through the kitchens, follow me . . .

> *They start to run as before. More chase music from Kevin.*

Uncle Erraticus What's happening now?

Uncle Oblivious What are they doing?

Great Aunt Repetitus They're getting away again, you idiots . . .

Uncle Erraticus Stop them!

Uncle Oblivious Stop them!

Great Aunt Repetitus Stop them!

Nell Here we are, through here . . .

Fred We're out! We're in the forest . . .

Uncle Erraticus They're outside!

Uncle Oblivious They've got into the forest!

Uncle Erraticus They've escaped!

Uncle Oblivious What are we going to do?

Great Aunt Repetitus Don't worry, leave it to me . . . It always has to be me in the end, doesn't it? And even as they ran through the forest – a great wind arose . . .

Howling wind noise from Kevin.

And try as they might, they could not run against such a wind. They found themselves being blown backwards . . . back . . . towards the castle . . .

Nell Flavius, help me . . . hold on . . .

Fred It's no good . . . it's too strong . . . I can't . . .

Great Aunt Repetitus And then the whole forest was alive with whirling leaves and twisting twigs and stinging sticks and bristling branches which tore and scratched at them as if trying to cling on to them for ever . . . and the hurricane grew stronger and stronger and stronger until suddenly –

A loud creaking sound.

Nell Look out! Mind the tree!

Fred Watch out for the tree!

Great Aunt Repetitus And the highest tree in the forest came crashing down on top of them both.

A final crash. The wind dies. Silence. Fred and Nell lie motionless on the ground.

Great Aunt Repetitus (*satisfied*) There!

Uncle Erraticus Are they –?

Uncle Oblivious Dead?

Great Aunt Repetitus Oh, no . . . Not yet . . .

Nell (*groggily*) Flavius –?

Fred Uh?

Nell Can you move? I can't move – something's . . . The tree's on top of me . . . I can't move.

Fred Just a minute, I'll – I'll try and . . .

Great Aunt Repetitus But try as they might, they could never hope to move the tree. And as they lay there, they heard someone coming towards them, singing . . .

Bethany (*singing*)
As loud as you scream, as much as you shout,
Once you're in here, you will never get out,
Without any doubt, you will never get out,
Never get out, never get out . . .

Nell (*over this, in a whisper*) It's the witch . . .

Fred The witch . . .

Nell I love you, Flavius . . .

Fred I love you, Nell . . .

Bethany appears.

Bethany Hallo, kids. What's the problem here?

Nell We're trapped, can you –? Could you –? Please?

Bethany Good heavens, yes. Oh dear. Hang about. Hup!

Great Aunt Repetitus And with her little finger the witch lifted the tree off them . . .

More creaks from Kevin.

Bethany Hey *voilà*!

Fred (*trying to rise*) Thank you. We're so –

Bethany No, no . . . Please. Don't get up. You must rest, both of you. You look so sweet lying there. Do you know what you remind me of? Babes in the Wood. You lie there and sleep. (*bending low over them*) And if you're both specially good – you'll get a goodnight kiss. Like this . . . (*She kisses Nell on the forehead.*) . . . and this . . . (*She kisses Fred.*) . . . There!

Great Aunt Repetitus And as the witch kissed them both on their foreheads . . .

Uncle Oblivious (*muttering*) Foreheads! That's the word . . .

Great Aunt Repetitus (*glaring at him*) . . . and as she kissed them she drew from inside their heads all the secret dreams they'd ever dreamt and all the secret loves they'd ever treasured. And pursing her lips, she blew them clear away into the bright morning air . . . Then Molly no longer remembered Jonas . . . and Jonas forgot Molly. And likewise Flavius forgot Nell and Nell forgot Flavius . . . So for each of them, the other no longer existed . . .

Uncle Erraticus Brilliant!

Uncle Oblivious Bravo!

Great Aunt Repetitus (*as she rises*) And the StoryPlayers, their tale told, gathered up their belongings and departed slowly for another place, for another story . . .

*The Players, except for Fred, slowly leave the stage.
Albert replaces the sign that says 'STORIES TOLD HERE
TODAY AT 10.30 A.M.' They are followed by the Story-
Tellers, moving as they speak.*

Great Aunt Repetitus And not one of them remembered
Flavius. Nor did Flavius remember them. In fact,
wherever he was, the witch had taken so much of his
memory, he couldn't even remember his own name.
Indeed, he became convinced that his name was Fred.

Uncle Erraticus Fred?

Uncle Oblivious Fred?

Great Aunt Repetitus Why not? It's as good a name as
any other.

They all go out, leaving Fred sitting as at the start.

Fred (*to no one in particular*) I've been waiting here a
very long time indeed. (*reflecting*) At least, I think I have.

Nell enters. She carries her bundle as before.

Nell (*seeing Fred*) Oh, hallo.

Fred Hallo.

Nell Why, it's – Isn't it –? Yes. Aren't you –?

Fred Fred.

Nell No, you're not. Surely you're . . .?

Fred Fred. My name's Fred.

Nell Well. Alright, then. I'm Nell.

Fred How do you do?

Nell Fred? (*She stares at him.*) Are you *sure* that's your
name?

Fred Don't start that again, please.

Nell Strange. It must have been another story, mustn't it?

Fred What?

Nell Another time. Yes. It was a happy time, I know that.

Fred (*suspecting she is slightly deranged*) Oh, yes? Good.

Nell So anyway what story are you in at the moment, Fred?

Fred Story? I'm not in a story

Nell Oh, but you must be.

Fred What story?

Nell Whoever's telling it. The story by the person who made you up.

Fred Made me up? What are you talking about?

Nell Invented you. The reason you're here is because someone somewhere is telling a story about you. You knew that, surely? If you don't mind my saying so, you're not very well informed are you, Fred? You don't seem to know much.

Fred I know plenty of things, never you mind.

Nell What, for instance? You don't even look as if you know what you're doing here.

Fred I know what I'm doing here.

Nell What?

Fred I'm doing here – waiting – waiting patiently for these stories to start. When are they going to start? I've been waiting here for ages.

Nell How long? Exactly?

Fred (*puzzled*) I don't know. Exactly. Does it matter? Hours and hours. Days and days. I don't know. Years and years. For ever.

Nell For ever after. Fascinating. You know, I'm not certain yet if I'm appearing in your story or you're appearing in my story. But the fact is we're both in the same story now. Obviously. And the story is apparently that I should come on here ahead of the others in order to meet you alone. Presumably. Why?

Fred No idea.

Nell Why to meet you? There must have been a reason. We shall see, won't we? This must have an ending or they couldn't have started it. How exciting Which one of them could possibly have told it like this? It must have been one of them . . .

Fred One of who?

Nell Well, either . . .

Before she can answer, though, the other StoryPlayers, Bethany, Talitha, Jenkin and Albert, enter as before.

Nell Ah! Here they are

Bethany Here we are.

Jenkin Here we are.

Talitha Here we are.

Albert Are we? Thank heavens.

Nell Everyone, this is Fred.

Jenkin (*coolly*) Oh, yes?

Talitha Oh, how lovely. Another character.

251

Bethany (*looking Fred up and down appreciatively*) Another character. Delicious.

Albert Not before time.

Fred Hallo . . .

Nell Fred, this is Bethany . . .

Bethany Hallo. He seems familiar, doesn't he?

Talitha Yes, he does rather. I'm Talitha, hallo.

Fred (*a bit overwhelmed*) Hallo.

Talitha But I can't think where we could have met him, Bethany, can you?

Bethany No. But he's not someone you'd forget, is he, Talitha?

Talitha Not at all.

Bethany (*to Nell*) What did you say his name was, Nell?

Nell Fred.

Bethany Fred?

Talitha Fred?

Bethany No.

Talitha No.

Albert I knew a Fred once.

Nell Did you?

Albert (*indicating Fred*) But it wasn't this one.

Nell No?

Albert No, this particular Fred died when he was fifty-seven. Eaten by a giant.

Talitha Sad.

Jenkin Personally, I have never known anyone called Fred, alive or dead. But you are familiar . . . (*He walks away and starts to unpack his bundle in a distant corner.*)

Fred Good. Well, are we –? Are you all going to tell us a story then. Now you're here?

They all look at him blankly.

Please?

Albert Oh, no.

Bethany No.

Nell No.

Talitha No.

Jenkin Certainly not.

Bethany We're not the Story *Tellers* . . .

Nell We're Story *Players*.

Bethany Quite different.

Talitha Quite, quite different.

Albert Quite, quite, quite different.

Fred Alright then, who is telling these stories, if you're not?

Talitha They are, of course.

Bethany Who else?

Fred Who?

Nell Either Great Aunt Repetitus . . .

Albert If you like hearing things twice . . .

Talitha Or Uncle Erraticus . . .

Albert When he can remember to get it right . . .

Bethany Or Uncle Oblivious . . .

Albert If he can remember anything at all.

Talitha He forgot on the way here.

Bethany That's why we're late.

Nell (*to Fred*) Don't worry, they'll be along shortly.

Talitha They're quite elderly.

Bethany *Extremely* elderly.

Jenkin They're all half dead. Well, I'm ready. I don't know about the rest of you.

Talitha Well, now you're going to have to wait, Jenkin, aren't you?

Nell Because the Storytellers aren't here, are they?

Bethany Why don't you make one up yourself, Jenkin?

Talitha Yes, off you go, Jenkin.

Nell Come on, Jenkin . . .

Albert Go for it, Jenkin.

Jenkin If you think I'm doing anything just so you lot can snigger . . . I can wait. Anyway, we haven't even got . . . Where is he?

Bethany (*alarmed*) Oh no . . . . . .

Albert (*equally so*) Oh.

Nell (*alarmed*) Oh no . . .

Jenkin (*equally so*) Oh.

Fred What's the matter?

Talitha (*agitatedly*) Oh, oh, oh . . .

Nell (*to Jenkin*) What have you done with him?

Fred Done with who?

Nell Kevin on Keyboards, of course.

Albert What are we going to do?

Nell Now, don't panic. Everyone spread out and look for him.

Albert Spread out!

Talitha Spread out!

Bethany Spread out!

Jenkin Spread out!

They all spread out.

Fred (*still mystified*) I'm still not quite certain who we're looking for?

Nell Kevin on Keyboards. Who do you think? Honestly! Don't you know *anything*?

Albert Kevin on Keyboards! Come on, call him, you lot.

Bethany Kevin on Keyboards!

Nell Kevin on Keyboards!

Talitha Kevin on Keyboards!

Jenkin Kevin on Keyboards!

Fred Kevin on Keyboards! (*to Nell*) What does he look like?

Nell Well, obviously he looks exactly like . . .

Bethany Shh!

Talitha Listen!

Albert Shhh!

Jenkin Shh! Everyone.

A distant squeaking noise, approaching.

Nell That's him. (*calling*) Kevin on Keyboards!

All (*shouting*) Kevin on Keyboards!

The roar of an engine, the squeal of tyres and Kevin on Keyboards arrives. He screeches to a halt at the edge of the stage.

Fred (*recovering from the sigh*t) What is it?

Nell Kevin on Keyboards.

Albert This is Kevin. This is his keyboard.

Fred Is he a story teller?

Bethany Not really, no.

Talitha But he does help tell the stories, don't you Kevin?

Kevin presses a note and a voice from somewhere says 'YOU BET I DO, HONEYCHILD.'

Nell Kevin, this is Fred.

Fred Hallo, Kevin, how do you do?

Kevin presses a key and plays a chorus of 'hallo's'.

Bethany That's just his way of saying hallo.

Talitha I think he likes you.

Fred (*to Kevin*) You know, he seems familiar. I've met him before.

Nell Have you? That's interesting. Where?

Fred I can't think where.

Nell Try and think, Fred. It could be important.

Albert (*to Fred*) Were you ever a woodcutter? Maybe that's where we've met?

Fred No, I don't think so.

Albert A miller? A blacksmith? A magic shoemaker?

Fred No. I'm sure I'd have remembered.

Nell He doesn't remember anything, Albert. Who is he? Why do we all know him?

Talitha Someone should have given him some thoughts, surely?

Bethany And memories . . .

Talitha And ideas.

Bethany Careless. It wouldn't have taken long, would it?

Albert As the Swineherd once said to me . . . Ideas cost nothing.

Nell (*touching Fred lightly on the cheek*) You poor thing. We'll find out about you. Don't worry.

Fred (*frowning, taking her hand*) Nell . . .?

Nell Yes? What is it, Fred?

Fred Nell . . . Oh, Nell . . . (*He looks round the group.*) Bethany . . .?

Bethany Yes . . .

Fred Talitha?

Talitha Yes.

Bethany He's remembering . . .

Nell Sssh!

Fred Albert . . .?

Albert That's me.

Fred Jenkin . . .?

Jenkin Yes.

Nell Who are you? Who are you *really*, Fred . . .

Fred I'm F – Fl – Flav – ius. Fla – vius . . .

Nell Flavius?

Bethany Flavius?

Talitha Flavius?

Albert Flavius?

Jenkin Flavius?

Nell (*overjoyed*) Oh, Flavius . . .

> *She throws her arms round him. Fred is a little bewildered.*

Albert (*with a whoop*) Flavius!

Bethany (*likewise*) Flavius!

Talitha (*likewise*) Flavius!

Jenkin (*likewise*) Flavius!

> *Kevin strikes up a wild jig. The four dance wildly for a moment. Nell and Fred watch amused.*

Fred Just a minute! Just a minute! Before we celebrate too soon. Remember, we are not, as they say, clear of the wood. We have not yet dealt with the StoryTellers. They are still telling stories for us and they are capable of telling more.

Albert True.

Talitha What do we do?

Nell Flavius?

Jenkin Flavius?

Fred Leave them to me

Kevin plays a fanfare.

Albert Here they come!

Bethany Here they come!

Talitha Here they come!

Jenkin Here they come!

Nell They're coming!

They all stand back respectfully. Fred follows suit. The Storytellers enter together as before. The Players stand motionless, waiting.

Great Aunt Repetitus Here we are, then.

Uncle Erraticus Here we are.

Uncle Oblivious Here we are.

Great Aunt Repetitus Time for stories!

Uncle Erraticus Stories!

Uncle Oblivious Stories!

A fanfare from Kevin on Keyboards. The three
Storytellers hobble to their positions outside the acting
area where they seat themselves. The Players gather at
the edge of the stage, and wait expectantly. Fred
stands with them.

Albert (*as they do this, cheerfully*) What happens now?

Nell What do we do next?

Bethany What's going to happen?

Talitha Flavius?

Jenkin Flavius?

Fred Shhh!

Great Aunt Repetitus And the first story will be told
by . . . (*She pauses dramatically.*)

Nell Wait for it!

Fred Me.

Great Aunt Repetitus What?

Uncle Erraticus What?

Uncle Oblivious What?

Great Aunt Repetitus How dare you?

Uncle Oblivious Who is he?

Uncle Erraticus No idea.

Fred Once upon a time, there were three old Storytellers – Great Aunt Repetitus, Uncle Erraticus and
Uncle Oblivious . . .

Great Aunt Repetitus Eh?

Uncle Erraticus Eh?

Uncle Oblivious Eh?

Fred And these three Storytellers had so outlived their welcome that they decided never to tell stories again. Ever.

Uncle Oblivious What's he saying? What's he saying?

Fred And so Uncle Oblivious said to the Players:

Uncle Oblivious I'm awfully sorry. I'm not going to tell any more stories ever – I'm just going to go and lie down for the next 150 years if you'll excuse me . . . What am I saying? I'm not saying that. Who's saying this . . . Goodbye . . . Who am I saying? I'm not saying this. Goodbye. Not goodbye. Yes, goodbye.

Players Goodbye!

   Uncle Oblivious goes off, looking rather dazed.

Fred And then Uncle Erraticus, who had been watching all this . . .

Uncle Erraticus Oh, no, oh, no. Not with me you don't, young man

Fred Decided it was time to stretch his legs and up he got and almost immediately he banged his foot –

Uncle Erraticus (*doing so*) Ow!

Fred And then, would you believe, his knee.

Uncle Erraticus Ooo!

Great Aunt Repetitus Erraticus!

Fred And then his head –

Uncle Erraticus Ouch!

Fred And then his elbow!

Uncle Erraticus Oook! . . .

Great Aunt Repetitus Erraticus! What are you playing at?

Fred Which made him hop up and down like a deranged rabbit . . .

Uncle Erraticus (*hopping about*) You can't do this to me . . . I forbid it!

Fred And, would you believe it, the poor man jumped up and down so furiously that eventually his trousers caught fire.

Smoke starts to come from Uncle Erraticus.

Great Aunt Repetitus Erraticus!

Uncle Erraticus Oh, no, no, no . . . Help . . .

Fred And he ran from that building and into the nearby duck pond and was never seen again. Bye!

Players Goodbye!

Fred turns to Great Aunt Repetitus.

Great Aunt Repetitus I hope you don't think you can frighten me, young man, because you can't. I'm a far better story teller than you are. If you don't believe it try me . . .

Fred You're not that good.

Great Aunt Repetitus Good enough for you.

Fred Why do you think I'm still here? Why hasn't Flavius disappeared like you planned for him to disappear? Ever after? Tell me that?

Great Aunt Repetitus You're still here because one of those two old fools made a mistake . . . Probably

Oblivious. He forgot. He's always forgetting. He forgets everything. He brought you back.

Fred It wasn't Uncle Oblivious.

Great Aunt Repetitus Erraticus then. What does it matter? Erraticus made one of his mistakes. He makes mistakes all the time. You're another of them . . .

Fred He's not the one, either.

Great Aunt Repetitus Who else? Who else could possibly –? (*staring at him*) Me? Don't be ridiculous.

Fred Remember, you're the one who tells stories that go in circles. You're the one who kept bringing me back – and back – and back . . .

Great Aunt Repetitus It can't be . . . It can't be me . . .

Fred It is . . .

Great Aunt Repetitus I don't . . . I don't believe you . . .

Fred And so Great Aunt Repetitus started to tell her last story . . .

Great Aunt Repetitus You're lying . . . you're a little liar . . .

Fred There was once . . .

Great Aunt Repetitus There was once . . . you can't do this to me . . .

Fred An old woman . . .

Great Aunt Repetitus An old woman . . .

Fred Who told stories that went round and round . . .

Great Aunt Repetitus Round and round . . .

Fred And that was all there was . . .

Great Aunt Repetitus And that was all there was once an old woman who told stories that went round and round and that was all there was once an old woman who told stories that went round and round and that was all there was once . . . etc.

She goes off still reciting her tale and getting faster and faster. Kevin accelerates her story even more.

Fred Bye!

Players (*as she goes*) Goodbye!

Albert Free!

Bethany Free!

Talitha Free!

Jenkin Free!

Nell We're free.

Fred Wait! One last story. A very short one . . . Are you all ready?

All Ready.

Fred Once upon a time . . .

All Once upon a time . . .

Fred There was a group of players . . .

All There was a group of players . . .

Fred Albert . . .

Albert Albert . . .

Fred Bethany . . .

Bethany Bethany . . .

Fred Talitha . . .

Talitha Talitha . . .

Fred Jenkin . . .

Jenkin Jenkin . . .

Fred Kevin on Keyboards . . .

Kevin plays: 'Kevin on Keyboards'.

Fred And not forgetting Nell . . .

Nell Not forgetting Nell . . .

Fred And they all, every one of them lived . . .

All . . . every one of them lived . . .

Fred . . . happily . . .

All . . . happily . . .

Fred . . . ever . . .

All . . . ever . . . AFTER!!!

And with a whoop they all run off.
Curtain.

MY VERY OWN STORY

Characters

Scene: Here, there and everywhere
Any old time.

My Very Own Story was first performed at the
Stephen Joseph Theatre in the Round, Scarborough,
on 10 August 1991. The cast was as follows:

The Storytellers
Percy Parton Peter Bourke
Peter Patchett Crispin Letts
Paul Peel James Simmons
The Keyboard Player John Pattison

The Donkey
Rupert James Simmons
Gorff Robert Austin
Yerp Jeffrey Chiswick
Mrs Yerp Elizabeth Kelly
Frederick Glyn Grain
Leonora Rebecca Lacey

The Enchanted Suitor
Frederick Peter Bourke
Alicia Anna Keaveney
Cecilia Isabel Lloyd
Emilia Elizabeth Rider

The Sorcerer's Daughters
Varius Crispin Letts
Cecilia/Alicia Isabel Lloyd
Alicia/Cecilia Anna Keaveney
Emilia Elizabeth Rider
Denzil Gary Whitaker
Basil Robert Austin
A Village Boy Jeffrey Chiswick

Director Alan Ayckbourn
Musical Director John Pattison
Designer Juliet Nichols
Lighting Jackie Staines

Act One

The keyboard player is in place and already playing.
Percy sticks his head round the curtain and signals. The
keyboard player plays a fanfare. Percy enters.

Percy Thank you, thank you. You're very kind. Splendid.
Marvellous. My name is Percy Parton and may I say
straight away how delighted I was to receive your
invitation to come along here today to entertain you
with this, my very own story. Please remember, ladies
and gentlemen, if you will, that what you are about to
witness here in a few moment's time is my very own
personal, individual, singular and utterly original
narrative. Remember where you heard it first – from
me, the horse's mouth. (*He laughs.*) But seriously, enough
of that and, as we often say in the magical world of the
theatre, on with the show. May I first of all introduce to
you the people who will be assisting me today. Taking
care of music and melody, on keyboards, Mr Reg Cord.

The keyboard player plays a fanfare and
acknowledges the audience.

Secondly, those most important people who will be
taking part in my very own story – ladies and gentlemen
– the actors!

The actors come on, bow briefly and go off again.

Now, do bear with me, ladies and gentlemen, I have
outside in the taxi – which is still ticking over incidentally – one or two small props and additional items
which we will be using to assist us with our storytelling.

I won't be one moment, I promise. Perhaps in the meantime I could ask Mr Cord, if he would, to entertain you with a selection of brief musical moments. Won't be one second. Don't go away. Thank you, Mr Cord.

As Percy goes off, the keyboard player begins to play again, as at the start. After a moment, from a different direction, Peter sticks his head round the curtain. He signals to the keyboard player who plays a fanfare. Peter enters.

Peter Thank you, everyone, so very much. You're most kind. I must apologize for being a tiny bit late. Blame the traffic. Hallo, my name is Peter Patchett and may I say, right at the start, how delighted I was to receive your invitation to come along here today to entertain you with this, my very own story. Never forget, ladies and gentlemen, if you will, that what you are about to witness here in just a second or two will be my own personal, unique, singular and quintessentially original narrative. Avoid cheap imitations, insist only on the original – yours truly! (*He laughs.*) But enough mirth for the present and, as we often say in the wondrous world of the theatre, let's get this show on the road. May I first of all, though, introduce you to the people who will be assisting me today. Taking care of music and melody, on keyboards, Mr Bill Notes, ladies and gentlemen.

The keyboard player plays a fanfare and acknowledges the audience. He looks a bit puzzled.

Secondly, those people who will be taking part in my very own story – ladies and gentlemen – the players themselves!

The actors come on, bow briefly and go off again. They also look a little puzzled.

Now, you're going to have to excuse me just one second, ladies and gentlemen. I have to fetch one or two small properties and technical items from my van outside, I'm afraid. I won't be one moment. I do so apologize. Meanwhile, I will ask Mr Notes if he'd be good enough to entertain you with a few lingering magical musical moments. Won't be one second. Stay right there. Take it away, Mr Notes.

As Peter goes off, the keyboard player begins to play again, as at the start. After a moment, Percy hurries back with a suitcase of props, he puts them at one side of the stage.

Percy Won't keep you long. Carry on, Mr Cord.

Percy hurries off. From a different direction, Paul sticks his head round the curtain. He signals to the keyboard player who plays a fanfare. Paul enters, rather breathless.

Paul Look, I'm terribly late I know and I do sincerely beg your pardon, all of you. I'm afraid we have British Rail to thank for this. My name is Paul Peel and, believe me, I'm delighted to be here at long last. Thank you for asking me. And for your patience. I won't waste a moment longer of your time. Just quickly to put you in the picture. What you're about to hear is my incomparable, unparalleled, supremely distinctive, highly individual, very own story. Beware of cheap imitations, insist on the original – me. (*He laughs.*) But – no time for jokes, let us, as we show business people are wont to say, ring up the curtain. But before we do that, I must first introduce to you the people who will be assisting me today. Taking care of music and melody – on keyboards, ladies and gentlemen, Mr Brian Tune.

The keyboard player plays a fanfare and acknowledges the audience. He looks still more puzzled.

275

And now those special people who will be playing various roles in my very own story today – ladies and gentlemen – the performers!

The actors come on, as before, bow briefly and go off again. They now seem thoroughly confused and a bit cross.

Listen, I'm afraid I'm going to have to crave just one more smidgin of your patience. I've got a couple of bags of stuff outside I have to bring in before we can start, I do beg your pardon. So I'm going to ask Mr Tune here if he'd mind playing you a few myriad melodies, just for a quick second. Would you mind most awfully, Mr Tune? Thank you. Won't be a tick.

As Paul goes off, the keyboard player begins to play again, as at the start. After a moment, Peter hurries back with a box of props, he puts them at one side of the stage.

Peter (*smiling at the audience*) Nearly there. Keep going, Mr Notes.

Peter goes off. Percy comes on. He has another case. He puts it at the side of the stage with the other.

Percy (*smiling at the audience*) That's the lot. Just going to pay the taxi. Thank you, Mr Cord, keep up the good work.

Percy goes off. Paul comes on with a bag of props which he puts at the side of the stage.

Paul One more. Hang on. Carry on, Mr Tune.

Paul goes off. Peter comes on with another box of props which he puts with the first.

Peter That's it. Sorry to keep you. Just got to lock the van. Bravo, Mr Notes, thank you.

Peter goes off. Percy comes back.

Percy Alright now, thank you for waiting. And thank you, Mr Cord, thank you, Reg. A big hand for Reg Cord, ladies and gentlemen.

Percy leads the applause. The keyboard player acknowledges this.

Thank you, thank you. Now. Pay close attention, if you will. My very own story. Let us take a second to imagine, ladies and gentlemen, if you will, that we are in a dark, dark wood. Imagine that.

Percy pauses dramatically, eyes closed. Peter returns.

Peter (*without noticing Percy*) Thank you, ladies and gentlemen, you've been very patient, thank you again and a special big thank you to Mr Notes for keeping us all entertained. Ladies and gentlemen, on keyboards, Mr Bill Notes. Thank you.

Peter leads the applause. The keyboard player acknowledges this. Percy stares in amazement.

Thank you so much, you're very generous. Now, gather round everyone please for this, my very own story. It started one bright September morning when I was –

Percy Hey! I say. Oy!

Peter What?

Percy I say – do you mind?

Peter Sorry. Do you mind?

Percy I'm saying, do you mind?

Peter Look, do you mind?

Percy No, no, I'm asking, do you mind . . .

Peter That's what I'm asking you, do you mind . . .

Percy No, I' m the one who's doing the asking. Do you mind?

Peter Well, yes, I do mind. I certainly do mind, if you don't mind.

Percy Me? I mind. Indeed I do mind. Never mind asking me if I mind, I'm asking you, do you mind?

Peter How many more times, yes, I do. I mind very much.

Percy Well, so do I. So mind out of the way.

Peter Mind it, now, mind it.

Percy No, you mind it, mate, you're the one to mind it. I've a good mind to give you a piece of my mind in a minute, mind.

Peter I don't mind. See if I mind. You're out of your mind, anyway. I've half a mind to –

Percy A mind to what? A mind to what?

Peter Never mind. (*muttering*) Mindless git.

Percy (*threateningly*) Now, mind your language!

Peter Mind your own business!

> *They stand facing each other antagonistically. Paul returns with his second bag. He fails to notice the other two.*

Paul Thank you so much, ladies and gentlemen, and I do promise you that will be our last delay, the very last one. And under the circumstances I think a specially big hand for our noble keyboard player, Mr Tune, is in order. Ladies and gentlemen, Mr Brian Tune

*Paul leads the applause. The keyboard player
acknowledges this. Peter and Percy stand stupefied.*

Thank you so very much. Now, without further delay,
off we go – my very own story, chapter one. Imagine if
you will one wet afternoon in June. I was just returning
from –

Percy and Peter (*together*) Oy! I'm sorry . . .

Paul (*puzzled*) Sorry?

Percy No, I'm sorry . . .

Paul You're sorry? Sorry, I'm the one that should be
sorry, surely –

Peter There's no point in being sorry now, is there?

A slight pause as they stare at each other.

Percy (*muttering*) Well, this is a sorry state of affairs

Paul Sorry?

Percy Sorry, I was just . . .

They look at each other. Another pause.

Peter I think we ought to sort this out, don't you?

Percy We should.

Paul It's perfectly simple. I've every right to be here and
you two haven't. That's the long and the short of it.

Percy Is it now?

Paul Yes.

Peter Really?

Paul It most certainly is.

Percy Please excuse us one minute, ladies and gentlemen.

Peter One moment . . .

Paul Just one second. Music please, Mr Tune –

Percy Mr Cord . . .

Peter Mr Note . . .

The keyboard player, rather bewildered, starts to play feverishly.

Percy (*rather quickly*) Quiet!

Peter *Quiet!*

Paul QUIET!!!

The keyboard player stops playing.

Percy Listen, this can be sorted out very quickly. There's obviously been a double – triple booking here. Quite easily sorted out. No need for aggravation, I'm sure. After all, we're all members of the wonderful brotherhood of showbusiness . . . (*He produces a contract from his pocket.*) . . . here we are, legal proof . . . if proof is needed . . . (*reading*) This agreement between on the one hand the theatre company hereinafter known as the employer and the undersigned hereinafter referred to as the entertainer . . . (*skipping a bit*) . . . diddly-diddly-doo . . . I, Percy Parton, do hereby agree . . .

Peter (*reading from an identical contract he has produced*) . . . I, Peter Patchett, do hereby agree . . .

Paul (*doing likewise*) . . . I, Paul Peel, do hereby agree

Percy . . . to abide . . .

Peter . . . to abide . . .

Paul . . . to abide . . .

Percy . . . by . . .

Peter . . . by . . .

Paul . . . by . . .

They stare at each other.

Percy (*grabbing Peter's contract*) Let me see that . . .

Peter (*grabbing Paul's contract*) Let me see that . . .

Paul (*grabbing Percy's contract*) Let me see that . . .

A pause while they study the respective documents, muttering through the small print.

Percy (*grabbing Paul's contact from Peter*) Let me see that . . .

Peter (*grabbing Percy's contract from Paul*) Let me see that . . .

Paul (*grabbing Peter's contract from Percy*) Let me see that . . .

A pause while they study the respective documents as before.

Percy That seems . . .

He hands Paul's contract back to Peter.

Peter . . . to be . . .

He hands Percy's contract back to Paul.

Paul . . . in order

He hands Peter's contract back to Percy.

All . . . yes.

They glance at the contracts, realize they have the wrong ones and exchange yet again.

All . . . yes.

Peter This needs thinking about.

Percy Yes.

Paul Yes.

Peter Mr Note . . .

Percy Mr Cord . . .

Paul Mr Tune . . .

*They ponder. The keyboard player starts to play
again. He has barely started when:*

Percy Just a moment!

The keyboard player stops.

Peter (*startled*) What?

Paul (*similarly*) What is it?

Percy Listen, we are faced with a problem, right?

Peter Correct.

Paul True.

Percy Now, I may be wrong but it seems to me we have
far too many storytellers here.

Peter Two . . .

Paul . . . too many.

Percy So. (*to Peter*) Either you leave . . .

Paul Hear! Hear!

Peter Absolutely not . . .

Percy (*to Paul*) Or you leave . . .

Peter Brilliant.

Paul Out of the question . . .

Percy Or I leave . . .

Peter and Paul Good idea.

Percy – which we won't even bother to discuss.

Slight pause.

Peter So we're all staying.

Percy Exactly.

Paul Precisely.

Peter Well, we can't tell three stories, can we?

Percy Take all night.

Paul Right.

Peter In that case, we'd better all tell the same story.

Percy Well, you're certainly not going to tell my very own story.

Paul Nobody tells my very own story but me.

Peter Well, I was thinking we might tell my very own story, actually.

Percy Your very own story?

Paul Certainly not. It's yours.

Peter Just an idea.

Slight pause. An Actor appears from offstage.

Actor Excuse me . . .

Percy Yes?

Peter Yes?

Paul What is it?

Actor Will we be starting soon . . .?

Percy In a minute . . .

Actor . . . only the lads are getting a bit restless . . .

Peter . . . two seconds . . .

Actor . . . only we've been bowing a lot, you see, but not a lot of acting . . .

Paul Literally, half a second . . .

Actor Sorry to trouble you.

Percy Not at all.

The Actor goes off again.

Paul I think –

Percy Yes?

Peter Yes?

Paul I think the only way around this, is to decide it by chance.

Percy We could draw for it.

Peter Lots?

Percy Well, once or twice. Just till we decide.

Paul I've got it. The yes or no game. We all keep talking but none of us can say yes or no. If we say yes or no, we're out of the game. Last one in wins. What about that, then?

Percy and Peter No.

The keyboard player makes a gong sound as he does on all subsequent 'yes's and no's' during the game.

Paul Right, you're both out. I win.

Percy We weren't ready.

Peter Not ready.

Percy Anyway, it's a stupid game, you can never win it.

Paul Yes, you can.

Gong.

Percy Right, that's you out.

Paul I wasn't playing.

Percy (*to Peter*) You heard him, he said it, didn't he?

Peter Yes.

Gong.

Percy Right that's you out too, I win.

Peter I wasn't ready.

Paul He didn't say anything, did he?

Percy Yes, he did.

Gong.

Paul Right, that's you out . . .

Percy Just a minute, just a minute . . .

Peter Alright. Start again. This is the real start. OK? The real start of the game. Both ready?

Percy (*carefully*) I am ready.

Paul I am quite ready. (*Silence.*)

Peter Somebody say something.

Percy Why?

Peter Because we can't decide the game unless somebody says something, can we? (*Pause.*)

Paul Very nice weather, isn't it?

Percy When?

Paul Lately.

Peter Where?

Paul Up – there – in the sky. (*Pause.*)

Peter (*suddenly, to Paul*) Sorry, did you say something?

Paul No.

   Gong.

Peter Out!

Paul That wasn't fair.

Percy Out!

Peter Just me and you.

Percy Just us. (*A silence.*)

Peter (*suddenly, as before*) Sorry. Did you say something?

Percy Who, me?

Peter Yes.

   Gong.

Percy Out!

Peter That was cheating.

Paul Out!

Percy I win. Now, my very own story –

Peter What do we do, then?

Paul What happens to us?

Percy I don't know. Goodbye, then.

Peter Goodbye?

Percy Off you go.

Paul Go?

Percy So long.

Peter But we –

Percy Cheerio.

Paul We –

Percy Ta-ta.

Paul and Peter leave reluctantly.

Paul (*returning momentarily*) What about all our –

He indicates the bags of props etc.

Percy Later. You can collect them later.

Paul finally leaves.

Ladies and gentlemen, at long last My Very Own Story.
It is a tragic Victorian tale entitled, *The Donkey*.

Music and light change.

Imagine it is night time in a dark wood, a few days
before a Christmas, many long forgotten years ago. It
is bitterly cold, a sharp, slicing, biting wind; thick snow
lies on the ground. Snow so deep that it is now almost
impossible to make out the rough cart track that winds
between the trunks of the huge tall trees. Very few
people venture this way in weather such as this and
rarely if ever at night. Yet it was along this very path on
that day before Christmas Eve that I, Rupert Fellowes,
found myself travelling alone. I was intending to spend
the holidays with my brother and his family. They had
recently moved away from our home and we had
consequently lost touch. I was now anxious to see both

him and his wife and most especially my angelic little nephews and nieces for whom I had bought a whole trunk load of gifts and presents. I confess though that, when I set out, I had no idea what a remote and god-forsaken district they had chosen for their new home. Difficult to reach even in mid-summer, the recent snowstorms had made their village all but inaccessible. Indeed few local coachmen would agree to venture out at all and I had nearly given up hope of finding a driver. Then one particular fellow named Gorff approached me and offered his services. Had I not been so anxious for transportation, I might have realized that his willingness to convey me concealed an evil and ulterior design.

At this point the 'coach' enters. It is driven by Gorff, an evil-looking coachman. In the back is Paul muffled up and unrecognizable in coat, scarf and hat. He is being shaken about as Gorff struggles with his horses.

Gorff (*cursing*) Gwaaaan . . . Gooworrn . . . gwaaarn, yer bleezers . . . yup . . . yurr . . . gworrn . . .

Percy This Gorff was certainly an evil enough looking fellow but I prided myself on never judging others on first appearances. The journey was, though, one of the most thoroughly uncomfortable I had ever undergone. Gorff's coach could well have benefited from care and attention, his horses from food and better treatment, and his passengers from a little consideration.

Gorff Whooyer . . . whooa . . . wheeerr . . . whooorrrr! (*He reins back the horses and the coach stops.*)

Percy Unexpectedly, the coach pulled up with a shud-dering suddenness. I must confess the abrupt lack of motion was a considerable physical relief. I wondered what the cause of our stopping might be. I leant out of the window and called to the man.

Paul I say – I say, what's happening? Why have we stopped, coachman?

Percy The man Gorff, by way of reply, climbed down off the box seat, muttering incomprehensibly.

Gorff climbs down, muttering.

Gorff Mun git down wearn stuckinasnow . . .

Paul What's that you say?

Gorff Stuckinasnow . . . (*gesticulating to demonstrate*) Stuckin! Stuckin!

Paul Stuckin? Oh, stuck in . . .

Gorff Ar. Stuckinasnow

Paul Ah! Stuck in the snow. Oh yes, quite. I see. Are we? Oh, dear . . .

Gorff Git darn. Mun git darn.

Paul Mun git darn?

Gorff Ye mun git darn.

Paul Mun git darn?

Gorff *Ye* mun git darn.

Paul You mean e mun git darn? Ah. Mun git darn?

Percy I confess to a certain difficulty understanding the fellow.

Gorff (*insistent*) Git darn.

Paul Git darn? Git darn? What on earth can he mean? Oh, you mean get down. You want me to git darn?

Gorff Git darn on the grarn.

Paul On the grarn. Right. (*He climbs out.*)

Percy It was bitterly cold out of the coach.

Paul Brrr!

Gorff Mun pushem. (*demonstrating*) Pushem, see?

Paul Pushem, yes. You want me to pushem, do you?

Gorff Ar. (*He moves off and starts to climb up again.*)

Paul Righty-ho. What are you going to do?

Gorff Pullem. Oi mun pullem.

Paul Oh, I see. You're going to pullem. I'll pushem, you pullem. Fair enough.

Gorff Uroit!

Paul Say when. I'm ready. (*He braces himself against the back of the coach.*)

Gorff Uroit!

Paul Er – right.

Gorff (*whipping up the horses*) Giddy – or – arrr! Hup!

> He moves off rapidly. Paul falls over in the snow. Gorff exits.

Paul Grooo!

Percy And to my horror, before I could prevent him, the fellow had whipped up the horses and in a trice had galloped into the night, leaving me face down in the snow.

Paul Hoy!

Percy I clambered to my feet and shouted after the fellow cursing him roundly in no uncertain terms.

Paul (*calling after Gorff*) Rogue! Villain! Scoundrel!

Percy But to no avail. My voice was all but lost in the
increasing blizzard. I looked around me for signs of
assistance but I was completely alone and helplessly lost.
The knave had taken everything I owned. My hip flask,
my travelling rug, all my luggage and, worse still, all the
Christmas presents intended for my angelic little
nephews and nieces.

Paul Blackguard! (*He shivers.*)

Percy I knew if I failed to find shelter soon I would
swiftly perish from the cold; but in which direction to
walk I had little idea. I was, I confess, hopelessly lost
now, as the last evidence of the cart track disappeared
under ever deepening snow. I walked for what seemed
miles and miles; but for all I know, in circles.

Paul Help! Help!

Percy The cold wind sliced like a dagger through my
clothes, my limbs grew wearier, my voice weaker . . .

Paul (*feebly*) Help!

Percy And I resigned myself to death . . .

Paul sits huddled for a moment.

Then – all of a sudden – I caught sight of something. A
distant glimmer, a glint of – could it be lamplight – yes –
through that thick curtain of snowflakes . . . something!
I struggled to my feet . . . I was feeble now and had
reached the limit of my strength. Somehow I managed to
stagger towards that ray of light, of hope, of life itself . . .

*Paul does all this simultaneously with the narration.
He stops now.*

The source of light was from a lamp illuminating the
doorway of a large stone building – not quite a castle

but certainly a house of some considerable size. Summoning my last gram of strength I crawled to the portal and knocked upon the door.

Hollow knocking. Paul waits.

It seemed an age before anyone answered.

Mrs Yerp, a housekeeper, opens the door. Rattling of chains and bolts and a final creak.

Mrs Yerp (*suspiciously*) Yes?

Paul (*faintly*) Excuse me . . . I . . . I'm so sorry to trouble you I . . . I'm sorry I . . .

Percy But at that point my strength finally gave out.

Paul faints at Mrs Yerp's feet.

Mrs Yerp (*alarmed*) Mr Yerp! Mr Yerp!

Yerp, the family retainer, hurries on.

Yerp What's the matter, wife?

Mrs Yerp Help me. Help me with him, here.

During the next, Yerp and Mrs Yerp carry Paul inside. As they do this, Leonora pushes on a chaise on which they lie him.

Percy Whilst I was still unconscious they must have carried me inside, I do not recall. How long I remained thus I cannot tell. But my next memory will remain with me for the rest of my life. When I awoke I found myself lying on a chaise-longue beside a log fire. As I opened my eyes fully, there standing before me with a look of such tender compassion, a manner so demure and gentle, was the most beautiful woman I had ever seen in my life.

Leonora Help me to remove his outer garments, Mrs Yerp, they're soaked through . . .

Mrs Yerp Yes, madam . . .

Leonora Yerp, please build up the fire, he must be kept warm.

Yerp Yes, ma'am.

They remove Paul's coat, hat and scarf, revealing him for the first time.

Paul (*groaning*) Aaah!

Leonora He's regaining consciousness, quickly . . .

Paul (*groggily*) Who – who – waaa . . . way . . .

Leonora We must fetch blankets . . .

Percy (*recognizing Paul for the first time*) Just a minute. Hold it a minute . . .

The tableau freezes.

You. Yes, you.

Paul Me?

Percy What are you doing in my story?

Paul What do you think I'm doing? I'm playing Rupert.

Percy Rupert? Who said you could play Rupert?

Paul They did.

Percy They?

Paul Them back there. They said I could.

Percy What's it got to do with them?

Paul They said to me you can play him, they said. You look a right Rupert.

Percy Rubbish. You don't look anything like him. Get off at once. Where's the real bloke? The one who's supposed to be doing him?

Paul He's playing cards.

Percy Playing cards? I'm paying for him. Get him out here.

Leonora (*coming out of character*) Oh, leave him alone, he's good, this one.

Percy (*startled*) What?

Mrs Yerp (*likewise abandoning her character*) He is. He's brilliant.

Yerp He's great.

Leonora He's better than the other one.

Mrs Yerp Great improvement.

Yerp Certainly is . . .

Paul Thank you very much . . .

Percy Listen, what are you lot playing at? What's going on here?

Leonora Oh, go on . . .

Mrs Yerp Go on . . .

Yerp Go on . . .

Percy Whose story is this, anyway?

Leonora Oh, get on with it . . .

Paul Yes, get on with it . . .

Mrs Yerp (*with him*) Get on with it . . .

Yerp (*with them*) Get on!

Percy (*trying to be heard*) Just a minute . . .!

> The other actors have gathered on the edge of the
> stage in varying stages of dress, several apparently in
> mid card game.

Actors (*variously*) Get on . . . get on with it . . . go on . . . etc.

Percy (*shouting them down*) Alright! *Alright!* ALRIGHT!

Silence.

(*sulkily*) But I should have been asked first. This is my very own story and I should have been asked.

The other actors go off again. The others resume their tableau.

Carry on, then. (*Pause.*) Where were we?

Leonora I was asking them to fetch blankets.

Percy Well, go on, then . . .

Leonora We must fetch blankets . . .

Mrs Yerp Yes, madam.

Leonora And more logs for the fire . . .

Yerp Yes, ma'am.

Yerp and Mrs Yerp go off.

Percy I gazed in wonder at this beautiful woman.

Paul Who are you? Where am I?

Percy (*muttering*) He's not right for Rupert at all.

Leonora My name is Leonora Stringer. You are in Deepwood House. Mrs Yerp found you on our doorstep, half dead. How did you come to be here, on a night like this?

Paul I was – I . . . (*He tries to get up but feels giddy.*)

Leonora No, don't try to stand, you're exhausted. You need food and then you must sleep.

Paul My name is Rupert Fellowes. I need to reach my brother's house tonight. They're expecting me . . .

Leonora Where does he live?

Paul In Thornglade Village. Is it far?

Leonora Not too far. But you can't possibly travel there tonight. You must at least wait until morning.

Mrs Yerp returns with a blanket.

Mrs Yerp, we will dine immediately, please.

Mrs Yerp Yes, madam. But what about the master?

Leonora He – will probably join us – in due course.

Mrs Yerp Very good, madam.

Leonora And Mrs Yerp . . .

Mrs Yerp Yes, madam?

Leonora You had better warn my brother we have company tonight.

Mrs Yerp Yes, madam. (*She goes out.*)

Paul You live with your brother, Miss Stringer?

Leonora (*frowning*) Yes. I do, Mr Fellowes.

Percy At the mention of her brother, her smooth and quite flawless complexion became marred by the hint of a frown. I was to note this phenomenon on future occasions whenever he was present or his name mentioned.

Yerp pushes on a dining table. Mrs Yerp follows with two chairs. One she places at the end and another in the centre of the table.

Yerp Dinner is served, madam.

Leonora Thank you, Yerp. (*to Paul*) Please, Mr Fellowes . . . (*indicating the centre chair*) Sit here.

Yerp goes out again. Paul rises and sways.

(*alarmed*) Can you manage?

Paul Yes, I'm fine, Miss Stringer. I'm perfectly fine.

Mrs Yerp (*offering her arm*) Sir . . .

Paul Thank you. Thank you.

Mrs Yerp guides him to the table. He sits. Leonora does likewise. Yerp returns with a third dining chair which he places at the head of the table. Mrs Yerp starts to serve dinner. Yerp assists her.

Percy The dinner was superb and my hostess never less than completely charming. Nonetheless I could not entirely ignore the frequent and anxious glances she gave either towards the doorway or to the empty chair at the other end of the table.

Paul It's a great pity your brother is missing this delicious meal. May I enquire, will he soon be joining us?

Leonora It is of no consequence either way, Mr Fellowes. Frederick – my brother wouldn't – couldn't eat this at all, I fear. He's on a rather strict and special diet.

Paul Oh, dear.

Leonora For his health, that is all.

Paul Can he not eat meat?

Leonora Oh, no. Nor fish, nor game nor most vegetables.

Paul How tragic. What is wrong with him?

Leonora He's –

Frederick enters. He crosses to the table and sits
without looking at either Paul or Leonora. He gazes
ahead of him with a tortured expression.

Percy But before she could answer the door burst open
and I caught my first glimpse of her brother, Frederick
Stringer. If two natures in a brother and sister could ever
be described as opposing then here indeed was a striking
example. The one temperament sunny and outgoing, the
other dark and withdrawn. The man entered the room
but chose to ignore both of us completely.

Paul (*half rising*) Good evening, sir.

Frederick ignores him.

Leonora (*gently*) Frederick, dear, this is Mr Fellowes.
(*Silence.*) He was trapped in the storm and lost his way.
(*Silence.*) He will be staying here for the night with us, if
that is satisfactory.

Percy But the brother sat as though unable to hear his
sister at all.

Paul (*to himself*) How could one ignore such a divine
creature as this?

Leonora You must excuse my brother, Mr Fellowes.
Sometimes he – he – is lost in contemplation.

Paul Do not let it trouble you for an instant, Miss
Stringer. I fully understand.

Mrs Yerp enters and starts to serve Frederick. Once
she has done this, she leaves.

Percy After the appearance of the brother, the meal took
on a more sombre tone as we lapsed increasingly into
silence. In the absence of conversation, I could not help
but observe the food that was being served to the
brother, Frederick. It was indeed singular fare. Large

helpings of what appeared to be nothing more nor less than long grass, prettily served from a silver salver and accompanied – could my eyes be deceiving me? – by a salad of common or garden thistles.

Paul (*incredulously*) Thistles?

Leonora I beg your pardon, Mr Fellowes? Did you speak?

Paul No, Miss Stringer. I was merely remarking on the delicious quality of the food.

Leonora Oh.

Percy It was not until the very end of the meal that Mr Stringer was to utter his first words.

Frederick Leonora, I note that we have company. I was not informed of this.

Leonora Oh, I am sorry, my dear, I did –

Paul (*getting up and extending his hand*) How do you do, sir. My name is –

Frederick (*rising abruptly*) Goodnight to you, sir.

He goes out. A silence.

Leonora You really must excuse my brother, Mr Fellowes, he is . . . he is . . .

Paul (*helpfully*) Lost in contemplation, perhaps?

Leonora (*gratefully*) Precisely. He contemplates more and more these days.

Paul An admirable quality and one we would all of us be wise to emulate, Miss Stringer.

Percy But secretly I observed the man to be both uncouth and ungallant. How could brother and sister be so different?

Leonora (*drifting to the door*) Allow me to show you to your room, Mr Fellowes, you must be quite exhausted.

Paul But for the stimulation and excitement of the company, madam, I confess I would have fallen asleep an hour ago.

Leonora (*smiling*) You are too kind, Mr Fellowes.

Percy She and I were getting on like a house on fire.

They both move away to a 'bedchamber' area – possibly the chaise-longue.

I allowed the delicate creature to lead me to my bedchamber.

Leonora If everything is to your satisfaction, I will bid you goodnight, Mr Fellowes.

Paul Please, Miss Stringer, I would much prefer it if you were to call me Rupert.

Leonora Very well. If you so wish you may call me Leonora.

Paul Leonora.

Leonora Goodnight, Rupert.

Paul Goodnight, Leonora.

Leonora goes off. Paul, in due course, lies down. Yerp and Mrs Yerp enter under the next and re-arrange the table for breakfast.

Percy Once she had gone, leaving me with only the delicate aroma of her perfume and the soft lingering memory of her final haunting smile, I fell upon the bed fully dressed and was instantly asleep. My slumber was uninterrupted but for one strange occurrence that awoke me just before dawn.

The distant braying of a donkey is heard. Paul sits up, startled. Yerp and Mrs Yerp listen too for a moment, then resume their tasks.

What on earth could have been the source of such an unearthly sound I could not begin to guess.

Paul lies back in his bed. Immediately a cock crows and he sits up again. Under the next, Leonora enters and sits at the table.

The following morning I awoke fully refreshed, dressed swiftly and hurried downstairs in search of breakfast. For I confess, despite last night's splendid repast, I was again ravenous.

Paul has arrived at the table. Under the next Mrs Yerp serves breakfast.

A little to my surprise, considering the hour, Leonora was already breakfasting.

Leonora Good morning, Rupert.

Paul Good morning, Leonora.

Percy Her complexion seemed a trifle pale, her manner somewhat distracted.

Leonora I trust you slept well?

Paul Extremely well, thank you. And you?

Leonora I – have had a little trouble lately in sleeping – I...

Paul Indeed. I am sorry to hear that. (*to Mrs Yerp*) Thank you.

Leonora It is nothing, I assure you. It will pass, I expect. (*softly*) As most things do in time. (*A slight pause.*)

Paul (*brightly*) Certainly your brother does not seem to share your affliction.

Leonora (*startled from her reverie*) What?

Paul Your brother. Frederick. I conclude, from his absence at this table, that he sleeps better than any of us. (*He laughs rather nervously.*)

Mrs Yerp stares at him sharply.

Unless of course he is already up and about.

Leonora (*her eyes closed*) He is indeed up. And about.

Paul I see. I apologize, then. (*He laughs.*) Perhaps –

Leonora gives a barely controlled sob.

(*concerned*) Miss Stringer . . . Leonora . . .

Paul attempts to place his hand on hers to console her. At his touch, Leonora rises and rushes from the room. Her crying can be heard, receding along the passage. Paul rises as if to follow.

Mrs Yerp (*rather firmly*) Indian or Chinese tea, sir.

Paul – er Chindian. Inese, rather. I mean . . .

Mrs Yerp A little of each, sir.

Paul sits.

Paul Mrs Yerp, is there anything . . .? Is there?

Mrs Yerp Nothing that need concern you, sir.

Paul It's just that Miss –

Mrs Yerp She'll be perfectly alright, sir, I can assure you. The minute you've gone.

Paul Me? It is I who am the cause of her upset? Surely not.

Mrs Yerp My advice, sir, for what it's worth is to quit this house as soon as possible.

Paul Indeed?

Mrs Yerp It's a damned house, sir. Lived in by a doomed family.

Paul I don't understand. Miss Stringer seems to me –

Mrs Yerp Mr Yerp, my husband, he set off for the village at five o'clock this morning. He'll be back with a horse for you by noon if he don't get trapped by the snow meantimes.

Paul Seven hours to ride to the village and back? Is it that far?

Mrs Yerp He won't be riding there, sir. Only riding back.

Paul Then how is he getting there? Not walking, surely?

Mrs Yerp Aye.

Paul You have no horses here?

Mrs Yerp No, sir. The master and mistress won't have them. Won't have them on the property.

Paul Why on earth not?

Mrs Yerp That's their choice, sir. It's not for us to question.

Paul But what if there was an emergency? What if you needed, say, a doctor. Do you hope to walk to the village in the event of a crisis?

Mrs Yerp If there's a crisis then we runs, sir. Will there be anything further you require?

Paul No, no . . . A splendid breakfast. Thank you, Mrs Yerp.

Mrs Yerp Thank you, sir.

Paul rises. Mrs Yerp pushes the table away. Paul moves out into the 'grounds'.

Percy There being no further sign of my host or hostess I resolved, since the weather appeared to have improved, to walk a little in the gardens. Although covered in snow, this gave the house and the outbuildings an almost fairy-tale beauty. For the life of me, I could detect nothing in the least damned, let alone doomed about the place. I did not venture far for fear of getting lost but the grounds were quite large enough to provide me with an exhilarating two hour walk around their perimeter. When I returned, expecting to find Mr Yerp back from the village with my horse, I was to be disappointed. There was no sign of the man.

Mrs Yerp has entered. She clears the chairs.

Paul It is now past noon, has Mr Yerp not returned?

Mrs Yerp No, sir.

Paul Oh, dear . . .

Mrs Yerp The snow'll probably be deep around Keeper's Lug.

Paul I see. It's just my brother is expecting me. Was expecting me. Yesterday.

Mrs Yerp I daresay my husband's trying his level best, sir. (*She goes off.*)

Paul (*after her*) I have no doubt.

Percy I determined, rather than wait about, to walk the perimeter back the other way. Thus I took another two hour stroll around the grounds. When I returned, to my dismay, there was still no sign of the wretched Yerp.

I had to conclude that he had in all probability fallen into a snowdrift.

Paul (*calling*) I say . . . I say . . .

Mrs Yerp appears.

Mrs Yerp Sir?

Paul Is there still no sign yet of him?

Mrs Yerp No, sir. 'Fraid not. He'll be stuck in Swine's Bottom, most like.

Paul But it will soon be dark. I really must start on my way. Have you no other transport of any kind?

Mrs Yerp None at all, sir. Like I said. Excuse me. (*She goes.*)

Percy Pleasant as they were, I could not face another two hour walk around those grounds. Instead I decided this time to explore closer to the house itself. It was whilst I did this that I discovered in a high stone wall a small concealed entrance that had previously escaped my notice. Unable to resist curiosity I tried the handle, half expecting the door to be locked. To my amazement it opened easily and upon stepping through it I found myself in a small walled paddock. The snow here had all but been cleared, a not inconsiderable task. But for me the source of far greater interest was the creature standing motionless in a far corner of the enclosure, its eyes fixed intently upon me. It was – to my utter amazement – no less a beast than a donkey. I cried out in surprise:

Frederick enters as 'the donkey'. He stands watching Paul.

Paul Good heavens!

The donkey brays.

(*coaxingly*) Come on then. Come on, girl. Boy.

Percy Why they had lied to me was a mystery. Why had they told me that they had no transport, nothing that could carry me to the village? When it was clear even to one as untutored as myself that this sturdy little creature was more than adequate for the task. In a moment, my mind was made up. The hour was now late and if I was to avoid travelling in darkness I must leave this very minute. Having no luggage was, as it transpired, an advantage. I resolved to borrow this creature temporarily in order to reach the village. There I would leave it for Mr Yerp to recover. There could surely be no harm in that. But first to catch the beast, who seemed from what I knew of such creatures, unnaturally shy.

Paul (*coaxing 'the donkey'*) Come on, boy. That's it, boy – I'm not going to hurt you . . .

A sequence where Paul coaxes and tries to catch Frederick, 'the donkey'. Frederick backs away braying, Paul tries to corner him. At last he succeeds.

Percy He was an evasive brute but at last I succeeded –

Paul Got you! Success. Now, to mount you.

Paul struggles to climb on Frederick.

Percy I must confess the task proved extremely difficult. It was the most reluctant of steeds.

Paul Come on! Come on! Whooaa! Whoa! Steady! Easy!

A lot more braying as Paul finally 'mounts'.

Alright, my beauty. Just as far as the village and then I'll set you free again, I promise. You have my word. Yup there!

Percy But scarcely had we taken three paces outside the paddock . . .

Mrs Yerp rushes on.

Mrs Yerp (*agitatedly*) NO!!! No, you mustn't! You can't!

Paul I'm sorry, Mrs Yerp. I can wait no longer, I fear. The beast will be returned, I promise.

Mrs Yerp No, please sir, no. You mustn't, please. If you do that you'll . . .

Frederick suddenly rears up and gallops away, Paul holding on tightly.

Percy But before the wretched woman could finish, the donkey suddenly reared up and set off at a most terrifying gallop . . .

Paul (*alarmed*) Whooa!

Percy Indeed I was, until that moment, unaware that a mere donkey was capable of such speed . . . Out of the garden we galloped, across a meadow and then with barely a second's pause, into the deepest part of the forest . . .

The donkey brays triumphantly.

Paul Whoooa! Whooa! Whooa! Where are we going? Where are you taking me, you brute?

Percy By way of reply the donkey merely brayed louder and increased the pace of its gallop. It was as if the beast was enchanted. On and on we strode and just as I had given up all hope of ever stopping again . . .

The donkey gives a final bray and rears up, hurling Paul on to the ground where he lies. The donkey, too, collapses nearby.

Paul (*as he falls*) Aaaaah!

Percy How long I lay unconscious I do not know. When I awoke it was dark . . .

> *The lights have dimmed and Leonora, Yerp and Mrs Yerp have entered with lanterns.*

Leonora Thank God, he's still alive . . .

Mrs Yerp The snow broke his fall else he'd be a dead 'un.

Leonora Find my brother. Yerp, we must find my brother. He cannot be far away . . . (*calling*) Frederick! Frederick!

Yerp (*moving off slightly*) Mr Stringer, sir! Mr Stringer!

> *Paul groans.*

Leonora Rupert . . .

Percy For the second time in twenty-four hours, I was to awaken to the sight of this angel of mercy.

Paul Leonora, I –

Leonora No, don't try to stand, Rupert. You've had a bad fall.

Yerp (*calling*) He's over here, ma'am. Over here.

Leonora Is he alright?

Yerp Yes, ma'am. He's still breathing.

Leonora Oh, thank God.

Mrs Yerp The Lord be praised.

> *They move away from Paul and gather round Frederick.*

Percy I wondered for a moment why there should be so much relief and divine gratitude at the survival of what appeared to me to be an extremely foul-tempered, headstrong donkey. I am, of course, not insensitive myself to our dumb friends, but for this particular creature I was fully prepared to make an exception. Imagine my astonishment then, when I saw that the creature around whom they were all anxiously gathered was no donkey but rather the body of my unsociable host of the previous evening, Frederick Stringer.

Frederick I'm alright. I'm perfectly alright. Leave me alone, I tell you.

Leonora Frederick . . .

Frederick (*sharply*) I said leave me!

Percy His temper seemed not to have improved one iota.

Paul (*staggering to his feet*) Mr Stringer – how do you come to be here as well?

Leonora It's alright, Rupert. It is not your concern.

Paul But I demand to know. How is it that he is here like myself, injured in the snow? You must tell me. Leonora! I demand to know.

Percy But to this day, no satisfactory answer was I ever to receive. How Frederick came to be lying near me in the snow and what became of that extraordinary donkey will I fear remain a mystery, ladies and gentlemen, for ever more.

> *Percy appears to have finished. He marks the end of his story rather dramatically with a slight pause. The keyboard player plays a final flourish.*

Paul Is that it, then?

Percy Yes.

Paul Not much of an ending.

Leonora It never is.

The Others (*gloomily*) No . . .

Percy What are you complaining about? It's a mystery story. It's a classic Victorian mystery story.

Paul You might at least solve the mystery.

Percy If I did that it wouldn't be a mystery story, would it?

Paul What are you talking about? There's plenty of mystery stories where the mystery gets solved – Sherlock Holmes. He solves his mysteries.

Leonora Yes. Hercule Poirot . . .

Yerp . . . Inspector Morse . . .

Mrs Yerp . . . Columbo . . .

Percy (*angrily*) Well, it doesn't get solved in this one, so there. That's it! Enough. The end of my very own story. Finish. Goodbye. Thank you very much. Hope you've enjoyed it. Come back next week. I'll have my props back and all.

> *He moves to start gathering up his stuff. Barely has he started when Peter appears. We hear his voice before we are aware of him.*

Peter Chapter Two. The Mystery of Deepwood is revealed. Just as I had given up all hope of learning the secret of Deepwood House, Frederick stepped forward with a cry –

Percy Just a minute.

Peter What?

Percy What are you doing?

Peter Telling the rest of the story.

Percy You can't do that.

Peter Why not?

Percy It's ended. I finished it.

Peter You may have finished it, I haven't. I'm carrying on.

Percy You can't do that. It's my story.

Peter It was your story. It's not any more. You just said, you've finished with it. You've thrown it way. He just said that, didn't he? Didn't he just say that?

The Others Yes.

Peter There you are, they agree with me. Good bye. Nice to have seen you.

Percy This is illegal. This is unlawful. You can't do this.

Peter Just watch me . . .

Percy (*going off*) You haven't heard the end of this, you know. You haven't seen the last of me.

Peter Bye!

The Others Bye!

Percy goes off, leaving his props.

Peter To continue. Chapter Two. The Mystery of Deepwood is revealed. Just as I had given up all hope of learning the secret of Deepwood House, Frederick stepped forward with a cry –

Frederick It's no use, Leonora. We cannot conceal this secret a moment longer. He must be told the truth, he deserves that at least.

Leonora But Frederick . . .

Frederick Leonora, but for the snow Mr Fellowes would be surely dead. Since by some miracle he has been spared, he should be rewarded at the very least with the truth . . . Are you strong enough to walk, my friend?

Paul Yes, I think so . . .

Leonora Here, take my arm, Rupert

Paul Thank you, Leonora . . .

Peter And thus we made our way slowly back to the house, Yerp leading the way, followed by the three of us – Mr Fellowes our uninvited guest, my loyal loving sister Leonora, myself, Frederick Stringer – and finally Mrs Yerp bringing up the rear. Throughout our walk back I observed our guest relying greatly on the support of my sister's arm – though I suspect if truth be told the support was more spiritual and emotional than physical. For it did not take one of much perception to deduce that the two were clearly in love. Alas, as things were at present, their love was a fruitless and futile thing. As we walked, I tried to explain to Mr Fellowes the nature of the curse that had been brought upon our family – that I had brought upon our family, for in all this it cannot be emphasized too strongly that my dear, precious, sweet-natured sister was entirely innocent.

Frederick Mr Fellowes, I would have you know, sir, that I am to blame for all that has happened here. Many years ago, I behaved foolishly. I was punished quite rightly for this behaviour. My punishment continues to this day. Over twenty years. Twenty years. Will it ever end . . .?

Leonora Frederick . . .

Frederick It's alright, my dear. The simple fact is, Mr Fellowes, that due to some spell that has been put upon me, by day, during the hours of daylight, I am transformed into that creature you earlier saw and – tried to ride . . .

Paul The donkey. *You* were the donkey? Is this possible?

Frederick It is not only possible, Mr Fellowes, it is the truth. By night I resume my normal shape as you see me now. Though my appetites, alas, remain those of a beast. And by day . . . I am, as you witnessed me – that – thing in the field.

Paul How did this occur? Who could possibly have done this heartless thing to you? And why?

Frederick (*shaking his head*) It is a long story. I couldn't . . .

Leonora The tragedy is, Rupert, that even as a donkey my brother is unable to enjoy himself or give innocent pleasure to others. As you yourself discovered, he is a creature that none may ride or even stroke.

Frederick No sooner are they upon my back than all the fires of hell burn through me. I must shake them from me and kill them or perish myself.

Paul Even a child may not ride you . . .

Leonora No man, woman or child.

Frederick Save one.

Leonora (*softly*) Save one.

Yerp Do you want to stop for thistles, Mr Frederick?

Frederick No, Yerp, no. Not now, let us go on.

Paul You mention there is one who alone can ride you. Who is this man?

Frederick It is no man but a woman, Mr Fellowes. It is none other than the woman I betrayed.

Paul And is it she who put this spell upon you?

Frederick No. It was not she.

Paul Then who? I am acutely curious to know, Mr Stringer.

Frederick It is a sad and complicated tale but if you so wish, I will tell you . . .

Leonora Frederick, is this wise, my dear?

Frederick (*shaking his head, sadly*) Where is the harm now, Leonora, where is the harm?

The group make their way off during the next.

Peter And as we walked through the snow, retracing our tracks back to the house, I, Frederick Stringer, told him my story – my very own story. And that story – which I shall entitle *The Enchanted Suitor* – I shall relate to you, ladies and gentlemen, should you be good enough to return in a few moments time. We shall expect you. Please, do not be tardy.

He bows and goes off.
End of Act One.

Act Two

Peter comes on.

Peter And now, ladies and gentlemen, my very own story – a tale of contemporary times that I have entitled *The Enchanted Suitor* – being the sad cautionary account of one Frederick Stringer, landowner and part-time donkey. When he was younger, twenty years younger than he was in our last story, Frederick was really a very handsome, extremely good-looking young man.

Percy comes on as Frederick when young. He smiles around him.

He had only to step outside his door for young – Hey!

Percy Carry on.

Peter What are you doing back here?

Percy Young Frederick, what else.

Peter You can't do young Frederick.

Percy Why not? They said I could.

Peter Who said you could?

Percy Them back there. That lot. They knew you wanted a handsome bloke. They took a vote. I won hands down.

Peter Where's the real young Frederick?

Percy Playing cards.

Peter This is disgraceful.

315

Percy Carry on. I'm ready.

Peter (*muttering*) This is *my* very own story. You're not my idea of young Frederick.

Percy Come on, carry on. Frederick was really a very handsome, extremely good-looking young man . . .

Peter . . . he was also unfortunately extremely conceited. He had only to step outside his door for young women practically to swoon away at the sight of him.

> *As he speaks two young women walk past Percy and nearly faint with excitement. Percy preens himself.*

The problem with young Frederick was – like a number of very, very good looking people – he didn't really have much time for other folk at all. The only person he really loved was himself. His greatest pleasure was to stand in front of the mirror.

Percy (*standing in front of the mirror, admiringly*) Oh! Oh, you devil. You dashing devil, you! Mmm. Mmm.

Peter So, although many girls fell in love with him . . .

> *One of the young women returns and gazes adoringly at Percy.*

He had no time for them, however beautiful they might be . . .

Percy Shoo! Shoo! Go away, woman!

> *The woman runs off wailing.*

Wretched thing!

Peter He was extremely thoughtless and insensitive. And as for plain women . . .

> *A plain woman comes on.*

He had no time for them at all . . .

Percy Uurrrgggh!

The plain woman goes off weeping.

Peter In fact, there was very little to be said in Frederick's defence except that he was young and had been born naturally handsome and gifted and therefore probably didn't know any better. But he was soon to learn. For Frederick, although he didn't yet know it, was about to fall in love. Hopelessly in love. It started like most love stories – completely by accident . . .

Cecilia enters. She is carrying some tiny parcels. She fails to see Percy. They collide.

Cecilia Oh!

Percy Whoops!

Cecilia I'm so sorry

Percy No, *I'm* sorry . . .

Cecilia No, it was my fault . . .

Percy No, it was *my* fault . . .

They both catch sight of each other and tail off as they speak.

Percy and Cecilia No, it was very definitely . . . my . . . fault . . .

They stare at each other without moving. Music.

Peter Now for Frederick, having a stranger staring adoringly at him like this was no new experience. But to undergo the same emotion himself – here was a novelty.

Percy I'm – I'm . . . I'm Frederick Stringer.

Cecilia How do you do? I'm . . . I'm Cecilia Butterworth.

Percy (*dreamily*) Hallo.

Cecilia (*dreamily*) Hallo. Frederick Stinger . . .

Percy Stringer.

Cecilia Stringer. Sorry.

Percy That's quite alright, Miss Butterscotch.

Cecilia Worth. Butterworth.

Percy I'm sorry. Will you ever forgive me?

Cecilia Of course. Of course, of course, of course . . .

Peter And they went on like that in similar vein for a very long time but we won't bother with all that now because unless you happen to be in love yourself it does tend to get a bit boring. So, anyway, Frederick walked Cecilia Butterworth home and very generouly offered to carry all her extremely heavy parcels.

Cecilia (*admiringly*) You're so strong!

Percy laughs carelessly.

Peter When they reached her house, number forty nine Hollyhock Street, to show how grateful she was to him, Cecilia invited Frederick inside for a cup of tea. It was a delightful little semi-detached house, tastefully furnished and as clean and neat as a new pin. Frederick thoroughly approved.

Cecilia Mummy!

Peter Cried Cecilia.

Cecilia I'm home!

Alicia hurries on.

Alicia Darling, I wondered where on earth you'd – (*seeing Frederick*) Oh.

Percy Hallo.

Cecilia I've brought someone home.

Alicia Oh, yes. How lovely. Mr – ?

Percy Stringer. Frederick Stringer.

Cecilia Mr Stringer picked me up, Mummy. After I'd fallen over.

Alicia Oh, how simply sweet of him.

Cecilia I dropped all my parcels but he picked them up too.

Alicia Lovely.

Cecilia And then he carried them home.

Alicia Super. Would you like some tea, Mr String?

Percy Stringer –

Alicia Sorry.

Percy Yes please, if it's no trouble, Mrs Buttermere –

Alicia Butterworth.

Percy Yes, sorry.

Alicia Do sit down.

Percy Thank you.

Alicia Darling, keep Mr Stringer entertained. Perhaps you could show him your pictures.

Cecilia Oh, mummy, he doesn't want to see those.

Alicia I'm sure he'd adore to see them.

Cecilia No, no, no, no.

Alicia Do you care for pictures at all, Mr Stringer?

Percy Pictures? What sort of pictures are these?

Alicia Little pictures. She draws them herself. She's really frightfully talented, everybody says so. But she's unbelievably modest. I keep telling her she's got to push herself more. You need to push yourself, darling.

Cecilia Oh, mummy.

Alicia You tell her to push herself, Mr Stringer.

Percy I will, I will.

Alicia Won't be a tick. (*She goes out.*)

Percy What a charming mother you have.

Cecilia Oh gosh, heavens, gollyhoppers, she's ghastly. She's so embarrassing sometimes . . .

Percy Rubbish. I bet your father's amazing as well, isn't he?

Cecilia No, daddy's – daddy's gone. He's no longer with us.

Percy Oh, I'm sorry. Did he die recently?

Cecilia No, he's not dead, he just – he just doesn't live here any more. He's gone off. He got – well, I think he got a bit cheesed off with us really and he sort of took off.

Percy How frightful for you.

Cecilia Yes, it was a bit. It was worse for Mummy, of course.

Percy Just the two of you then now, is there?

Cecilia Well, and Em of course.

Percy Em?

Cecilia My sister Em. Short for Emilia. I expect you'll meet her. She's a super person, you'll love her. Very warm and friendly. Look, you don't really want to see my pictures, do you?

Percy Of course.

Cecilia Oh, but they're terrible, they're awful, they're ghastly, they're absolutely blush-making.

Percy I bet they're not. Come on, don't be so modest. Push yourself.

Cecilia (*needing no second invitation*) OK, I'll go and get them. Wait there. (*as she goes*) Look out of the window if you want to. Feel free. (*She dashes out.*)

Percy Thank you.

Peter Left alone in the front room, Percy took advantage of Cecilia's offer and looked out of the window. He saw a neat little garden, with a tidy little lawn and a trim little fence. There were some smart little flowers standing in spruce little rows, and some clean, orderly, just a little tiny bit but not all *that* much crazy paving.

Percy How absolutely lovely.

Peter So absorbed was he with the view that Percy failed to notice someone entering the room. It was Cecilia's sister, Emilia. Emilia, as Cecilia had intimated earlier, was the warmest and friendliest person you could possibly hope to meet. She was also one of the plainest.

Emilia Hallo, there.

Peter Frederick turned to see who it was. As I have told you, lack of beauty in others affected him deeply. He reacted to the sight of the poor girl with his characteristic sensitivity.

Percy Uurrgghh!

Emilia Oh!

Percy Sorry.

Emilia That's alright. I'm – it's always happening. You're a friend of Cecilia's, I presume. Hallo, I'm her sister, Emilia.

Percy (*hardly looking at her*) Hallo, I'm Frederick. It's awfully good to meet you. I've heard so much about you.

Emilia I expect you've been hearing how warm and friendly I am.

Percy Yes, yes, I have. You bet.

Emilia Yes, I thought you might somehow. I also dance, you know. Classical, modern and tap.

Percy How clever . . .

Emilia Waste of time, really. Nobody ever wants to watch me do it.

Percy What a shame. I would.

Emilia You wouldn't, you know. You say you would but if I started dancing for you now, you'd just stare at your feet or at the floor.

Peter Frederick, though, was anxious not to antagonize the sister of the girl he had secretly already decided to marry.

Percy I bet I wouldn't you know. I'd love to see you dance. Really I would.

Emilia Really? OK. You asked for it. Classical, modern or tap?

Percy Well. Bit of each would be nice.

Emilia OK. Here goes. Hold on to your hat. A-one, a-two . . .

The keyboard player strikes up. Emilia starts to dance for Percy. He stares at her for a second, then hurriedly at the floor.

Peter (*over this*) Poor Frederick became fearfully embarrassed. Not only was the poor girl distressingly unattractive to look at but she danced like a baby hippo. Fortunately, rescue was at hand . . .

Alicia enters with a small tea table.

Alicia (*sharply*) Emilia, stop that immediately.

The music stops. So does Emilia. She looks embarrassed.

That's better. Now sit down at once and stop showing off. You're embarrassing everyone.

Emilia (*softly*) Yes, Mummy. (*She sits apart from them her head hung low.*)

Alicia I'm afraid Emilia here is a dreadful show-off, Mr Stringer. I hope you weren't too dreadfully embarrassed.

Percy Not at all, Mrs Butterworth. I was thoroughly entertained. Thank you, Emilia.

Emilia flashs him a quick smile of gratitude.

Alicia (*dryly*) Really? One lump or two?

Percy Two, thank you.

Alicia Hand round the tea, Emilia. Do something useful with your life for heaven's sake.

Emilia Yes, mummy. (*She hands round the tea awkwardly.*)

Alicia Emilia rather fancies herself as a dancer, Mr Stringer, but I can't say I'd give much for her chances with the Royal Ballet, would you? (*She laughs.*)

Percy (*embarrassed*) I – I . . . I really wouldn't know . . .

Alicia Well, I'm not an expert but I'm sure there must be some upper limit on the size of feet for a start, don't you think? Careful, darling, don't spill them . . .

Emilia Sorry, Mummy . . .

Alicia She's unbelievably clumsy. I don't know where she gets this clumsiness from either, I'm sure.

Cecilia enters with her 'portfolio'.

Cecilia Hallo. Sorry, everyone . . .

Alicia Oh, come in, darling, you're just in time for tea.

Cecilia Super. Hi, Em . . .

Emilia Hallo.

Cecilia You've met Frederick?

Emilia Yes.

Alicia Em's been keeping him entertained. In her inimitable manner.

Cecilia Oh. Sorry, I took so long. I couldn't decide which ones to show you so I've brought down the lot.

Alicia What does it matter, they're all equally good. I don't think I could choose my favourite even if you forced me. Emilia, pass this to your sister. Come along.

Emilia dutifully passes the cup to Cecilia who places it on the floor beside her. She proceeds to open her portfolio of dull watercolours. Emilia resumes her seat in the corner. Alicia swells with pride. Percy tries to enthuse.

Now, Mr Stringer, tell me what you think of these. Be honest, you can be perfectly honest, can't he, Cecilia?

Cecilia Oh don't, please, no don't. Most of these are just dreadful, I know they are.

Peter In fact, Cecilia was wrong in only one respect. All the pictures were equally dreadful. Frederick was no art expert but even he could tell at half a glance that the woman he loved, the girl he would willingly lay down his life for, had about as much artistic talent as a disoriented snail. And yet, love being what it is . . .

Percy Oh, oh, oh, oh. Oh. Now, these are quite extraordinary. What a unique talent!

Alicia Now, what did I say . . .

Cecilia Oh . . .

Percy Absolutely remarkable. So fresh. So untouched by the taint of commercialism.

Alicia Yes, yes, yes . . .

Percy Unencumbered by dull formal training or the rigid restraints of technique. Yours is a true, innate talent, Cecilia.

Cecilia (*modestly*) Thank you.

Alicia There, Cecilia, listen to that. That's someone who knows about these things.

Percy Oh, please, I really know nothing . . .

Alicia Enough to recognize talent.

Percy Oh, yes. Enough to recognize that, I trust.

Peter And at last Frederick took his leave of the family, reflecting that he would probably in time grow to love Cecilia's pictures, who knows? And if not he would never, he was certain, ever grow tired of her glorious face.

Alicia and Emilia have gone off under the last; Alicia with the tea things, Emilia with the portfolio.

Over the next few days, Frederick and Cecilia, spent every hour they could together, celebrating and cementing their new found love.

Frederick and Cecilia dash hither and thither being terribly happy together. Music under.

Less than a month later, one summer's evening, Frederick plucked up the courage to ask Cecilia to be his wife. He had seldom been so happy, never so in love with another. Why, whole days passed without him looking in a mirror at all. It had to be the real thing. Cecilia, needless to say, said yes.

Alicia re-enters. Emilia follows at a distance.

They broke the news to her mother who was overjoyed. In fact, everyone was happy. Or nearly everyone. As usual, nobody noticed Emilia; the plain, clumsy, talentless good hearted Emilia as usual was quite ignored. Preparations for the wedding were soon under way. All mothers love weddings and Alicia loved them more than most mothers.

A great deal of rushing about with parcels and fabrics, etc.

Two days before the big day, something rather odd occurred. Frederick had popped round to their house to deliver some particular paper doilies that Alicia had asked him to collect. Cecilia was out somewhere, probably at the hairdressers. She had already spent several days in the hairdressers recently for she wanted to look just right for her walk down the aisle. When

Frederick arrived though, Alicia seemed in an unusually solemn and serious mood. She asked Frederick if she could have a word with him alone in the front room.

Percy Of course. What's it about? Nothing serious, I hope?

Peter It seemed, frankly, a little late to ask if his intentions were honourable.

Alicia Sit down, Frederick. I want to say something to you.

Percy Yes, Alicia?

Alicia The point is – I don't want Cecilia to be hurt. Ever.

Percy Hurt?

Alicia You're positive you love her?

Percy Of course!

Alicia You'll always love her and care for her?

Percy How can you doubt that?

Alicia I'm sorry. I have a – I have a reason.

Percy Something to do with me? Something I've said? Something I've done?

Alicia Oh, no . . . I'm sure you mean what you say. It's only . . . It's just, Frederick, that people sometimes turn out differently from how you expect, that's all. You see?

Percy How do you mean?

Alicia They just do. You marry them and then you turn round and they're different. I can't really explain it.

Percy I don't see this at all. What are you trying to tell me?

Alicia You're sure you wouldn't be happier with, say, Emilia?

Percy (*appalled*) Emilia?

Alicia Yes.

Percy Absolutely not. Me and Emilia? Emilia and me? Certainly not. That would be quite . . . I mean, she has a marvellous warm and friendly nature, I know, but I could never love her. I love Cecilia. She's the most beautiful creature in the world.

Alicia Whereas Emilia isn't.

Percy Well, frankly no. She has this lovely nature but –

Alicia Yes. Well, I can say no more then, Frederick. Nothing I can do will make you reconsider.

Percy You want me to reconsider?

Alicia I want you to be certain. Because I'm not sure you're going to be happy with Cecilia, Frederick. I have this dreadful forboding.

Percy Nonsense. (*He stares at her.*) There's something else, isn't there? Something you haven't told me, Alicia? What is it?

Alicia Nothing. At least, nothing that any one of us can do a thing about, I'm afraid. (*She kisses him suddenly on the forehead.*) Take care of yourself, Frederick, I beg you. I'm really dreadfully fond of you, you see. (*breaking from him, a little overcome*) Excuse me. I must unpack the confetti.

    She hurries out. Percy stands bewildered.

Percy What on earth did she mean by all that?

Peter Frederick was deeply puzzled. What *could* she have meant? Marry Emilia instead? What a suggestion.

Why he could barely bring himself to look at the poor girl. Whereas Cecilia – he could gaze upon her for ever. And just think, the day after tomorrow he would be able to do so. Till death them did part. Oh, happy man!

The next is re-enacted as it is narrated.

And soon enough, all doubts put firmly aside, the wedding day came. The sun shone brightly on the couple. The bride looked perfect – her hair just right. Even Emilia, the bridesmaid, managed to look – well, almost presentable – though she did trip over once or twice. Then on to the honeymoon, a perfect, love-filled, sun-drenched honeymoon. No second thoughts so far. And so back to their own little house, number forty-one Hollyhock Street, just four doors down from the in-laws. A few weeks later, Frederick was standing in his front room gazing out of his window. He tended to gaze out of his window quite a lot these days. Mainly to avoid looking too much at the walls of their home, every inch of which were covered by his wife's watercolour pictures. Frederick was learning to live with them but they were, he had to confess, an acquired taste. One that he had not personally yet acquired. So he gazed as usual out of his window, noting with some pride his neat little garden, with its tidy little lawn and its trim little fence. He derived some pleasure in observing their smart little flowers standing in spruce little rows, and their clean, orderly, just a little tiny bit but not all *that* much crazy paving.

Cecilia pokes her head round the door.

Cecilia Supper's ready, darling.

Percy (*thoughtfully*) Righto, darling. (*He turns to her. Startled*) Ah!

Cecilia What is it, darling?

Percy Nothing. You've done something new to your hair, have you, darling?

Cecilia No.

Percy To your makeup?

Cecilia No.

Percy Something's different.

Cecilia No, darling. Silly. Come on. It's on the table.

She goes out.

Peter But as Frederick made to follow her, he felt rather peculiar. Could it be that his wife was growing – less attractive? Surely not. She was after all the most beautiful woman in the world – and yet . . . Something about her was – just for a second – was almost *un*attractive. No. He was imagining things. He was losing touch with reality. He looked out of his window again to reassure himself that all was well. And at that moment, he saw someone passing in the street. A woman, faintly familiar. And yet quite unfamiliar, for this was someone – for a recently married man at least – disquietingly attractive. Just for a second, that was.

Emilia walks by.

For then as she turned and saw him watching her she smiled at him. A warm and thoroughly friendly smile. And he saw at once it was Emilia. Plain old, clumsy old Emilia. Warm and friendly, maybe, but . . . not beautiful. Never. Attractive perhaps in – certain lights but compared with Cecilia . . . What nonsense!

Percy shakes his head and smiles.

But as the weeks went by, as regards his wife, the feeling wouldn't quite go away. In fact some days she looked positively ugly.

Cecilia enters, scowling.

Cecilia Look, darling, are you going to fix it or not?

Percy Yes, I'm just coming, darling.

Cecilia Well, it's leaking all over the place, darling. I thought you said you were going to fix it.

Percy I will, I will, darling. I've only just got home from work, you know . . .

Cecilia (*flouncing out*) Well, it's alright for some then, isn't it?

Peter But then, these little tiffs are common enough in any marriage and soon pass. And Frederick continued to work hard and save what money he could for that magic day when they would start a family. And Cecilia worked hard to keep the place nice for them, thinking up little improvements to make their little home even prettier. And she and Frederick even decorated the spare bedroom as a nursery for the child they fully expected to start any day now.

Percy and Cecilia have entered. They sit apart. She is sewing. He is reading. They both seem very unhappy. The clock strikes.

The only major problem to all this was that, after a year of marriage, Frederick could no longer bear to look at Cecilia at all. She had grown most unbelievably plain. And as you recall, the one thing that Frederick could not abide was plain people. In fact, looking in the mirror of late, he detected a certain diminishing in his own good looks. No, impossible.

Percy (*rising*) Well, I'll – I'll be off to bed then, dear.

Cecilia (*coolly*) Alright, dear.

Percy Are you coming up, dear?

Cecilia Not quite yet, dear.

Peter Thank heavens for that, thought Frederick.

Percy Righty-ho . . .

Peter Said Frederick, rather too cheerfully.

Percy 'Night night, then.

Cecilia I see.

Percy What?

Cecilia No, nothing.

Percy What is it?

Cecilia Not even a goodnight kiss now, I notice.

Percy Oh, no, right. Here you are.

Cecilia (*pushing him away*) No, I don't want one now. It's no good now, is it?

Percy Come on, come on. Don't be silly, dear.

Cecilia No, I don't want you slobbering all over me. Go away, go away . . .

Percy What on earth's got into you? You're impossible these days . .

Cecilia (*hysterically*) Don't you start telling me I'm impossible – you're the one who's impossible, not me. You're the one who can't even bear to look at me. Who can't even bring himself to kiss me unless I beg him to. You're the one. I can't help it if you don't find me attractive. Don't blame me, it's not my fault, is it? I knew this would happen, I knew it would, they all said it would . . .

She rushes out, weeping bitterly. Percy stands amazed.

Peter Poor Frederick was quite staggered at this sudden outburst.

Percy Good Lord.

Peter Partly because he had had no appreciation of how clearly he had allowed his real feelings to show.

Percy Heavens!

Peter He decided the best thing was to go for a walk. Allow his wife time to cool down. Poor Frederick was quite unaware that so far as cooling down was concerned, women invariably took far longer to do so than men. It was a bright moonlit evening and Frederick set off along the street intending to walk around the local park. That very park where a year ago he had walked and talked and dreamed with Cecilia. Ah me! But he had gone less than a few hundred yards when he spied coming towards him an apparition of such beauty, such grace, such divine enchantment, that he stopped dead in his tracks. Who could she be, this vision of loveliness?

Emilia has entered. Percy has stopped dead and is staring at her.

Emilia Oh, hello, Frederick.

Percy (*amazed*) Emilia.

Peter Frederick at that moment fell in love all over again.

Emilia What are you doing out at this hour?

Peter The moonlight picking out the soft, gentle contours of her face, sparkling in her hair like spun moonbeams . . .

Emilia Frederick?

Peter Her eyes so clear and bright, brimful of warmth and friendliness . . .

Emilia Frederick, are you alright?

Percy (*hoarsely*) Yes.

Emilia Are you sure? You look terrible. Here, come inside for a minute. I've just come back from my evening down at the Mission. Come on, take my arm . . .

Peter Not only warm and friendly and beautiful but she worked for the poor . . . Oh, perfection. She led Frederick into the house.

Emilia Mummy's out at the moment. Sit down. Would you like some tea? I'll make us a pot.

Percy No, no . . . I'll . . . be fine . . .

Emilia Shall I pop round and fetch Cecilia? Is she at home?

Percy Yes, she is. But no. Don't bother. I'll be fine. Please, Em. Sit down.

Emilia Sure?

Percy Please.

Emilia Right.

    She sits. A pause. Percy stares at her.

What on earth are you staring at?

Percy Would you – would you do something for me?

Emilia Of course. What is it?

Percy Would you – would you dance for me, Emilia?

Emilia Dance?

Percy Yes.

334

Emilia For you?

Percy Please.

Emilia But I'm awful. Everybody says I'm awful. I can't dance. I've no talent.

Percy I think you have. (*Pause.*) Please.

Emilia Well, alright. If you're sure. If it'll make you feel better. (*She rises.*) Classical, modern or tap.

Percy I really don't mind. Anything. I just want to watch you – moving.

Emilia Well, OK. It'd better be classical then. It's a bit quieter. It's getting rather late.

The keyboard player plays something soft and romantic. Emilia moves and sways gently. Percy watches her.

Peter And as he watched her, Frederick was suddenly gripped with a compulsion to dance with her – even though Frederick had never before danced classical ballet in his entire life, the urge to partner Emilia became irresistible . . .

Percy and Emilia dance for a second or two together. At the finish they embrace and kiss. They freeze thus under the next.

But Frederick as he embraced his sister-in-law in the front room of his mother-in-law's house had overlooked another vital fact concerning women in general and wives in particular. That when their lives become difficult or their marriages impossible they invariably run home to mother.

Cecilia enters with a small suitcase. She sees Emilia and Percy and screams. The lovers part hastily.

Cecilia (*flinging down her case, beside herself with fury*) I knew it. I knew this would happen. You – you little hussy . . .

Emilia Cecilia . . .

Percy Cecilia, I'm sorry, I –

Cecilia I knew you'd do this. I knew you would. Mummy said you would and you've done it! I'll never forgive you for this. Never!

> *She rushes from the room. Alicia passes her in the doorway.*

Emilia Cecilia . . .! Oh heavens. Oh Lord. Oh gosh.

> *She runs out after her sister taking the case with her. Percy smiles lamely at Alicia.*

Alicia (*shaking her head*) Oh dear.

Percy I've ruined everything now, haven't I?

Alicia I'm afraid you have rather.

Percy Burnt my boats.

Alicia Completely.

Percy Both boats.

Alicia You've sunk the entire navy, Frederick.

Percy (*sitting down*) Oh. How can anyone be so stupid? What a fool I am! What a fool!

Peter And Alicia, though she did not bother to contradict him, at least had the decency not to say, I told you so. Though she had every excuse to do so. And the moral of the story is this. Before you marry anyone, not only examine them very, very closely but do make sure you examine yourself as well. That is if you don't want to make a complete and utter ass of yourself.

Percy starts braying like a donkey. The keyboard plays a flourish.

Percy Is that it?

Peter That's it.

Percy That's not much of an ending.

Peter What do you mean?

Percy You complained about my ending, this one's much worse. No ending at all.

Peter It's a perfectly good story. It's a simple, modern morality tale, that's all.

Percy You might at least finish it.

Alicia Yes, I think you ought to finish it.

Peter It is finished! Look, I'm not arguing. That's my very own story and that's it. It's finished. Thank you very much, ladies and gentlemen, hope you enjoyed it. Goodbye and thank you.

Peter starts to move off. As he does so Paul, who has appeared unobserved, takes up the narrative.

Paul Chapter Three. The true story of the Butterworth family. Frederick turned to Alicia. Only she could tell him how to extricate himself from his plight –

Peter Just a minute.

Paul What?

Peter What are you doing?

Paul Telling the rest of the story.

Peter You can't do that.

Paul Why not?

Peter I've just said. It's ended. It's finished.

Paul You may have finished it, I haven't. I'm carrying on.

Peter You can't do that. It's my story.

Paul It was your story. It's not any more. You've finished with it. Anyway, you carried on his story. Why shouldn't I carry on yours? Fair's fair, isn't it?

The Others Yes.

Paul There you are, they agree with me. Good bye. Nice to have seen you.

Peter This is disgraceful. You can't do this.

Paul Here I go . . .

Peter (*going off*) You haven't heard the end of this, you know. You haven't seen the last of me.

Paul Bye!

The Others Bye!

Percy goes off, leaving his props.

Paul And Frederick turned to Alicia and begged her to tell him how all this had befallen him. For he knew that with her, surely, lay the secret.

Alicia Alright, I'll tell you

Paul Said Alicia.

Alicia If truth be told the fault does lie with me.

Paul And her eyes filled with tears as she began to speak. And so begins my very own story, a fantastical magical tale of long, long ago which I shall entitle *The Sorcerer's Daughters*.

Alicia Many years ago, Frederick, when I was much younger – about the age my daughters are now – I was a very pretty little thing – is that hard for you to imagine, Frederick?

Percy No, not at all . . .

Paul Cried Frederick gallantly, if a little untruthfully.

Alicia I suppose I looked rather like Cecilia does today.

Cecilia comes on as the young Alicia.

And in due course I fell in love as one does and married the most handsome of men – not unlike you, Frederick –

Percy Thank you.

Alicia Or as you used to be. But this man was not only handsome and rich, he was also a sorcerer.

Percy A sorcerer?

Alicia Yes, you smile but it's true. Such people do exist. Though they're very secretive and unless you marry them you'd never find out that they were one.

Peter has entered under the last dressed as Varius. He is hooded in a wizard's cloak. He moves to Cecilia who runs to greet him.

His name was Varius and he was a white wizard. His spells were always for the good. Including the spell he cast upon me when we first met. Oh, we were so happy, you cannot imagine, Frederick . . . He was the most remarkable of men . . .

At this point he throws back the hood to reveal his true identity. He is about to kiss Cecilia when Paul interrupts.

Paul Oh, no . . .

Peter Fair's fair . . . They said I could back there.
They've got to a very exciting point in their card game.

Paul Alright, carry on. (*muttering*) Anyone less like a
sorcerer.

Cecilia Looks alright to me.

Alicia Better than the one out there . . .

Cecilia Much . . .

Paul Get on with it . . .

Alicia He was the most remarkable of men and ours was
truly the happiest of marriages. It was not, as I say, until
we did marry that I realized that my husband had
magical powers. But since he used those powers only for
good and never to harm anyone – that made me all the
happier. And in a year or two, I presented him with two
daughters . . .

> *Cecilia presents Peter with two babylike bundles.
> During the next they both go off together with the
> babies, delighted.*

. . . whom we christened Cecilia and Emilia.

Paul And young Frederick listened spellbound as Alicia
continued to relate her story.

> *During the next, Alicia and Percy go off.*

Because they were so rich they lived in this huge castle
where the children played happily all day long. For they
both had the run of the place – all except for one room
which no one was allowed to enter, not even their
mother. This was the room where the sorcerer, Varius,
kept his spells and potions – a secret room only he and
he alone could enter. The sorcerer's code is a strict one –
for if anyone other than they themselves found out their

secrets, then the penalties laid down by the Imperial Grand Society of Sorcerers were too terrible to mention.

Cecilia and Emilia enter together, under the next, playing with a ball.

And Cecilia and Emilia grew up to be beautiful and strong and healthy – Cecilia favouring her mother's looks and Emilia her father's.

Alicia, now as herself, enters with Peter. They watch their children proudly.

And Alicia and Varius were the proudest parents there ever could have been.

Peter stays for a second and then goes off again.

If there was one single cloud in the sky, it was this. Alicia was a most ambitious mother. She wanted not just beautiful children, but the most beautiful children in the whole world. And she wanted them, eventually, not to marry ordinary, decent, honest men but the richest, most handsome princes in the kingdom.

A village boy comes on and ogles the girls as they play.

And if an unsuitable boy should even approach them . . .

One of the girls drops the ball. The village boy picks it up and holds it out for them to come and retrieve.

She would quickly shoo them away.

Alicia shouts at the village boy. He drops the ball and runs. During the next she beckons her daughters over to her and reproaches them.

And she would reprimand her children most severely for talking with common, rough boys. And both being children who loved and trusted their mother, they believed her and so the next time a common, rough boy dared to come near them . . .

The village boy reappears. The girls shoo him away. Alicia looks on approvingly. Events mirror the next speech.

. . . neither girl would have anything whatever to do with him. Of course, their father knew nothing of this, but if he had done he would have been very angry but maybe, just maybe, he might have stopped all the dreadful things that were about to happen. In due course, the girls grew up and put aside childish games and became mature, beautiful sophisticated young women. What parent could have asked for more? Alicia, the proudest of mothers, doted on her girls. She adored them. Their every wish was her command. They were, if truth be told, terribly, terribly spoilt. And yet, beautiful as they were, Alicia felt that somehow they could be still more beautiful. Tall as they were, wouldn't it be lovely if they were just a mite taller? A fraction more elegant? A tiny bit more charming? Surely her husband could arrange that? A couple of quick spells. After all, he'd cured them of measles, hadn't he? But Varius refused and said no, magic wasn't to be used for personal gain and certainly not for foolish things like that. The girls were quite beautiful enough and they should thank their lucky stars and be content with the way they were. In fact, he got quite firm with her. So she had to pretend to make the best of it. Because although it happened very rarely, if her husband ever did lose his temper it was a terrible thing to behold and it often rained for weeks afterwards. And then, one day, Varius had to go away for a while to attend the Society of Sorcerers' Annual Conference up north. He bade his family farewell and told them to take good care, he'd only be gone a week or so. And off he went. That same evening when both the girls were in

bed, Alicia began to think. What would be the harm,
she thought, in using just a tiny spell? If it helped her
daughters? After all, she was only thinking of them. It
was perfectly natural in a parent. Who wouldn't, offered
half a chance? She was sure she'd be able to work a
spell as simple as that. She'd seen Varius do it and it all
looked perfectly simple to her. So she crept upstairs to
his study – she knew where he hid the key, she'd already
spied on him – and she very cautiously opened the door
and entered the forbidden room. It was like a treasure
trove – books piled high against the walls. Vats of
strange coloured liquid, glass jars with things in she
couldn't begin to guess what they were. Ugggh! Dusty
bottles. Dusty dishes. An awful lot of dust.

Alicia Uggh!

Paul Finally, Alicia found what she was looking for. The
spell book . . .

Alicia (*thumbing the pages, muttering*) B for Beautiful –
Banshees . . . Bats . . . Beetle Juice . . . Ah . . . Beautiful . . .
Brackets see also Irresistible. Irresistible. Even better
(*She turns more pages.*) Incubi . . . Invisibility . . . Irresistible. To become Irresistible, prepare the following in a
large jar: (*She begins hurriedly to assemble the
ingredients, muttering to herself, under the next.*)

Paul The mother worked feverishly for although she
knew full well that her husband was away, she had the
uneasy feeling that none the less someone, somewhere
was watching her.

A cat miaows. She jumps.

Alicia Out of the way, damn cat! Right. Stir the
ingredients well. (*She does so.*) Good. Now, pour the
mixture over the pillow and inhale overnight. That's it
then. That's it. Simple. Nothing to it.

343

Paul And the mother crept out of the study, being careful to re-lock the door, and tip-toed along to her daughters' rooms, where she ever so gently, being careful not to wake them, poured the magic mixture on to each of their pillows.

Alicia (*softly*) There! Sleep well, my little beauties.

Paul In the morning, when the girls awoke and came down for breakfast, they seemed to Alicia no different than before.

Alicia (*muttering*) I must have got it wrong.

Paul But later on, when they both went for their stroll in the garden, she witnessed the results for herself.

The village boy comes on, catches sight of Cecilia and Emilia, grasps his throat and drops dead. They walk on oblivious.

The potion worked better than she'd dared hope.

Alicia I must have made it a bit strong. Never mind.

Paul Over the next few days, Alicia decided to introduce her new irresistible daughters to a few possible suitors. It would be up to the girls themselves to choose the one they wanted to marry. After all, who could refuse them now? They were irresistible. So Alicia invited the kingdom's most eligible princes, all fabulously rich good-looking young men from every corner of the realm.

Denzil comes strutting on, dressed up to the nines, he stands arrogantly. He catches sight of Emilia and his mouth drops open.

Emilia (*smiling*) Hallo.

Denzil Arrgghhh!

Paul The potion really was most effective.

Cecilia (*smiling*) Hallo.

Denzil (*spinning round*) Arrrggg! Arrrgghh!

Paul In fact rather too effective . . .

Emilia Here!

Cecilia No, here!

Emilia No, over here!

Cecilia Come on!

Emilia Come on!

> *Denzil spins this way and that unable to choose between them. The girls continue to tease him.*

Paul The problem was, as Alicia soon discovered, that although the daughters were irresistible, gradually they lost their hearts. And to each of their suitors they became as cold and uncharitable as the North Wind itself.

> *Cecilia and Emilia lead Denzil a dance.*

Alicia (*uneasily*) Now, girls, that's enough . . .

Denzil Yes, please. Mercy . . . I give in . . .

Alicia You must let Prince Denzil sit down.

Cecilia We don't want him to sit down.

Alicia Why ever not?

Emilia Because he doesn't please us.

Cecilia He revolts us.

Emilia He disgusts us.

Cecilia He repels us.

Emilia He appalls us.

Cecilia Go away.

Emilia Go away.

Denzil But, ladies, I beg you . . .

Emilia and Cecilia GO AWAY!

Denzil, startled, rushes off. The girls laugh.

Alicia (*reproving*) Now that was no way to treat a crown prince, was it, you naughty girls?

Paul But every prince was treated just the same – in fact, worse and worse . . .

Alicia (*announcing*) Girls, look. Prince Basil is here.

Basil enters. He is as arrogant as the other one.

Basil Good afternoon, ladies, I – (*seeing the girls*) Aaaarrgghhh!

Alicia These are my daughters.

Cecilia (*smiling*) Hallo, fatty.

Emilia (*smiling*) Hallo, ugly.

Basil (*spellbound*) Arrrgghhh!

Alicia Now, now, girls. (*whispering*) He's incredibly rich. Be nice to him.

Cecilia Alright.

Emilia If you say so.

Cecilia Come here, spotty. Do you want to play a game, then?

Emilia Going to play a game, wart face?

Basil Anything, anything to please you, ladies.

Cecilia Blind man's buff.

Emilia Super.

Basil is blindfolded.

Cecilia Don't wriggle.

Emilia Hold still, silly little man.

Basil You're both so beautiful.

Cecilia Of course we are. (*sharply*) Don't touch me!

Emilia We know we are. (*sharply*) Don't touch!

Cecilia (*spinning him around*) Alright. Whichever one of us you can catch you can kiss.

Basil (*ecstatically*) Ah!

Emilia (*softly*) Maybe. (*loudly*) Off you go, then.

Alicia Now, girls, you must let Basil catch one of you.

Cecilia Possibly.

Emilia Perhaps.

Cecilia Who knows? (*calling*) Basil!

Emilia Who can tell? (*calling*) Basil!

Basil reacts to their voices but they dodge him with ease. The girls exchange glances.

Cecilia Hey! This way, podgy.

Emilia This way, lumpy.

They lure him towards an exit.

Cecilia That's it.

Emilia That's the way.

Alicia Carefully, now, carefully.

Cecilia Come on, then. Run to me now, Basil.

Emilia Run to me, Basil.

Cecilia and Emilia Now, Basil!

Basil rushes at them. They step aside at the last minute. He disappears.

Alicia (*alarmed*) Oh, no!

A great cry of Basil falling. A splash.

Cecilia Oh, dear!

Emilia He's fallen off the battlements.

Cecilia Into the moat.

Emilia Poor old Basil.

Cecilia (*calling*) Bad luck, Basil!

Alicia You naughty, naughty girls. You wicked girls, you did that deliberately. You're both of you heartless children. I've a good mind to give you no supper. You wait till your father gets back. He'll hear about this.

Cecilia We don't care.

Emilia We'll push him in the moat as well.

Cecilia See if we don't.

Alicia (*to herself*) Oh dear.

Paul But before their mother could say another word they had flounced away to torment more village boys. Alicia was horrified. For she realized that this was all her fault. And although she had threatened it, she was secretly quite frightened to think what Varius would say when he returned. He did, as I say, have a terrible temper when roused. So that night the mother once again crept into her husband's study and searched frantically for some antidote to the Irresistible Spell. But she could find none

348

Alicia (*desperately thumbing through the book*) Repellent . . . Repulsive . . . No, I can't use those. What if I got the strength wrong again? No one would ever want to look at my lovely children then. Oh, what am I going to do? What shall I do?

Paul She could do nothing. And so the daughters, day by day, grew steadily more cruel and heartless without a single thought for anyone, man or woman. They destroyed marriages, they wrecked young love wherever they could; they stole grooms from brides, husbands from wives, only to discard them again instantly with never a second thought for the unhappiness they had caused. Far and wide hearts were broken. People lived in fear of them now. For not a single soul who loved or was in turn loved was any longer safe from this wicked pair. Then one day, word reached the family that a stranger had arrived in the kingdom. A prince, richer and more handsome than all other princes. What is more, he had asked to meet the irresistible daughters, for their fame by now had spread beyond the kingdom. Their mother was very excited.

Alicia Now, girls, this time, please . . .

Cecilia (*casually*) Alright. We'll see him . . .

Emilia (*casually*) For a second . . .

Cecilia Show him in then, mother.

Alicia Oh dear. Don't do anything dreadful to him, will you? Do try. For me. (*She goes off.*)

Emilia What shall we do with this one then?

Cecilia Drown him?

Emilia Done that.

Cecilia Drive him mad with desire and make him jump into the fire.

Emilia Done that as well. Twice.

Cecilia Oh yes, so we have.

Emilia I know. We'll make him give us all his money –

Cecilia By asking him trick questions –

Emilia Which he could never answer –

Cecilia Yes.

Emilia And then make him pay a forfeit –

Cecilia Yes!

Emilia To – drink the moat.

Cecilia Through a straw.

Emilia Until he explodes.

Cecilia Yes. Shhh! He's coming.

Peter enters. He is still Varius but is masked and disguised. Alicia ushers him in.

Alicia Girls, this is Prince Nemo.

Cecilia (*smiling*) Hallo.

Emilia (*smiling*) Hallo.

Peter (*as Varius, bowing*) Your servant, young ladies.

Cecilia (*puzzled, to Emilia*) Why didn't he go aaarrrggh?

Emilia (*puzzled, to Cecilia*) I don't know.

Cecilia What is it you want?

Emilia And why are you wearing a mask?

Peter I have come to pay court to you. The mask is so that you will not be influenced by my devastating good looks but only by the sincerity of my nature.

Cecilia (*to Emilia*) He thinks a lot of himself, doesn't he?

Emilia (*to Cecilia*) He certainly does. We'd better pull him down a peg or two, hadn't we? (*loudly*) If you have come to pay court to us you must first prove your intelligence by answering two questions, one from each of us. Do you agree to that?

Peter I agree.

Alicia Simple questions now, girls.

Cecilia We have decided to be generous so you may have as many guesses as you like. But for every guess you make you must give us money. Do you agree?

Peter I agree.

Emilia If you fail to guess either one of the questions you must also pay a forfeit which we shall devise. Do you agree?

Peter I agree.

Cecilia Very well. The first question shall be mine. It's very simple. You have merely to guess the date of my birth. But wait! The date and time to the exact second. For every second you are wrong you will pay me one piece of gold. For every minute, ten pieces of gold. For every hour a hundred. For every day a thousand. And for every year you are wrong a million pieces of gold. Do you agree?

Peter I agree.

Cecilia Proceed then. You have plenty of time.

Emilia Plenty of time.

Alicia Really, girls, that's quite impossible. Even I don't know –

Cecilia Shhh, Mother!

Emilia Shhh!

Paul The strange prince appeared to think deeply for a moment.

Cecilia (*impatiently*) Come on!

Emilia (*impatiently*) Come on!

Peter Cecilia, you were born eighteen years ago. On the thirty-ninth second of the fifty-first minute of the eighth hour of the fifteenth day of the seventh month. (*A silence.*) Am I correct?

Cecilia (*shaken*) You might be.

Emilia (*softly*) He is, you know

Alicia (*loudly*) He is. He's right. I remember now.

Paul There was no denying it, the unknown prince was absolutely correct.

Cecilia That was a very, very lucky guess indeed. You must now answer my sister's question.

Peter I will try.

Alicia Oh, girls, surely the prince has done enough – ?

Emilia (*firmly*) Next question. Are you ready?

Peter I am ready.

Emilia Very well. Mine is also a simple problem. You have merely to guess my middle name. You may have as many guesses as you wish. For the first guess you pay me one piece of gold. For the second two pieces of gold. For the third, four. For the fourth, eight. For the fifth guess, sixteen. And so on. If you continue to guess wrongly or when you finally give up, then you pay the forfeit. Which I warn you will probably be your life. Now go ahead. (*Silence.*) Aren't you going to have a guess?

Cecilia (*smirking*) Perhaps he can't think of any names.

Peter I was simply wondering.

Emilia Wonder away.

Peter I was wondering what could possibly be the middle name of a young woman so empty, so cold, so unfeeling, so heartless. Surely the answer is that, like her very self, there is nothing at the centre at all. Thus my answer to your question is equally simple. I look where your heart should be and find nothing there but emptiness. Likewise with your names. You have no middle name, Emilia.

Alicia He's right!

Emilia (*in fury*) How did you know that? Somebody told you. (*to Alicia*) You told him, didn't you? I'll get you for this.

Cecilia We'll get you for this.

Alicia No, no, girls. It wasn't me. I promise it wasn't me who told him.

Emilia Get her!

Cecilia Get her!

Alicia No!

The girls advance on their mother.

Peter (*with a roar*) STOP!!!

353

A vast clap of thunder. The women freeze in their tracks. Peter removes his mask with flourish.

Alicia (*in a whisper*) Varius . . .

Cecilia (*likewise*) Father . . .

Emilia (*likewise*) Father . . .

Peter stares at them Another rumble of thunder.

Alicia (*softly*) Your father is angry.

Peter I am. Very angry. And very sad. Sad that I am unable to trust my own family, my own wife. Unable to trust her not to meddle in things that do not concern her.

Alicia You know . . .?

Peter Of course I know, woman. Even though I was a thousand leagues away, I knew the very second you unlocked the door and stole into my study. Oh, Alicia . . .

Alicia I'm sorry. It's all my fault. Don't blame the girls.

Peter I blame only myself. For allowing such greed, such vanity to destroy my own family. The people I cared for most in the world . . .

Cecilia What will happen to us?

Emilia What are you going to do to us, father?

Cecilia Please don't punish us, we didn't mean . . .

Peter Cecilia, you have created your own punishment long ago. You have worshipped your looks and neglected your nature, child. Well, keep your looks for as long as they last. Indeed, you will need to fight to keep them. For I will tell you this. Anyone who loves you, will love only those looks. Once they tire of that beauty or it begins to fade, they will discover nothing beneath it but emptiness. And then and only then will they perceive the

354

true beauty in your sister here. But too late. They will have already chosen.

Cecilia Oh.

Emilia And me? What about me?

Peter Emilia, you are condemned to live eternally in your sister's shadow. You have chosen to put aside your true beauty – in that case, let it remain for ever hidden where most men, being as they are, will never think to look for it. Instead, they will choose your worthless sister.

Emilia Oh.

Peter And for those foolish men themselves who cannot perceive beauty that is more than skin deep, such asses by night deserve to be no more than donkeys by day. Let them bray away in a field until they finally come to their senses.

Alicia How long must this last?

Peter Until at least one of you loves selflessly and is herself selflessly loved.

More thunder.

Alicia What about me? I'm your wife.

Peter Take your children and go, woman. I've finished with you.

Alicia Finished with me? What do you mean?

Peter Go!

Alicia It's pouring with rain . . .

Cecilia Mother, come on . . .

Emilia Mother . . .

Alicia Don't I get any settlement? Any alimony? How do we live?

Peter Try working.

Alicia Work?

Cecilia Mother . . .

Emilia Mother . . .

Peter You'll be provided for, don't worry. Go on, leave me. Before I grow really angry.

> *A big clap of thunder. The women hurry out. Peter glares at the sky.*

Paul The sorcerer was as good as his word. He rehoused his family in number forty-nine Hollyhock Street. A pleasant little property but a bit of a come down from a fifty bedroomed castle, I must admit. I suppose as sorcerers go he was fairly pleasant about it, but it has to be said that at the end of the day, they're not the easiest of people to live with. So unforgiving, really.

> *Percy and Alicia have re-entered.*

And with a long bitter sigh, Alicia finished her story. The end.

Peter (*taking over the narrative*) And Frederick, who had listened intently to all this, now fully understood the curse that had fallen on him when he had betrayed his wife.

Alicia Do you understand now, Frederick?

Percy Yes, I do.

> *Cecilia and Emilia enter. Emilia is consoling Cecilia.*

Peter He said, a trifle uneasily. For Frederick felt a deep sense of shame, not least because he had behaved so boringly and predictably just as the magician had prophesied he would.

Percy Oh fool, fool. (*He brays.*)

Peter And he ran from the room past his wife and her sister. For he could no longer bear to look at either of them.

> *Percy gives a final bray as he goes. In a second the women, too, go out.*

And he sold the house and contents in Hollyhock Street, divided the cash, gave his wife custody of the water-colours and moved away to a dark, distant forest where he pooled resources with his sister and bought a large deserted mansion. And there he lived for the rest of his life, by day a donkey, by night a lonely bitter man with only Leonora for company. The end.

> *Paul, Frederick, Leonora, Yerp and Mrs Yerp enter walking as before.*

Percy (*taking up the narrative again*) And as Frederick finished his tale, the lights of the house came into view.

Paul What a remarkable story.

Leonora Every word of it is true, Rupert.

Paul I do not doubt it, Leonora. What is to be done, then?

Frederick There is nothing to be done. Nothing. Come, there are the lights of the house. Let us get out of this bitter cold.

Percy I could see that the brother had lapsed into his former gloom once again. Probably as a result of re-telling his tragic story. I was destined, anyway, to spend another night in that doom-laden house for it was now far too late to think of travelling. My poor brother and sister-in-law and my angelic little nieces and nephews would have to be disappointed; but with luck I would join them on Boxing Day although without, I fear, the presents I had intended for them, poor mites. It was my fervent hope that the villainous coachman, Gorff, was even now choking to death on my stolen sweetmeats and rich plum pudding. I slept fitfully that night, my dreams filled with warlocks and witches and donkeys and – yes, I have to confess – with Leonora whose divine countenance dominated everything. My bedroom overlooked the driveway and finally I was awoken by a heavy knocking on the front door.

Heavy knocking.

And a few seconds later by excited, raised voices.

Mrs Yerp and Alicia, now playing an older Cecilia, enter.

Mrs Yerp . . . and I say you can't just barge your way in here, madam . . .

Alicia Great heavens, woman, I've driven all night, through the most appalling conditions. You have to let me in.

Percy I dressed quickly . . .

Mrs Yerp The mistress is still abed and the master's – elsewhere. They can't be disturbed. You'll have to wait . . .

Alicia Oh, this is impossible. You don't seem to realize how urgent this is –

Mrs Yerp Nothing to do with me . . .

Paul May I be of assistance, Mrs Yerp?

Mrs Yerp It's alright, sir. It's not a problem. This here lady's just come visiting, that's all.

Alicia Ah, sir, I fear I do not know your name but please tell this – woman to let me in. I assure you my business is of a most urgent nature.

Paul I am Rupert Fellowes, at your service. May I enquire your name, madam?

Alicia My name, sir, is Mrs Cecilia Stringer, if that means anything to you at all.

Percy I caught my breath.

Paul It certainly does, madam. Kindly let the lady pass, Mrs Yerp, I can vouch for her. Madam, I am but a guest here, yet I will see to it that Miss Stringer or her brother is awoken at once.

Alicia Sir, I thank you . . .

Mrs Yerp They wouldn't want that, sir, I assure you . . .

Leonora appears and soon, from another direction, Yerp.

Percy But before I could argue further with the woman, Leonora appeared at the top of the stairs. I fear we had disturbed her.

Leonora What is the matter? Oh –

Mrs Yerp Madam, this woman's been trying to –

Paul This *lady*, Leonora, is none other than . . .

Alicia I am Cecilia Stringer. You are Miss Leonora Stringer, are you not? I am your sister-in-law, Miss Stringer.

Leonora So it would appear. What do you want here?

Alicia To see Frederick. To see my husband.

Leonora He is no longer your husband.

Alicia Indeed –

Leonora You have no relationship to this family any longer. I must ask you to leave.

Alicia But surely, you could not –

Leonora Please leave, Miss Butterworth.

Alicia I am Mrs Stringer and I am staying until I have spoken to my husband .

Leonora He would not wish to see you, I assure you. Good day. Mrs Yerp, please show this lady out.

Mrs Yerp Yes, madam.

Leonora Miss Stringer, I beg you. Please. Let me see him. Sir, if you have influence at all, intercede for me, I beg you.

Paul Leonora, I must plead on the lady's behalf. Her distress is pitiful to behold. I apologize if I seem to you –

Leonora What would be the point, Rupert?

Paul There can be no harm in seeing him, surely. After all, it is past dawn and he is presumably . . . What could be the harm? She has travelled a long way. Please. For my sake.

Leonora Very well, Rupert. For you I will reluctantly grant her request.

Alicia Thank you, thank you.

Leonora It is against my better judgement, it must be said. Yerp, is the master . . .?

Yerp He's already out in the paddock, ma'am. He's had his hay.

Leonora Thank you. You will be able to see for yourself, Mrs Stringer, the depths of shame and indignity which your marriage has heaped upon my brother.

Alicia I realize. I already realize, believe me.

They all move out into the grounds.

Percy We walked together to the paddock. I attempted to lift the mood of the party with some light conversation.

Paul You travelled alone, Mrs Stringer?

Alicia Yes, indeed. My sister Emilia would have accompanied me but my mother these days suffers from ill health and we could not leave her entirely alone.

Paul Nothing too serious I hope?

Alicia No, but she is of an age now, of course, when such things occur. But she still looks well and most days she is bright and cheerful. She has a naturally strong constitution which fortunately I have inherited. In fact, many observe that now I am older we are not dissimilar in looks.

Paul Then your mother must indeed be an attractive woman, Mrs Stringer.

Percy We reached the hidden door to the paddock.

Leonora I do not know what you intend to do now you are here, Mrs Stringer, but please be quick.

Alicia I will, Miss Stringer.

Percy Although I pride myself on being a normal, strong, masculine, unromantic man, the scene I was about to behold all but brought tears to my eyes.

They enter the paddock. Frederick enters as the donkey. He stands watching them. Alicia steps forward.

Mrs Stringer and the donkey stood staring at each other. The woman wore an expression of such tender and touching sadness, it was almost unbearable to behold. As for the donkey, at first it seemed that he failed to recognize her. Until –

Frederick brays loudly.

The creature let out such a bellow that could only be interpreted as one great joyous cry of greeting.

Alicia Frederick!

Alicia runs forward and embraces Frederick.

Percy Without another word, the woman rushed forward to embrace the creature, wrapping her arms around its neck and kissing it passionately on the muzzle. In an instant a remarkable and miraculous transformation took place. Where once the dumb creature had been, restored to his natural shape and size now stood the joyful figure of Frederick.

Frederick Cecilia!

Alicia Frederick, oh, Frederick.

They embrace. The whole group are now somewhat overwhelmed.

Percy I have to report that I was not the only one to be moved by these events.

Alicia Oh, Frederick. You didn't forget me?

Frederick How could I forget, Cecilia? Forgive me.

Alicia With all my heart.

They embrace again.

Percy Indeed so moved was I by this sight and also anxious not to embarrass the reunited couple, that I turned to make some light converation with Leonora.

Paul Miss Stringer, may I ask you –

Leonora Oh, yes, yes, yes, Rupert. My answer can be none other than yes!

She throws herself into Paul's arms. After a second he responds.

Percy There had been it seemed a small social misunderstanding between us but one that I was more than happy to overlook. The habit, moreover, appeared to be catching.

Yerp Oh, Mrs Yerp!

Mrs Yerp Mr Yerp.

They too embrace. Peter enters as Varius.

Paul At that moment, hovering in the sky, the spirit of Varius, the sorcerer appeared.

Peter Cecilia, you have at last found unselfish love. The spell is now broken.

Thunder.

Percy Just a minute, who's telling this story . . . ?

Peter And as for Emilia, she too was finally free to find true love . . .

Emilia enters.

And she did so almost immediately with a certain Albert Haskins a few doors down at number twenty-five Hollyhock Street. A very eligible bachelor who not only worked for the gas board but was an extremely accomplished ballroom dancer . . .

Percy (*indignantly*) Look, what is going on here?

Peter But the main reason Emilia loved Albert Haskins was that he looked exactly like the younger version of her sister Cecilia's husband, Frederick.

Emilia (*looking at Percy and holding out her arms*) Darling!

Percy (*not prepared to argue*) Oh, alright then, what the hell . . . (*running down to join her*) Darling!

They embrace. Cecilia enters.

Paul And as for Varius himself, well, wouldn't you know it, he ran off with a girl who was young enough to be his daughter –

Cecilia (*running to Peter*) Darling!

Peter Darling! (*They embrace.*)

Paul But then sorcerers have all the luck.

Percy So finally, remember this, ladies and gentlemen, if you will . . .

Peter Whichever way you look at it . . .

Paul Whichever story you choose to believe . . .

Percy (*indicating Peter*) His . . .

Peter (*indicating Paul*) Or his . . .

Paul (*indicating Percy*) Or his . . .

Percy However they may start . . .

Peter However they might continue . . .

Paul You'll find they all tend to finish up much the same in the end . . .

Percy . . . the end . . .

Peter . . . the end . . .

Paul . . . the end . . .

Everyone . . . THE END!

The keyboard player strikes up some music. The company dance, bow and finally exit.
  Curtain.

THE CHAMPION OF PARIBANOU

Characters

The Sultan
Houssain, his first son
Ali, his second son
Ahmed, his third son
The Grand Vizier
Murganah, his daughter
Nouronnihar, a princess
Safia, her maid
Salim, her father's emissary
Paribanou
Nasuh, her servant
Schaibar, the stranger
A Highwayman
An Innkeeper

*A land in the forgotten past
or the undreamt future.*

Suggested doubles

Safia *and* Paribanou
Schaibar *and* Salim
Innkeeper *and* Nasuh
Highwayman *and* Sultan

The Champion of Paribanou was first performed at the
Stephen Joseph Theatre, Scarborough, on 29 November
1996. The cast was as follows:

The Sultan Malcolm Rennie
Houssain Andrew Mallett
Ali Howard Saddler
Ahmed Jonathan McGuiness
The Grand Vizier Adrian McLoughlin
Murganah Pauline Turner
Princess Nouronnihar Eleanor Tremain
Safia Kate Farrah
Salim Colin Gourley
A Highwayman Malcolm Rennie
Schaibar Colin Gourley
An Innkeeper Wolf Christian
Paribanou Kate Farrah
Nasuh Wolf Christian

Director Alan Ayckbourn
Design Roger Glossop
Costume Design Elaine Garrard
Lighting Mick Hughes
Fight Director Wolf Christian
Music John Pattison

Act One

SCENE ONE

The Sultan's Palace Grounds.
    The Vizier enters in a hurry. He is elderly and rather flustered.

Vizier (*calling*) My lord Houssain! My lord! Prince Houssain!

> *Houssain appears from high up, as if in a tree. He has been reading a book. He is the lean, rather scholarly one of the Sultan's three sons.*

Houssain Hallo? Somebody want me?

Vizier My lord Houssain! Please!

Houssain What's the problem?

Vizier My lord, it's noon.

Houssain (*unconcerned, gazing at the sky*) Good heavens! So it must be.

Vizier Thursday.

Houssain Right.

Vizier The third month of the second moon . . .

Houssain Thank you so much for reminding me, Grand Vizier. Good day to you.

Vizier My Lord, please, the Princess . . .

Houssain Princess?

Vizier . . . arrives in a few minutes. Your father is expecting you and your brothers in the palace at noon

373

to greet her on her arrival. This has been arranged for weeks. For months. For years. The clock has just struck twelve *and not one of you is there! NOW PLEASE!*

Houssain Oh. You mean Princess . . .

Vizier . . . Her Highness the Princess Nouronnihar . . .

Houssain . . . Nouronnihar. Quite. Couldn't she just . . . meet the others . . .? I've . . . I've got a lot of reading . . .

Vizier (*imploringly*) My lord!

Houssain Alright, I'm coming. Princess Nouronnihar . . . Oh, if there's one thing I loathe it's princesses . . . (*He starts to climb down from the tree.*)

Vizier Do you know where your brothers are, my lord?

Houssain Haven't the faintest idea. If you're looking for Prince Ali, I should start in the maids' quarters . . .

Vizier (*muttering to himself*) The maids' quarters . . . Why didn't I think of that? The maids' quarters . . . of course!

The Vizier moves on. Houssain is gone.

The maids' quarters. (*calling up to a window*) Prince Ali! My lord! Prince Ali!

Ali appears at the window, shirtless. He is the good looking, well built and (it has to be said) rather vain brother.

Ali Shhh! Quietly! You'll wake her husband!

Vizier Her husband!

Ali Only joking . . . What do you want, it's only – first thing in the morning . . .

Vizier It is noon on the Thursday of the third month of the second moon . . .

Ali Thanks very much. Goodbye! (*He makes to withdraw.*)

Vizier My lord . . .

Maid (*off, sleepily*) Ali . . .

Ali (*to the Vizier*) Cheerio!

Vizier . . . please . . .

Maid (*off*) . . . come back to bed . . .

Ali Coming, my love . . .

Vizier The Princess Nouronnihar!

Ali (*puzzled*) The Princess Nouronnihar?

Vizier The Princess Nouronnihar.

Ali Oh, that Princess Nouronnihar. Arrived, has she?

Vizier Imminently. Your father is awaiting you.

Ali Well, tell him – Can't you tell him I'm . . .?

Vizier No, my lord. *You* tell him. He'll probably only have you beaten; me he'll execute!

Ali Good thinking. I'll just get my shirt.

Vizier Please, where pray is your younger brother?

Ali Ahmed? Who knows. In the clouds? Dreaming? Playing his life away? I'll tell you what, though . . . wherever your daughter is – he won't be far away . . . Find Murganah, you'll have found Ahmed. Bet you! (*as he withdraws his head, to someone inside*) Alas, my love! I have to go . . .

Maid (*off, disappointedly*) Oh! Ali!

   Ali goes. The Vizier moves on.

Vizier (*annoyed with himself*) Find Murganah, you'll find Prince Ahmed. Where else! (*calling as he goes*) Murganah! Where are you, girl? Murganah!

The Vizier goes off. As he does so, two figures appear. They are fighting with practice swords. Both are wearing protective helmets so are indistinguishable. One is the boyish figure of Murganah. She is young and athletic and clearly the superior fighter. Her opponent, Ahmed, is furiously defending himself. It is good natured, almost playful as Murganah toys with him.

Murganah (*inviting Ahmed to attack her*) Yes? Come on . . . come on . . .

Ahmed falls for the trick and makes a lunge at her. She twists away, easily evading him. Ahmed loses his balance and falls over.

Ahmed Aaah! Not again . . .

Murganah disarms him.

Every time!

She holds her sword above him as if to make the final coup de grâce.

Murganah And . . . die!

Ahmed (*rather overdoing it*) Aaaarrrrhhh! Aaaarrrggghhh! Ugghh!

Murganah takes off her helmet and sits on the ground beside him now, laughing and laying aside her sword.

Murganah You never learn, do you?

Ahmed I'm hopeless, hopeless . . . Every time. Same old trick. I've never won. Not once.

Murganah Lucky you have me to look after you then, isn't it?

Ahmed Yes, but I'm . . . That's the problem. I'm supposed to look after you . . .

Murganah Who says?

Ahmed Well, it's a fact. I'm the man. I'm supposed to look after you.

Murganah Because I'm the woman?

Ahmed Yes.

Murganah Why can't the woman look after the man?

Ahmed I don't know. They just don't. They're not supposed to. I'm supposed to look after you. That's the way it is.

Murganah But you can't look after me, can you?

Ahmed I know.

Murganah You're useless.

Ahmed That's the problem.

Murganah So I'll have to look after you then, won't I?

Ahmed (*a little unhappily*) Yes. Thank you.

Murganah For ever.

Ahmed Yes.

Murganah As blood twins.

Ahmed Yes.

Murganah No one else?

Ahmed No.

Murganah Ever?

Ahmed No.

Murganah Swear?

Ahmed (*hesitating*) I can't.

Murganah You won't?

Ahmed I'm a prince . . .

Murganah So?

Ahmed Princes have to – There's things they have to do. They can't always choose.

Murganah Why not?

Ahmed You know why. It's the way it is . . . We're not free. None of us are.

Murganah I am. I'm free. I obey nobody. I am answerable to no one but myself.

Ahmed No, you're not. You're the Grand Vizier's daughter, you have as much responsibility as anyone else. You're –

Murganah I'm not his daughter. I'm adopted.

Ahmed Nonetheless . . .

Murganah I'm a child of the forest. I told you. I was abandoned by wolves. My mother found me wrapped in tiger skins, hidden under the leaves. I was wild like an animal . . .

Ahmed Murganah!

Murganah What?

Ahmed Come on. We don't know this for certain.

Murganah I do. (*She looks at him for a second.*) Ahmed, do you love me?

Ahmed (*hesitating*) Yes . . .

Murganah I love you.

Ahmed I know.

Murganah Then what else can matter? (*He stands defiantly. Yelling*) Let them all come. I'm ready for you!

The Vizier enters.

Vizier Murganah!

Murganah (*startled*) Father!

Vizier What are you playing at? Look at the way you're dressed! Look at your clothes. You're a disgrace. What on earth do you think you're doing, girl? If your stepmother was alive she'd drop dead with shame.

Murganah What's wrong?

Vizier You know perfectly well. I've told you a hundred times. You're not a child any more, you're a grown woman, Murganah. So try and behave like one and not like a street urchin.

Murganah How do you know? Maybe I am a street urchin. How do you know what I am?

Vizier That's enough! My lord Ahmed, the Princess Nouronnihar is arriving at any minute. Your father says will you please assemble with your brothers in the Grand Drawing Room immediately.

Ahmed Goodness, is that today?

Vizier (*wearily*) My lord, you knew it was today. Twelve noon on the Thursday of the third month of the second moon. I wrote it down for you . . .

Ahmed Oh, yes.

Vizier And Murganah. I've arranged for you to attend on the Princess as her maidservant during her stay here.

Murganah Attend on her? Me?

Vizier Yes. It's about time you learnt something useful, girl. Up to your room and get changed. Come along both of you, please. Hurry! Please! (*He goes.*)

Murganah (*in a fury*) I'm not attending on her. I'm not a servant. How dare he! Who does he think I am?

Ahmed (*gently*) Murganah!

Murganah I'm nobody's servant! I'm me! I'm free!

Ahmed Murganah . . . We all have a role to play. I have one and so do you.

Murganah Oh, Ahmed . . . (*She suddenly clings to him, tearfully.*) What's going to happen to us, Ahmed?

Ahmed I don't know.

Murganah You'll marry this princess, I know it . . .

Ahmed (*surprised*) What?

Murganah You'll see her and fall straight in love with her. I know you will.

Ahmed Nonsense. I'm not marrying a princess . . .

Murganah Then why is she here?

Ahmed I don't know.

Murganah To arrange a marriage. Why else do princesses come visiting?

Ahmed Well, what if she is? I don't care. If she wants to marry someone, let her. She can marry Ali or Houssain . . .

Murganah And what if she prefers you? What if she wants to marry you?

Ahmed I'll tell her, no thank you.

Murganah No, you won't. Because you're not free. You've said so. You'll have to marry her, won't you? And then what's going to happen to us? To me? Heaven knows where I came from. Heaven knows where I'm going.

Ahmed Murganah. You always told me – courage. When I was scared, when we were both very little. At night. In the dark. When you were brave for both of us. Courage! Remember?

Murganah (*dully*) Yes.

Ahmed Then, courage. Come on. (*He makes to move off.*)

Murganah Ahmed, I'll tell you one thing. If another tries to take you from me, I will kill her. I swear it. You are my blood twin and no one will ever part us. Ever. I'll die first. (*He stares at her.*) I mean it, Ahmed.

Ahmed (*sadly*) I hope you don't. Come on. (*He goes.*)

Murganah (*to herself, holding up her sword as a cross*) I swear.

As she follows him the scene changes to:

SCENE TWO

The Sultan's Palace Grand Drawing Room.
Houssain and Ali, now more formally dressed, are
waiting. Ali is looking out of the window. Houssain
is reading his book.

Ali They're just arriving. She's getting out of her carriage.

Houssain (*without looking up*) Good

Ali I can't see what she looks like. She's all – covered up. Probably as plain as a pig. They're greatly over-rated, princesses. In my experience. Give me a kitchen maid any day.

Houssain Or preferably several.

Ali Jealous? I can't help it if women find me irresistible, can I?

Houssain My dear chap, you're welcome to all the women in the world. All I want is to settle down with a good book. Only people keep interrupting.

Ali How can you possibly read at a time like this? Our whole future's at stake. One of us is going to have to marry her.

Houssain Not me.

Ali Well, certainly not me.

Houssain Lucky old Ahmed, then.

Ali (*laughing*) If she wants Ahmed she'll have to deal with Murganah first. Don't fancy anyone's chances there. (*still looking out*) Hey, she's got this huge man with her. Must be her bodyguard . . . Father's greeting them . . . (*mimicking his father*) Pray welcome, princess, to our humble palace. All three hundred and twenty seven rooms . . .

A fanfare.

Look out! They're coming. Is my hair alright?

Ahmed enters, struggling into his jacket.

Houssain Come on, Ahmed. Where have you been?

Ali Playing soldiers with Murganah. I bet she beat you as usual.

Ahmed Possibly she did.

Ali Possibly she did. You couldn't beat a blind tortoise . . .

Houssain Leave him alone, Ali . . .

The Vizier enters, hurriedly.

Vizier Quickly, now. They're here, they're here!

Another fanfare.
The Sultan enters escorting the Princess Nouronnihar. The Sultan is elderly but impressive and incisive. A no-nonsense military man. Nouronnihar is followed in turn by Safia, her silent maid. We see little of Nouronnihar at first as both women are heavily veiled. Safia is to remain so throughout.
Following them is Salim, the Princess's escort.
He is, as described, a giant. Armoured, metallic, menacing and, as we are soon to discover, non-human, mechanical and slightly faulty.
The Princes bow to the Princess. Nouronnihar curtseys to the sons in turn.

Sultan May I first of all welcome you, Princess Nouronnihar, to our humble palace . . .

Ali (*muttering*) All three hundred and twenty seven rooms . . .

Sultan (*with a sharp look at Ali*) And to introduce my three sons. Houssain, my eldest. Ali, my second son. And finally Ahmed, my youngest.

Nouronnihar (*formally*) I greet you all.

Houssain The pleasure is ours, Princess, I assure you.

Ali I am utterly enchanted, Princess. I am yours to serve.

Ahmed Hi!

Sultan My youngest, as you observe, Princess, is still a boy. (*He glares at Ahmed.*)

Nouronnihar Surely not? To me he seems every inch a man.

Ahmed (*pleased*) Thank you very much. (*He smiles at her, gratefully.*)

Nouronnihar May I in turn introduce Salim, my escort and Emissary of my father, The Imperial Grand Ruler of Kawar And All its Environs. Salim brings greeting from my father and a message of friendship from the people of The Glorious Kingdom of Kawar. Salim! Speak the message.

Salim gives a sudden shudder and starts to deliver the message.

Salim Grook oorrr crake bying bong orse rrok bikk sprak soot wick bike toong ding rooot speckle ting coke . . .

Ahmed (*to Ali*) What's he saying?

Ali No idea . . .

Salim . . . harder creck creck sprenkle tack-tack-tack-tack-tack –

384

Salim appears to have got stuck. Nouronnihar hits him with the flat of her hand.

(*triumphantly*) Tacker-rackar! (*He gives a gurgle and stops.*)

Vizier Bravo. A most – moving and eloquent message.

Salim gives another gurgle.

Sultan I wonder if he'd mind saying that all again.

Nouronnihar I believe that would be difficult. Salim is, of course, mechanical.

Sultan (*startled*) Mechanical. Good gracious!

Nouronnihar On our way here we encountered several thunderstorms. He has become extremely rusty.

Vizier Perhaps some oil. (*calling*) Oil for the Emissary!

Sultan If I may be permitted, Grand Vizier . . .

Vizier I am sorry, sire . . .

Sultan We can oil him later. To the point of our meeting today. We are all of us aware, that in the past there have been some differences between your father, Princess, and myself. Between our own State and that of the Kingdom of Kawar there has been an unfortunate tension. Today it is our hope that through a union of our respective children, by means of the marriage of the Princess Nouronnihar with one of my sons, we shall build a new bridge of friendship and co-operation between our two peoples.

Vizier Hear! Hear!

Salim makes a grinding noise by way of consent. Nouronnihar hits him. He stops.

Nouronnihar It is indeed my father's dearest wish that this may be achieved. And, of course, my own.

Sultan As it is my sons. Boys?

Houssain Yes.

Ali Oh, yes.

Ahmed You bet.

Sultan It is for you to choose, Princess. The choice is yours. Take your time. You are welcome to stay as long as you wish. Get acquainted with them all. Although as a father I am possibly a little biased – may I say that I don't feel that any one of them will disappoint you.

Nouronnihar I am certain they will not. The choice will be very hard for me. Would you . . . Would you permit me, sire, to have a word alone with your sons.

Sultan Of course. (*roguishly*) The heart is impatient, eh?

Nouronnihar (*coyly*) I fear it is, sire.

Sultan Oh, I understand. I too was young once. Believe it or not. (*He laughs.*)

Ali (*laughing, to the others*) A likely story.

Nouronnihar (*laughing*) Oh, I do. I do believe it, sire.

Sultan Come, Vizier, let us leave these young people. I'm sure we can trust them to behave. Vizier, while they are talking tell the kitchens to prepare a feast for a hundred people. And a drop of our finest oil for the Emissary.

Salim makes a grinding noise.

I will see you at the feast, Princess.

Nouronnihar (*curtseying*) I look forward to it eagerly, sire.

The Sultan goes. Followed by the Vizier and Salim, who initially has trouble finding the door.
    An awkward silence.

Houssain Princess, before you jump to any . . .

Ali . . . hasty . . .

Ahmed . . . conclusions . . .

Houssain Make up your mind . . .

Ali Too fast . . .

Ahmed We ought to tell you . . .

Nouronnihar Listen, all of you. We need to talk – (*pulling at her veil*) Oh, hang on, I can't talk in this thing . . . (*She takes off her veil to reveal herself a pretty but determined young woman, very used to having things her own way.*) That's better. Now. We haven't much time. I take it you don't want this marriage, any of you? Any more than I do?

Houssain Well . . .

Nouronnihar Do you?

Ahmed No.

Ali Sorry, but –

Nouronnihar Don't be sorry. I certainly don't. When I get married, I need a better reason than this, I can tell you. To hell with my father. I'll marry who I want to marry and it certainly won't be one of you.

Ali (*slightly hurt*) Ah!

Nouronnihar So, what are we going to do? I take it your father will not be too pleased if you simply said no?

Houssain No.

Ali What about your father?

Nouronnihar My father? He'd probably have me executed

Ahmed Really?

Nouronnihar He had my sister executed for refusing to finish her tea. He's not the most forgiving of men . . .

Houssain What are we going to do, then? (*A silence.*)

Ahmed I have a thought. What if – what if you said that we were all so – undesirable that you didn't want any of us?

Nouronnihar I don't think that would solve anything. They'd simply say, bad luck you'll just have to choose the one you hate the least.

Ali No, that wouldn't work. They'd never believe that you hated me.

Nouronnihar (*coolly*) Really? Fancy yourself, do you?

Ali Doesn't everyone?

Ahmed What if – what if you said you'd fallen in love with all of us, then?

Nouronnihar Why? What good would that do?

Ahmed Just an idea . . .

Nouronnihar No, wait. It might work. What if you were all madly in love with me as well? Then – we would have to solve it – with a – with a what?

Ali With a quest. We three would have to go on a quest.

Houssain They always do in the books.

Nouronnihar Right.

Ahmed A quest for what?

Nouronnihar It doesn't really matter – something . . .

Houssain . . . something difficult . . .

Ali . . . something impossible . . .

Houssain That could take forever to find. Well, five years, anyway . . .

Ali Seven years . . .

Ahmed Ten years . . .

Nouronnihar For as long as they'll let us. Yes, this is good. I want each of you to find me – a – let's see – an object from beyond my wildest dreams. How about that?

Houssain Wonderful.

Ali Difficult.

Ahmed That ought to take some finding.

Nouronnihar But, wait . . . When you return, I shall find all your gifts unsuitable. You will have found nothing to please me.

Houssain Brilliant!

Nouronnihar Better make sure you don't.

Ahmed Then what happens?

Nouronnihar Then you'll all have to go on another quest. We can keep it going for years.

Houssain Inspired!

Nouronnihar One thing, though. This must remain a secret between the four of us. If anyone for a moment suspects that this is simply a deception – that we're not doing this because of our passionate love for each other, then we're done for. We must tell nobody.

Houssain Nobody.

Ali Nobody.

Ahmed Nobody at all?

Nouronnihar Nobody.

Ahmed Ah.

Nouronnihar See you don't. Or we're all dead. Are we sworn?

Houssain Sworn.

Ali Sworn.

Ahmed (*after a hesitation*) Sworn.

Nouronnihar Call them back, then. Let us hope they'll agree to the scheme.

Houssain goes to the door. Nouronnihar replaces her veil.

Houssain (*calling*) Hallo, there! We've finished.

The Vizier enters. He is accompanied by Murganah, now dressed for her maidservant duties.

Vizier You've decided? Already?

Nouronnihar No. I fear we have suddenly run up against a problem.

Vizier Really? Oh dear.

Nouronnihar It appears this has been a case of love at first sight.

Vizier Indeed. How magical. Between whom and whom, may I enquire?

Nouronnihar Between all of us.

Vizier (*rather taken aback*) All of you?

Nouronnihar (*indicating Houssain*) Between him and me . . .

Houssain And me and her . . .

Nouronnihar (*indicating Ali*) And him and me . . .

Ali And me and her . . .

Nouronnihar (*indicating Ahmed*) And him and me . . .

Ahmed (*after a quick look at Murganah*) And me and her . . .

Vizier Good heavens. But you've only been in here – five minutes. Surely . . .?

Nouronnihar Ah, but love does not wait, Grand Vizier. It swoops. It pounces, like a cat . . .

Houssain Like an eagle . . .

Ali Like a leopard . . .

Ahmed Like a duck . . .

Vizier (*uncertainly*) Yes. Well, this is very difficult. What are we to do? You can't all – marry each other. It wouldn't be – proper.

Nouronnihar We have a scheme.

Vizier You do?

Houssain We do.

Vizier What sort of scheme?

Ali We're going on a quest . . .

Ahmed Different quests.

Houssain We three.

Nouronnihar To find me something beyond my wildest dreams. He who finds the most magical, desirable object will retain my undying love . . .

Vizier I see. Yes, that's certainly a solution . . . How long do you think this quest might take?

Ahmed Ten years . . .

Vizier Oh, no . . .

Houssain Seven years . . .

Vizier No, no . . .

Ali Five years . . .

Vizier No, no, no . . . Your father will never agree to that.

Houssain How long do you think, then?

Vizier I should imagine one year. Maximum.

Ali One year?

Ahmed Oh.

Nouronnihar May I speak with the Sultan, Grand Vizier? I will plead for longer . . .

Houssain No, we'll speak to him.

Ali We know how to get round father . . .

Ahmed We'll talk him round.

Nouronnihar (*doubtfully*) Are you sure?

Houssain Leave it to us. (*to the others*) Follow me. All my love, princess, is for you . . .

Ali For you . . .

Ahmed (*with a glance at Murganah*) For you.

Houssain (*as he leaves*) Farewell! My love!

Ali (*as he leaves*) Farewell! My precious!

Ahmed (*making to leave*) Farewell! My . . . dear!

Murganah (*softly to Ahmed, as they leave*) I'll kill her . . .

Ahmed (*softly, to Murganah*) No . . .

Murganah (*to Ahmed*) . . . and I'll kill you . . .

Ahmed . . . you don't understand . . .

Nouronnihar (*sharply*) Who is that person, there?

Vizier Ah, Princess this is my daughter – my adopted daughter, Murganah, who will be honoured to serve you during your stay here . . .

Ali (*returning briefly, to Ahmed*) Come on . . .

Ahmed reluctantly leaves with Ali.

Nouronnihar *That* is to be my servant . . .?

Vizier She would deem it an honour . . .

Nouronnihar Then I would deem it an honour if she were properly dressed.

Vizier Is there something wrong with her dress?

Nouronnihar Why isn't she veiled? In my country a servant is veiled at all times when in the presence of her mistress in order to let her mistress's beauty shine unchallenged . . . Pull on your veil, girl, at once.

Murganah I'm not putting on –

Vizier (*sharply*) Murganah! (*more quietly*) Do as you're told.

Murganah Father, I cannot serve her. If you make me serve her – I promise I'll – I can't!

Vizier Excuse me, Princess. (*drawing Murganah aside, gently*) It is time you learnt to serve, Murganah. You cannot play for ever, child. You're grown up now. Like everyone else in the world, you have duties. For the next few months your duty is to the Princess. You will obey her every command. And devote yourself to her. Do you understand that?

Murganah (*who has bowed her head, almost inaudibly*) Yes . . .

Vizier Good. Now, do as she commands.

Murganah pulls up her veil obediently.

Princess, my daughter is happy and willing to serve you. Please forgive her indiscretion.

Nouronnihar Of course, Grand Vizier.

Vizier If you will excuse me, I must attend the Sultan and see what has been decided. I think I may have to cancel that feast. Until the happy day!

Nouronnihar Until the happy day!

Vizier Incidentally, Princess, your Emissary – Salim. He's – he's just walked through the wall of the dining room. Never mind. (*He laughs.*) What's a wall here or there, eh?

The Vizier leaves. Nouronnihar removes her veil and tosses it on the floor. She sighs a little impatiently.

Nouronnihar Why are all men such fools?

Murganah Not all of them are There are some who –

Nouronnihar Be quiet! How dare you speak in my presence! How dare you? Did I ask you to speak? In my country a servant who speaks out of turn has her tongue cut out. Do you know that? You speak once more unless you're spoken to and I'll see that happens to you. Do you hear? I said, do you hear me?

Murganah (*hissing*) Yes . . .

Nouronnihar Princess . . .

Murganah Princess . . .

Nouronnihar I hope you do. Come along, then.

Nouronnihar makes to leave with Safia.

(*to Murganah, indicating her veil*) And pick that up, then! At this rate you won't last a week.

Nouronnihar leaves. Murganah pulls back her own veil angrily. She is trembling with anger. She picks up the veil which Nouronnihar has discarded. In a violent motion she tears it in half.

Murganah I'm nobody's servant! I'm free!

Murganah goes. As she does so the scene changes to:

SCENE THREE

The Sultan's Palace Courtyard.
It is night. The sound of restless horses. The brothers are cloaked and ready to depart.

Ali This is a fine time to start on a quest. It's the middle of the night. I've got far better things I could be doing at this time of night.

Houssain You heard what father said. We start at midnight and we must return at midnight in six month's time.

Ali So much for seven years.

Ahmed So much for ten.

Ali Maybe she'll get fed up with waiting for us and marry someone else whilst we're away.

Ahmed Maybe she'll die.

Ali Maybe we will.

Houssain Let's get the horses . . .

A light appears at a window. Nouronnihar looks out.

Nouronnihar (*calling softly*) Good-bye!

Houssain Goodbye!

Ali See you in six months . . .

Ahmed Six months! I don't want to leave here for six months.

Nouronnihar Yes, you do. Goodbye! Bring me back something beautiful. Far beyond my wildest dreams . . .

Houssain We will, we will! I'm off to Bisnager, a city with the largest library in the world.

Ali And I to Persia where the wom – where there's some very nice people, so I've heard.

Ahmed I go to Samarkand, the land of magic and adventure. For a whole six months. On my own.

Houssain Farewell!

Ali Farewell!

Ahmed Goodbye!

Nouronnihar Farewell!

The three men go.

(*to herself, as she closes her window*) I hope you all fall down a deep well, you stupid oafs!

She goes in. The sound of the horses departing.
A cloaked, hooded figure slips from the shadows.
Although we cannot identify her, it is Murganah.
She hesitates, checking the coast is clear and then
hurries across the courtyard and off in the direction
that the men have taken.

    As this happens the scene changes to:

SCENE FOUR

The Inn in the Distance.
    A traditional Olde Inne with several tables. At one of
these, in a corner, sits Schaibar, dressed in black. His face
is always hidden by a deep hood. He pays no attention
to the ensuing scene but concentrates on a game of
patience he is playing with selected tarot cards.
    At another table sits the Highwayman. His features
which are visible are highly unsavoury. In a moment,
Ahmed enters.

Ahmed Whew! Cold out there! Good evening.

    Neither of the other two acknowledge him.

Is the landlord . . .? (*calling*) Landlord! We've been
riding since last night. Hardly stopped. Yes. (*calling
again*) Landlord! My horse is lame. Just a little. She
pulled up. Nothing serious. Tired, I think. (*The silence
is unnerving him.*) Landlord!

    The Innkeeper appears. He is almost as evil looking as
    the Highwayman.

Ah! Landlord! Yes?

Innkeeper Sir! Good sir! I'm so sorry. Can I be of
service?

Ahmed Yes. I was just telling these gentlemen . . . my horse is lame. I don't think it's serious but if someone could take a look.

Innkeeper Certainly, sir. Certainly. (*with a great yell*) MAXWELL! SEE TO THE MAN'S HORSE! (*in his normal tone*) Maxwell will see to it, sir. Would you care for a seat, whilst you're waiting. Maxwell is magic with horses, sir. He could do anything with them . . .

Highwayman Stewed, fried, boiled . . .

Ahmed I'm sorry . . .

Innkeeper (*laughing*) Ignore that gentleman, sir. Ignore him. He has a wicked humour. Wicked. A glass of fine ale, sir. Something to eat, perhaps?

Ahmed No, I haven't time for anything to eat, but I'd love a glass of ale, thank you.

Innkeeper A pleasure, sir. Have you a long journey ahead, then?

Ahmed Yes, indeed. I have to reach the frontier by dawn. Is it far?

Innkeeper Oh . . . a good twenty miles, sir. Long haul in the dark. In these parts. Would you not prefer to spend the night? We have rooms. Capacious rooms. Start fresh in the morning. Much safer, sir. (*to the Highwayman*) Eh?

Highwayman Much safer.

Innkeeper Treacherous round here after dark, sir. (*to the Highwayman*) Eh?

Highwayman Dreadful.

Ahmed Yes. Odd you should say that. We've had this feeling we've been followed. But I'll have to take my chances. I need to catch up with my brothers. They've ridden on ahead.

Innkeeper Then you're on your own then, are you, sir?

Ahmed Yes. On my own. Temporarily.

Innkeeper Glass of fine ale, sir?

Ahmed Thank you.

The Innkeeper goes off.

(*to the Highwayman*) Nice man.

The Highwayman ignores him. He has taken out a long knife and is intent upon cleaning his finger nails. Ahmed gets up, rather nervously. He wanders over to Schaibar's table. He stares over his shoulder at the cards.

Ah, now. Does that card go on . . .?

Schaibar, with a single, deft movement, turns over a row of face down cards. They are all identical. The Death Card.

(*nervously*) Ah, no, probably not. Sorry, my mistake.

He moves away to the fire as the Innkeeper returns with a tankard of ale.

Innkeeper Fine ale, sir.

Ahmed Ah, thank you.

The Innkeeper chooses a table with a chair with its back to the Highwayman upon which to put down the tankard.

Innkeeper Here, sir. Out of the draught.

Ahmed Thank you. (*He sits.*) How much do I owe you?

Innkeeper Just two grutts, sir . . .

Ahmed (*groping for his purse*) Two grutts, right. That's very reasonable. (*finding his purse*) Here we are. You may have to change a scrone. I don't think I've got anything smaller.

Innkeeper Oh, that'll be alright, sir. (*He takes the purse out of Ahmed's hand.*) I'll just take this. It'll be a lot easier.

The Highwayman gets up and moves behind Ahmed. Ahmed goes to grab the purse back. He grabs the Innkeeper's sleeve.

Ahmed Wait a minute! You can't do that. Give me that back . . .

The Highwayman grabs Ahmed's arms.

What are you – ? What's going on?

Innkeeper (*as they struggle*) The knife . . . Use your knife.

Highwayman Then hold him, why can't you?

Ahmed kicks out with his feet catching the Innkeeper in the stomach.

Innkeeper Ufff!

The Innkeeper collapses in a heap, totally winded. He drops the purse.
Ahmed wriggles free from the Highwayman and grabs back his purse.
He turns to run but the Highwayman, with the knife in his hand again, has Ahmed cornered.

Highwayman (*brandishing the knife dangerously*) Come on! Give it me, boy! Come on, then!

Ahmed No.

Highwayman Come on! I'll cut you, else. I'll cut you, boy. Come on.

Ahmed No. It's all the money I have.

Highwayman Alright. You asked for it . . .

The Highwayman moves in. Suddenly the front door bursts open. A masked figure stands there, sword drawn. The Highwayman turns, startled.

Who the – ? Who are you?

The figure advances with the sword. Ineffectually the Highwayman tries to fend off the stranger with his knife. A flick of the sword and he is disarmed, clasping his injured hand.

Aaaah! You'll be sorry for that.

Another lunge with the sword. He backs away.

Alright, then, steady! I'm leaving! I'm leaving! I tell you, I'm leaving! There's no need for that! (*He is backed out of the door. As he goes*) I'll be back.

The stranger closes the door and turns to Ahmed.

Ahmed Sir, I have to thank you. I have no idea who you are but . . .

The 'stranger' has removed her mask. It is Murganah.

Murganah!

Murganah Promised I would look after you . . .

Ahmed How did you get here?

Murganah How else? I followed you.

Ahmed I didn't recognize you. Dressed like that.

Murganah How do you expect me to dress in this part of the country at night? In a silk dress?

The Innkeeper groans.

You. Get up. And bring us some more ale.

Innkeeper He attacked me. Why should I bring him ale?

Murganah Because if you don't, I shall attack you.

Innkeeper You? Who are you?

Murganah Someone who doesn't like cheats or thieves and has been known to kill them on sight. Ale! And be quick about it!

The Innkeeper scuttles out.

You should take care, Ahmed. Your trouble is you trust everyone and treat them all as friends.

Ahmed How else am I to behave? Treat them all as enemies?

Murganah No. But you should be careful. Friends are rare. Real friends like me are precious. Value me, Ahmed. Instead of racing off on quests for Princesses with less brain than a dead maggot whom you don't even love.

Ahmed How do you know I don't?

Murganah Because I know you. Because you're my blood twin. You can't love her. Say it if you can. Tell me that you love Nouronnihar, if you dare.

Ahmed (*with difficulty*) I – I love – Nouronnihar.

Murganah (*staring at him, quietly*) You're lying!

Ahmed Please, Murganah, turn round and go home . . .

Murganah You're lying!

Ahmed One day I will explain everything to you –

Murganah You're lying . . .

Ahmed ... but at present I'm sworn to secrecy ...

Murganah You're lying! You're lying! You're lying! (*She snatches up the Highwayman's discarded dagger and holds it to Ahmed's throat.*) Tell me you're lying! If you're telling the truth, I swear I'll kill you, Ahmed.

Ahmed Then you'll have to kill me.

A silence. Murganah withdraws the dagger.

(*as calmly as he can*) I have to go now to find my brothers. Please don't follow us any further. One day you will understand what we are doing. One day you will forgive me.

Murganah (*softly*) You were my friend. I loved you. I loved you more than my life. You've betrayed me. You're now my enemy.

Ahmed Murganah, don't –

Murganah Get away from me –

Ahmed Murganah ...

Murganah (*with a cry*) Get out!

Ahmed leaves, sadly.

(*to herself*) Help me! By all the heavens, by all the darkest forces, by all that guide us by day, by all that seek to destroy us by night, help me! Help me! (*She plunges the knife into the table.*)

Schaibar throughout all this has continued calmly with his card game.

Schaibar (*without looking up, calmly*) That's no way to treat a good table.

Murganah (*having barely noticed him before, startled*) What?

403

Schaibar I think you're attacking the wrong thing. That table has done you no harm that I can see.

Murganah Who are you?

Schaibar Oh, just a passing stranger. You seem distressed, child. Have you a problem?

Murganah What is it to you, if I have? Mind your own business.

Schaibar Maybe I can help.

Murganah (*sarcastically*) How? By telling my fortune?

Schaibar Perhaps by shaping your fortune.

Murganah What are you saying? What is this nonsense?

Schaibar You called upon certain powers just now. To help you. Did you not?

Murganah I was – I was upset. I do that.

Schaibar Nonetheless such powers do exist. They're yours to control.

Murganah What powers?

Schaibar Powers such as these . . .

He makes a pass with his hand. Ahmed appears in an image. He seems to have lost his way.

Murganah (*amazed*) Ahmed! Where is he?

Schaibar On his journey. Lost, as usual . . . (*softly*) That way, Ahmed, that way . . .

Ahmed finds his way. The image fades.

Murganah By what trickery did you do that?

Schaibar Call it trickery, call it what you will. It can be yours. That's but a tiny fraction of what you can do.

Murganah (*whispering*) Could it give me wealth . . .?

Schaibar At only the smallest price . . .

Murganah Could it give me power . . .?

Schaibar With only the smallest sacrifice . . .

Murganah Happiness?

Schaibar At the cost of only the briefest tears . . .

Murganah My every wish?

Schaibar All that your heart secretly craves for . . .

Murganah Can be mine?

Schaibar Can be yours.

Murganah (*laughing, only half believing him*) Really? But in return? What do I have to give you in return?

Schaibar Yourself.

Murganah Myself? I see. What sort of bargain is that? I give myself to someone whose face I've never seen?

Schaibar You need give nothing now. Only at the end will I come to claim you. And at the end I will also show you my face. I promise.

Murganah The end of what?

Schaibar At the end of your worldly ambition.

Murganah If I have wealth and power and happiness and all that my heart desires, that could be years away . . .

Schaibar It could indeed. I can wait.

Murganah You may not even be alive.

Schaibar That is my risk.

Murganah considers.

Murganah (*still uncertain whether to take it seriously*)
Very well. I agree.

Schaibar Are you sure? Once we've sealed the bargain
there is no going back.

Murganah I am sure.

Schaibar Then give me your hand.

*Murganah removes her gauntlet and places her hand
in Schaibar's.*

By all the powers in me,
Where e'er they be,
I give to thee.

Murganah gives a cry and snatches back her hand.

It is done.

*Murganah is examining the palm of her hand. There is
now a black star imprinted on the palm.*

Murganah My hand! What have you done to my hand?

Schaibar A keepsake, lest you forget our bargain. Till
we meet again, Murganah. Enjoy your life . . . Use your
powers wisely. With them you can build. With them you
can equally destroy. (*He goes, melting into the shadows.*)

Murganah When shall I – ? (*She glances at her palm.*)
Nonsense. (*She sees there are three cards left on the
table, face down. She turns them over, one by one.*)
Death . . . death . . . death . . . (*Despite herself, she
shivers.*) Absurd. Right, let us see what we can do with
these powers.

*She waves her hand in the manner of Schaibar. An
image of Nouronnihar appears, similar to the earlier
one of Ahmed's. Nouronnihar is drinking wine from a*

406

glass, laughing and talking silently to someone we cannot see.

It works! Well, well, well, Princess. I hope the wine is good. (*Murganah makes another movement of her hand. The wine in Nouronnihar's glass changes colour. She sips her drink unaware that this is happening. She splutters silently and dabs at her mouth with her hand. The wine is evidently now very unpleasant. She laughs with delight. The image fades.*) Oh, yes! Oh, yes! Oh, Princess, beware. Revenge is sour!

The Innkeeper enters with two tankards on a tray.

Innkeeper Sorry about the delay. I had to change the barrel. (*seeing Murganah*) Ah. Where's your friend?

Murganah He's gone. As has the other gentleman.

Innkeeper What other gentleman?

Murganah The one who was sitting there just now.

Innkeeper There was no one there. Hasn't been all evening. Just you and your friend.

Murganah I see.

Innkeeper Now there's just you, is there? Just you and me. That's cosy. Want to share the ale, then?

Murganah No, you drink it.

Innkeeper Oh, come on. Be a bit friendly.

Murganah I'm going.

Innkeeper Well, you're paying for this, anyway. Might as well drink it.

Murganah I'm not paying. I haven't drunk any.

Innkeeper You ordered it.

Murganah Drink it yourself. Goodnight.

She turns to go. The Innkeeper puts down the tray and moves to intercept her.

Innkeeper Now just a minute, you're not leaving here till you pay me, one way or the other. Either in money or in kind, I don't care –

As the Innkeeper makes to grasp her shoulder, Murganah turns angrily and with the smallest of gestures send the man reeling backwards and crashing into a table.

(*winded again*) Ah!

Murganah Goodnight.

Murganah goes. The Innkeeper lies on the floor groaning.

Innkeeper Oh. I don't think I can get up for six months ...

The lights change to:

SCENE FIVE

The Inn in the Distance.
    It is a bright sunny morning, six month later. The Innkeeper is staggering to his feet when there is a loud knocking.

Houssain (*off, calling*) Innkeeper! Anyone at home?

Innkeeper Just a minute, just a minute. Come in, then.

Houssain enters. He has been travelling. He has a carpet under his arm.

Houssain About time. Are you open or closed?

Innkeeper Open. I was – I was asleep.

Houssain Asleep? At eleven o'clock in the morning? You ought to be ashamed of yourself on this fine spring day.

Innkeeper Spring? It's spring?

Houssain Yes, of course it's spring. April.

Innkeeper April.

Houssain Of course April. Bring me some ale.

Innkeeper Yes. (*He examines the two tankards still on the tray.*) I'll – get you some fresh. These are rather flat. Been standing a bit.

> The Innkeeper goes. Houssain, in a good mood, sings to himself.
> Ali enters. He carries a telescope.

Ali (*as he enters*) Anyone at – ? Houssain!

Houssain Ali!

Ali How was Bisnager?

Houssain Fantastic! Landlord!

> The Innkeeper returns briefly.

Innkeeper Sir!

Houssain Make that two ales.

Innkeeper Right away, sir. (*He goes.*)

Houssain No, Bisnager was beautiful. A library such as you've never seen. Book upon book upon book. I spent the whole six months reading. Never moved.

Ali (*incredulously*) Really? And what about your gift? For the Princess? Have you brought her something from beyond her wildest dreams?

Houssain Of course, on my last day there. (*He indicates the carpet.*) I bought it from this merchant. He must have thought it was his birthday.

Ali What is it?

Houssain What else? A magic carpet, of course.

Ali A magic carpet? Does it work?

Houssain Sssh! No, of course it doesn't. At least I sincerely hope not. Wouldn't do to bring her back something useful, would it? (*He laughs.*) And you? What have you brought from Persia?

Ali Ah, Persia. Oh, the women in Persia, such women. You have no idea, Houssain . . .

Houssain And I don't want to know, thank you. Tell me, what have you brought her? Is that a telescope?

Ali Do you mind? A *magic* telescope, please. Through which you can see all that you wish to see. In any direction for a thousand miles.

Houssain Really?

Ali No, you can't see a blessed thing. You can't even see your hand through it. I think it's broken. But it cost me a fortune. A totally useless gift, eh?

Houssain Well, possibly. I still think my carpet takes a bit of beating. (*realizing the joke*) Takes a bit of beating. (*He laughs.*) Did you get that?

Ali (*dryly*) Yes . . .

Ahmed enters.

Ahmed Houssain!

Houssain Ahmed!

Ahmed Ali!

Ali Ahmed!

Ahmed How are you both?

Houssain Never better. (*calling*) Landlord!

The Innkeeper returns briefly.

Innkeeper Sir?

Houssain Make that three ales.

Innkeeper Right away, sir. (*He goes.*)

Ali Now, Ahmed, what fantastic gift have you managed to purchase for our Princess? Can it beat my sightless telescope?

Houssain Or my non-flying carpet?

Ali What have you brought? Have you brought anything at all?

Houssain If not, that's cheating.

Ahmed No, I've brought something. Never fear. From the magical, wondrous land of Samarkand. (*He takes an apple from his pocket.*) See here.

Ali What's that?

Ahmed What does it look like?

Houssain It looks like an ordinary apple.

Ahmed No. There you're wrong. This is no ordinary apple. This apple, dear brothers, is enchanted. One bite and all ills, all ailments are cured. This is the perfect medicine for all diseases.

Ali Really?

Ahmed No, not really. All it'll give you is indigestion. It's about the only thing in Samarkand that is guaranteed non-magical. Impressive, yes? Isn't this the worst possible gift? A sour, ordinary, common or garden apple?

Houssain (*a bit dismayed*) Yes.

Ali (*likewise*) Yes.

Ahmed It seems I may have won.

Houssain Possibly. But remember. There's hope for us, yet. Only one of us has to marry her.

Ali Yes. Let's look on the bright side.

The Innkeeper hurries through to the front door.

Houssain Landlord, where's that ale?

Innkeeper A million pardons, sir. There's a magnificent coach outside. With a beautiful woman in it.

Ali Is my hair alright?

Innkeeper We very rarely get any magnificent coaches calling here, sir.

Ali What about beautiful women?

Innkeeper Oh, never, sir! Excuse me, please!

The Innkeeper goes out.

Houssain Now, while we're alone, remember. Until the Princess has chosen or not chosen, we must continue with the deception, telling no one. We must convince everybody we've done our best to win her. Even though we've done our best to lose her. (*He extends his hand.*) May the worst gifts lose, brothers!

All (*joining hands*) May the worst gifts lose!

The Innkeeper returns with an elegantly dressed woman. It is a transformed Murganah. The brothers gawk at her.

412

Ali (*recovering first and bowing*) My lady!

Houssain (*bowing*) Madam!

Ahmed (*in amazement*) Murganah!

Houssain (*looking up*) Murganah?

Ali (*looking up*) Murganah?

Murganah My lords! (*She curtseys.*)

Houssain Landlord! Four ales!

Innkeeper Right away, sir! Just changing the barrel. (*He goes.*)

Ali What's happened to you, Murganah? You've changed so much in six months.

Murganah I came in to a little – good fortune.

Houssain A large fortune by the look of it.

Ahmed You look – beautiful.

Murganah Thank you, Ahmed.

Houssain And how is the Princess?

Murganah Perfectly fit when I left her. And how have you all fared on your travels? Have you brought back priceless gifts for the Princess?

Houssain (*with a look at the others*) Oh, famously. We have some unique and spectacular gifts for her. A magic carpet.

Ali A magic telescope.

Murganah And what about you, Ahmed?

Ahmed (*sheepishly*) A magic apple.

Murganah An apple? You hope to win her with an apple?

Ahmed (*with a look at the others*) Yes. It's been done before.

Murganah (*coolly*) I see. May I look at the gifts? How does this telescope work?

Ali Ah, well, you merely have to imagine and you are able to see whatever you wish to see within a thousand miles radius. Apparently.

Murganah How wonderful! How does it work?

Ali (*looking through it*) Well, actually, it's not quite in working order yet, it's . . .

Murganah makes a gesture.

Ah!

Houssain What is it?

Ali I can see through it. I can see her.

Ahmed See who?

Ali The Princess Nouronnihar. I just thought of her and I can see her. It's amazing. I was certain it wouldn't work . . . It's incredible.

Houssain (*taking it from him*) Let me look.

Ali Can you see her?

Houssain Yes. It's Nouronnihar.

Ahmed What is she doing?

Houssain She's lying deathly still. There are people round her bed. She's ill.

Ahmed Ill? (*taking it from him*) Yes, I see her. She's not ill. She seems to be dying.

Ali Dying!

Murganah Poor thing!

Houssain Dying!

Ali (*taking back the telescope*) We can't let her die. Not after all she's –

Houssain (*cutting him off*) We must go to her at once. Before it's too late.

Ahmed The Palace is a day's ride from here. We may be too late.

Murganah Why not use your carpet?

Houssain My what?

Murganah Your magic carpet? That should get you there in time.

Houssain Ah yes. Well, the carpet, yes. It has – one or teething problems. It's not very reliable. Just at present.

Murganah May I see?

Houssain Yes, of course. By all means.

The brothers unroll the carpet.

As you see it's a perfectly ordinary looking rug but it does have these amazing powers. When they work.

Murganah So what do you have to do?

Houssain Well, we're all supposed to sit on it.

Murganah Sit on it? How?

Houssain (*sheepishly*) Like this.

Murganah All of you?

Houssain Yes. Come on you two.

The other two join him.

Ali (*as they do so, softly to Houssain*) It's not going to start flying, is it?

Houssain (*softly*) Of course it isn't.

Murganah Now what happens?

Houssain Well, apparently all you have to do is say, Carpet! Magic Carpet! Take me to the Sultan's Palace! And then it – Oh, good grief!

> *Murganah makes a gesture. The carpet is suddenly lifting off the ground with the three brothers on it.*

Ali Oh, no . . .

Ahmed Whey-hey!

Houssain We're flying! It works! (*dismayed*) It's not supposed to work!

Murganah Goodbye! See you at the Palace!

> *The Innkeeper enters.*

Innkeeper Sorry to keep you – four ales . . . What the . . .?

Murganah Goodbye!

Houssain Goodbye!

Ali Goodbye!

Ahmed Goodbye!

Innkeeper Who's paying for these ales? Come back!

> *The Innkeeper and Murganah fade from sight as the brothers start their flying journey.*

Ahmed This is amazing!

Ali I can't look down. I can't stand heights!

Ahmed Look, there's the forest!

Houssain Why did it suddenly work?

Ahmed And the river.

Ali Tell me when it's over!

Ahmed Wheeeee!

Houssain There's the Palace, look!

Ali Thank heaven!

Ahmed So fast! This is the way to travel!

Houssain Look out everyone we're coming down!

Ali We're going to crash!

Ahmed No, we're not. Don't be so . . .

Houssain Brace yourselves!

The carpet lands and we are in:

SCENE SIX

Nouronnihar's Bedside.
The Sultan, Salim, the Vizier and Safia are standing around the bedside.

Vizier (*as they arrive*) Good gracious!

Salim momentarily draws his sword to protect his Princess.

Sultan Houssain! Ali! Ahmed! What is the meaning of this?

Houssain I'm sorry, father, we heard the Princess was ill. We –

Sultan She is not ill, Houssain. The Princess is dying. I think you might have shown a little more consideration, rather than bursting in like hooligans . . . How did you get in here, anyway?

Houssain We – we . . .

Ahmed . . . had a lift . . .

Vizier A lift?

Ali Father, what has caused this illness? We met Murganah and she told us the Princess was perfectly fit a day or two ago . . .

Vizier (*worriedly*) Ah, yes. Murganah.

Sultan No. She's right. This illness suddenly struck the Princess, soon after Murganah left to meet you. The doctors say there is nothing – nothing that can save her, poor girl. Now please leave and show some respect.

Houssain (*softly, to the others*) What are we going to do?

Ali Well, at least we don't have to marry her.

Ahmed Don't say that. We can't just let her die.

Ali What can we do?

Houssain What about the apple?

Ahmed The apple?

Houssain Your apple . . .

Ahmed (*to Houssain*) That's no good. It's just an ordinary apple.

Houssain The others things worked.

Ali Mine was just an ordinary broken telescope . . .

Houssain Mine was just a useless old carpet . . .

Ali Go on!

Houssain Why not?

Ahmed moves towards the bed.

Ahmed Er . . . father . . .

Sultan What is it? Are you still here, boy?

Ahmed (*tentatively*) I have something that may help the Princess . . .

Sultan Help? What is it?

Ahmed It's a – it's a – magic apple . . .

Sultan A magic apple?

Vizier Did he say a magic apple? I thought he said a magic apple . . .

Ahmed Here! (*He shows the apple.*)

Sultan Don't be so ridiculous . . .

Houssain Please let him try it, father.

Ali It could work.

Sultan What, an apple?

Ahmed It's a magic apple.

Houssain Please!

Ali Please!

Ahmed It's worth a try.

Salim Try.

Sultan (*reluctantly*) I warn you, I shall be very angry indeed if this is some sort of joke.

Ahmed (*approaching Nouronnihar*) It's not a joke, father. I promise you.

Ahmed, assisted by Safia, props up the Princess's head and persuades her to nibble the apple. Nouronnihar coughs and splutters and spits it out.

Ahmed (*distraught*) It doesn't work.

Sultan Just as I suspected. Ahmed! You will come to my chambers in five minutes. I'm going to have you flogged and thrown in a dungeon, young man. And as for you two – bread and water for ten weeks.

Ali Ten weeks!

Houssain Father! What have *we* done?

Sultan (*as he goes*) For encouraging him. Five minutes, Ahmed!

Salim Fool!

The Sultan sweeps out with Salim.

Vizier (*as he follows*) Appalling behaviour. You should be ashamed of yourselves, all of you. (*He goes out.*)

Houssain Well, thank you very much.

Ali Bread and water for ten weeks. What will that do to my figure?

Ahmed Well, at least it didn't work . . .

Houssain Obviously it didn't work. You idiot!

Ali You fool . . .

Ali and Houssain go out.

Ahmed (*vainly after them*) But it was never supposed to – (*He is alone*) – work. (*He moves back to the bedside. To the unconscious Nouronnihar*) I'm sorry. If I could do anything I would, Princess.

Murganah has appeared in the shadows.

Murganah There's nothing.

Ahmed (*startled*) Murganah . . . How did you get here?

Murganah I have some very fast transport of my own.
There's nothing you can do for her, Ahmed. She's dying.
Your pretty little Princess is dying.

Ahmed She can't die. She's so young. I mean, I –

Murganah Love her?

Ahmed No. Yes.

Murganah You do?

Ahmed Yes.

Murganah Then you'd better kiss her goodbye.

Ahmed Murganah, if there's any way you can help . . .
I mean, I saw you with the telescope and the carpet . . .
I don't know how you did it but . . . Can't you do the
same with this apple? Make it work as it's supposed
to work?

Murganah What if I could?

Ahmed Please.

Murganah Why should I? Why should I save her life?

Ahmed Because we can't just let her die. We can't. Please
Murganah. If you love me at all . . .

Murganah Oh, love, love, love . . .

Ahmed Alright, not love. Common humanity.
Murganah. I beg you.

Murganah (*a fractional hesitation*) Try it again. Try your
apple again.

Ahmed Thank you.

*Ahmed tries the apple on the Princess as before. Safia
assists. Murganah gestures. This time the Princess
slowly revives.*

Nouronnihar (*drowsily*) Whar . . . whar . . . what . . .
what . . . what happ – where?

Ahmed It's alright, I'm here. It's alright.

Nouronnihar You? You're back? I've had such terrible
dreams. Frightening dreams. He was coming for me . . .

Ahmed Coming for you? Who was coming for you?

Nouronnihar The man – the dead man in the cloak . . .

Murganah (*startled*) Who?

Ahmed What is she saying?

Murganah Nothing. She's delirious . . .

Ahmed She's cured. (*calling*) The Princess is cured.
Come quickly, the Princess is cured!

Houssain, Ali, the Sultan, the Vizier return.

Houssain Cured?

Ali (*overlapping*) You mean it worked?

Sultan (*overlapping*) What is the meaning of this? What's
happened?

Vizier (*overlapping*) Cured? She's cured? It's a miracle.

Salim (*overlapping*) It has worked?

Nouronnihar Ahmed! You cured me?

Ahmed In a way, yes . . .

Nouronnihar Then you are the one I must marry.

Salim He is the one she must marry!

All (*except Ahmed*) Hooray!

Ahmed Ah, yes . . . But if we had not got here so swiftly on Houssain's magic carpet we would have been too late to save you . . .

Nouronnihar Then maybe it is Houssain I should marry.

Salim He is the one she must marry!

All (*except Houssain*) Hooray!

Houssain Ah, no but if we had not looked through Ali's telescope we would never have known you were ill. It was all entirely due to Ali . . .

Nouronnihar Then perhaps it is Ali I should marry . . .

Salim He is the one she must marry!

All (*except Ali*) Hooray!

Nouronnihar I don't know. I'm confused. Someone help me decide.

Sultan It appears we need another competition.

Houssain Oh, good.

Ali Another one?

Ahmed Where are we going this time?

Vizier Might I suggest, sire . . .

Sultan Grand Vizier?

Vizier Might I suggest – that rather than another quest, a test. The test of the arrows.

Sultan Of course! The test of the arrows! What a brilliant idea of mine! So be it. Follow me. And after this test is over, tell the kitchens to prepare a feast for two hundred.

*The Sultan, the Vizier, Nouronnihar, Salim and Safia
leave.*

Ahmed (*as they follow them*) What's the test of the
arrows?

Ali Search me.

Houssain Haven't the faintest idea.

Sultan (*off*) Follow me, boys!

Ali Follow him!

*Ali and Houssain leave. Ahmed is about to follow.
Murganah, unnoticed in the corner, calls him back.*

Murganah (*softly*) Ahmed . . .

Ahmed Murganah, I . . . Thank you.

Murganah (*amused*) For saving you from a flogging?
From keeping you from the dungeon?

Ahmed You know what I mean.

Murganah I promised I'd always look after you . . .
Now's your chance to do something for me.

Ahmed How do you mean?

Murganah It's the test of the arrows. Each of you must
fire an arrow up into the Mountain of Storms. He who
manages to fire his arrow furthest wins. You have only
to fire short of your brothers and one of them must
marry her. And then you'll be mine. Mine, Ahmed. As
it was meant to be. And I shall be yours.

Ahmed (*uncertainly*) Yes . . .

Murganah See how beautiful I have become for you,
Ahmed. I did this for you. Don't you think I'm more
beautiful than her? Than your little idiot Princess. Don't
you?

Ahmed Yes.

Murganah Then lose for me. I can make you rich, I can give you power, I can make you happy . . . Anyone who stands in our way. We can crush them. We can destroy them . . .

Ahmed Murganah . . . What's happened to you? You've changed so much. You've grown colder . . .

Murganah I've grown up, that's all. I've realized that in this life, what you want you take. You don't wait, you don't ask. You take. The world is made up of givers and takers. I am a winner and I take all. Join with me, Ahmed, and we'll win together. But first of all you must lose this contest. Come on.

Murganah goes out.

Ahmed (*as he follows her, worriedly*) Oh, Murganah . . .

As he goes, the scene changes to:

SCENE SEVEN

At the foot of The Mountain of Storms.
 Everyone is assembling. The Sultan, the Vizier, Salim, Nouronnihar with her Maid, Houssain, Ali and finally Murganah and Ahmed.

Sultan Very well. If we are all assembled, let the contest begin. My eldest son will fire first. Give the bow to Houssain.

The Vizier hands the long bow to Houssain.

Ali (*softly, to Houssain*) I bet I can shoot less far than you can.

Houssain Want to bet. Watch this.

425

Houssain draws back the bow and fires the arrow.
Murganah gestures. The others watch its flight
shading their eyes and ooohing and aaahing.

Vizier Heavens! It's gone for miles.

Sultan Good shot, Houssain! Didn't know you had it in you, my boy.

Ali (*amused*) Good shot!

Houssain I must have – I must have misfired.

Ahmed (*to Murganah*) How did Houssain fire that far? He normally hasn't the strength to lift up a bow.

Murganah It's a mystery to me. (*She smiles.*)

Salim He is the one she must marry!

Sultan Not yet, not yet, Salim! Ali, my second son. See if you can match Houssain's fine shot.

Ali I'll do my best not to – not to let you down, father!

Sultan Good boy!

The Vizier hands the bow to Ali who prepares to fire.

Ali Watch this, Houssain . . .

Ali fires. Murganah gestures. The others watch,
shading their eyes, and ooh and ahhh.

Vizier It's cleared the trees.

Sultan It's even better.

Ali Oh, no!

Vizier Amazing!

Sultan Brilliant shooting, lad!

Ahmed Oh, Murganah!

Ali Come back! Come back! You stupid arrow!

Houssain (*applauding sarcastically*) Well done!

Salim He is the one she must marry!

Sultan Not yet, not yet, Salim. So far, Ali is the winner. But come along, young Ahmed. Let's see what you can do.

Ahmed I'll try, father. I don't think I'll be able to beat my brothers.

Murganah I doubt it.

Sultan Never lose heart, boy. You can do it.

Ahmed is handed the bow. He prepares to fire.

Ahmed Right. Here I go.

He fires. A disappointed noise from the crowd.

Sultan Oh, come on, boy. That hasn't gone more than two – Good heavens. What's happening? Just look at that! I thought it had landed.

Vizier It must be the wind. A freak gust of wind. There it goes.

Everyone shades their eyes following the arrow. It goes higher and higher up the mountain. Much ooohing and aaahing.

Houssain Good shot!

Ali Well done!

Ahmed (*to Murganah*) Did I do that?

Murganah (*frowning*) No . . .

Ahmed Did you do that?

Murganah No. But somebody did.

Nouronnihar Bravo! (*bounding up to Ahmed*) The winner!

Salim He is the one she must marry!

Sultan Ah, no, no, Princess. Don't be too impatient. There is still the second half of the trial for them to complete. Grand Vizier!

Vizier Each contestant must now climb the mountain and further prove their prowess by retrieving his own arrow and presenting it to the Princess. May the best man win. It looks like you have quite a climb ahead of you, young Ahmed. No one has ever climbed that high on the Mountain of Storms.

Ahmed Oh, great.

Houssain Good luck, Ahmed. I'll be back for tea.

Ali Should make it home by supper time.

Houssain See you brother. Good shooting.

Ali (*clapping Ahmed on the shoulder*) Didn't know you had it in you. Bye.

> *Houssain and Ali go off up the mountain.*

Sultan You can see for yourself, Salim, what fine sons I've bred, eh?

Salim He is the one she must marry!

Sultan Yes, yes. All in good time, Salim. (*to the Vizier*) I think he may have gone wrong again, don't you?

Vizier I will have our workshops look at him again, sire. But they do tell me that rust has taken its toll.

Sultan Ah me! Well it happens to us all. Come along.

Vizier I think we may need to postpone the feast, sire, till they return.

Sultan Oh, really? I suppose we must. That's a pity . . .

The Sultan and the Vizier go off with Salim.

Ahmed Well, here I go.

Nouronnihar (*kissing him*) Good luck. I'll be waiting.

Ahmed Thank you. (*to Murganah*) See you soon.

Murganah does not reply.

Yes. Right. (*Ahmed goes off.*)

Nouronnihar (*seeing her*) Murganah? I hardly recognized you. If I've told you once, I've told you a hundred times, why are you still unveiled in my presence?

Murganah (*looking at her dangerously*) I'm sorry, Princess. (*She pulls up her veil.*)

Nouronnihar Once more, I'll have you punished. As I had to do with Safia there. Have you noticed how little she talks? There's a reason for that. She'd tell you if she could. (*brightening*) Do you know, assuming I have to marry one of them, which of course I have to sooner or later – I'm glad it's Ahmed. Assuming he gets down safely off that wretched mountain. I do think he's the sweetest of the three of them. I really do. Yes, I've made a good choice. Come along. It's getting cold. Yes, an excellent choice.

Nouronnihar goes out followed by Safia.

Murganah (*as she goes, to herself*) It could be your last choice, as well. (*with one last glance up the mountain*) Bring him down safely . . . bring him back to me and only me . . .

She leaves as the scene changes abruptly to:

SCENE EIGHT

Near the summit of The Mountain of Storms
A bleak mountainside not far from the summit. The
wind is getting up. Ahmed appears. He is breathless
from his climb. He pauses for a brief rest.

Ahmed How much higher? Where is it? Where are you,
arrow? I couldn't have shot it this far. Nobody in the
world could shoot an arrow to this height.

The wind increases.

It's getting difficult to see. The mist's getting thicker . . .
Just a bit higher. Nearly at the top . . .

He climbs a bit further. The wind increases to a howl.
Suddenly Ahmed is in the midst of a blizzard. He is
whirled this way and that.

Help . . . I can't stand up. Help! Help me!.

He starts to slip and slide, finally falling to his knees.
The blizzard continues to rage. Suddenly out of the
snow storm and the darkness emerges a rather
frightening looking figure, totally muffled against the
cold. Huge and rather menacing, a cross between a
Yeti and an Egyptian mummy. The figure approaches
Ahmed.

(*alarmed*) What the – ? Who are – ? Who are – ? Ah . . .

Ahmed faints clean away. As he starts to fall, the
figure catches him and effortlessly lifts the inert body.
As it carries Ahmed away into the blizzard, the lights
fade.
    Blackout.
    End of Act.

Act Two

SCENE ONE

Paribanou's Mountain Palace.

Her palace is a vast cave lit by torch light. Jewelled and glittering, beautiful but eerily empty. It is inhabited only by Nasuh, her servant, and by Paribanou herself.

Nasuh enters. Although he has removed his bulky outer protective clothing which made him appear even more giant-like, he remains a large powerful figure. He carries the inert body of Ahmed. In the shadows, almost indiscernible at this point, Paribanou appears.

Paribanou (*from the shadows*) How is he?

Nasuh Still unconscious.

Paribanou Take him to the chamber.

Nasuh starts to do so.

Do you think he will prove worthy?

Nasuh Who knows? He weighs less than a feather. I wouldn't care to stake my life on him.

Paribanou I think we may both have to, Nasuh. He could well be our last chance. Come, bring him.

She leads the way as Nasuh carries Ahmed off. As this happens, the scene changes to:

SCENE TWO

The Sultan's Palace.

The Sultan enters. From another direction, simultane-ously, the Grand Vizier also hurries on with Salim following.

Sultan Still no sign?

Vizier Sire, it has been two days now. Two days and two freezing nights. I fear no one could have survived on that mountain.

Sultan Then Ahmed is dead?

Vizier I fear so, sire. We have had search parties combing the hills. He must have climbed higher than the snow line.

Sultan But how could an arrow fired by an ordinary bow come to soar so high? It's inexplicable.

Vizier A freak wind, sire. That's all we can assume.

Salim If the boy is dead, then his brother must be declared the winner.

Sultan Oh, good, they got him working again. Yes, Salim, you are right. If Ahmed has perished, then it is Ali who must marry the Princess Nouronnihar. We will break the news to them. Send them here, Grand Vizier.

Vizier My lord, they are waiting outside for news.

Sultan Bring them.

The Vizier goes to the door and calls softly.

Vizier Please . . . will you all come in.

Houssain, Ali, Nouronnihar and Murganah enter.

432

Sultan I have sad news of Ahmed. I fear he has been lost on the mountain. We must assume him dead.

Ali turns to Houssain and they clasp each other for a moment in grief.
Nouronnihar clasps a hand to her mouth and gives a stifled cry. Only Murganah appears unmoved.

It would seem, under such sad circumstances, that Ali will receive the hand of Nouronnihar in marriage. There will be some appropriate days of mourning for Ahmed and the wedding will then be announced officially. God bless you both. God help us all.

Salim He is the one she must marry!

Sultan Oh, no. Not again!

The Sultan leaves, followed by the Vizier and Salim. A silence.

Ali Well. Would that these were happier circumstances to announce an engagement. (*to Nouronnihar*) I hope – I will try to be a good husband, Nouronnihar.

Nouronnihar Thank you. (*as she goes, tearfully*) I'm delighted to hear it. (*She goes out, weeping.*)

Ali What will you do, brother?

Houssain Me? What I always knew I would do. I shall become a hermit. I shall shut myself away somewhere in a remote place, far from civilization and I shall study my books. Try to unravel the mysteries of this world. Like why people as good and true as Ahmed should die so needlessly. (*He starts to leave.*)

Ali Won't you even stay for the wedding?

Houssain (*distressed*) I couldn't, Ali, I'm sorry. I must go straightaway. I'm sorry. I wish you every happiness, brother. Goodbye. (*He goes.*)

Ali Goodbye, Houssain. (*half to himself*) It seems I have lost two brothers in a single day. And what have I gained? A wife whom I suspect doesn't want me. What a bargain!

Murganah Nouronnihar will grow to love you. Never fear.

Ali You think so?

Murganah Give her time. And patience. Tenderness and encouragement.

Ali Encouragement?

Murganah Give her loving gifts. (*She produces a small ornamental jar.*) Like this.

Ali What is it?

Murganah Oranges. Preserved in rare spices. Spices with magical properties. Encourage her to eat one slice a day. I promise she will hour by hour grow more beautiful, more loving . . .

Ali Can that be so?

Murganah Take them as a wedding gift. I was saving them for my own wedding day but now – (*She breaks off, apparently overcome.*)

Ali Thank you, Murganah. I am very touched. (*He takes the jar from her.*) Thank you. (*He moves away.*)

Murganah (*as he goes*) One a day, mind. And watch the difference in her.

    Ali goes.

(*smiling to herself*) Just watch her grow.

    As Murganah leaves, the scene changes back to:

SCENE THREE

Paribanou's Mountain Palace.
  Ahmed is standing. Nasuh enters.

Nasuh Are you feeling stronger?

Ahmed A little, thank you. That was an excellent breakfast. My compliments to your cook, whoever it is.

Nasuh Me.

Ahmed Ah. Well, thank you. But would you please tell me where I am and who you are? What is this place? It's like a cave only – only as if it's made of rare jewels.

Nasuh It is the nature of the rock. It stores and reflects light. Light from many millions of years ago when the sun was so bright it saw fit to shine here.

Ahmed And you? How did you come to be here? More important, how did I come to be here?

  Paribanou has entered unobserved.

Paribanou You must ask your questions of me, not Nasuh. (*She steps forward for the first time into the light.*) Welcome, Ahmed.

Ahmed (*impressed*) Madam, I – I have not – I have not had the pleasure.

Paribanou My name is Paribanou.

Ahmed A princess?

Paribanou (*smiling*) No. Not a princess.

Ahmed Then who – ? How did you know my name? How did I – ?

435

Paribanou Leave us please, Nasuh.

Nasuh Mistress. (*He bows and goes.*)

Paribanou (*gently*) Sit down. We have much to talk about. But first I must explain a little. You are owed that. Do you like fairy tales, Ahmed.

Ahmed (*laughing*) Well. It depends. I used to.

Paribanou Listen to this one. And pay attention. Once upon a time there were two children. A sister and a brother. Their mother had died when they were very young and as a result the brother's behaviour was often very wild. They were brought up by their father, a good and powerful wizard in the most happy of kingdoms. One day it happened that the father had to leave them in order to make a journey. He left them in the care of the servants and before he went he bade them to be good and well behaved during his absence. If they were good, he said, when he returned he would reward them with wonderful gifts. And it happened that whilst he was away, although the daughter obeyed her father, the brother did not. Instead he meddled with his father's spell books, and not only tormented his sister but was cruel to the servants. In fact, he became so wild and uncontrollable that when the father returned the palace was all but in ruins. For by then the son, in his search for wealth and power, had sold his very soul to Schaibar himself . . .

Ahmed Schaibar?

Paribanou Schaibar, the Stranger from the Darkness who seeks to lead us all into that same Darkness. Anyway, the wizard could do nothing, realizing he had lost his only son for ever. And he became first sad and then angry with his daughter for just feebly standing by and doing nothing to stop her brother. And her punishment was to remain in a beautiful but lonely cave high on a mountain. A prison she could never leave until she learnt to stand up for what is right and to oppose all that is bad. And here she has remained to this day. Alone with only Nasuh for company. You are the first visitor this place has ever seen, Ahmed. Welcome.

Ahmed Why me?

Paribanou Maybe you were sent? Who knows?

Ahmed And your brother? What became of him?

Paribanou Alas, he has long ago gone to the Darkness. But there are others since who have made bargains with Schaibar. Others who seek to rule the world through uncertainty and fear.

Ahmed But how can you do anything if you're unable to leave this place?

Paribanou If I am ever to be free, then I need a Champion.

Ahmed A Champion?

Paribanou One such as you, Ahmed.

Ahmed Me? I'm no Champion, I'm afraid. I can't fight, I can't run, I can't climb. I'm not very brave and I'm frightened of spiders.

Paribanou You can shoot arrows, though.

Ahmed Yes. Yes, that's true. I can shoot arrows. But not much else, I'm afraid.

Paribanou You will learn. Nasuh will teach you.

Ahmed I really think he'd be wasting his time.

Paribanou Please, Ahmed. You're surely my last hope. Won't you consider it?

Ahmed It's just that there are dozens of others better qualified than I.

Paribanou There is only you. You've been sent. Please.

Ahmed (*considering*) I owe you my life. I acknowledge that. I suppose the least I can do is – You couldn't have found a worse man. That's all I'm saying. You're probably stronger than I am.

Paribanou Physical strength is not everything. There is a strength that lies within you, too. Is it a bargain?

Ahmed I am – yours to command . . . (*He extends his hand.*) Paribanou . . .

Paribanou (*taking his hand*) Come with me, my Champion, there is no time to lose.

They start to leave.

Ahmed (*as they go off*) I hope you know what you're doing.

As they leave the scene changes to:

SCENE FOUR

The Sultan's Palace.
Wedding bells. Nouronnihar comes on in her wedding dress which appears a trifle tight on her. Murganah fusses round her.

Nouronnihar (*in a frenzy*) . . . no, no, no. That's not right. You're not going to make it right doing that, are you, you stupid girl?

Murganah (*patiently*) Princess, please hold still. (*She tries to adjust the dress.*)

438

Nouronnihar This ridiculous dress. That stupid dress-maker. How could she make it two sizes too small? I mean look at it! I look absurd. I can't appear like this on my wedding day. People are simply going to laugh.

Murganah Princess, it hardly notices . . . It really doesn't!

Nouronnihar When I get hold of that dressmaker I'll have her head cut off. That'll teach her!

Murganah Princess, that would hardly be fair. You may have put on a tiny, tiny little bit of weight . . .

Nouronnihar Weight? Me? Put on *weight*? How dare you say that? Right, that's your tongue cut out!

Murganah (*unconcerned*) Yes, princess.

Nouronnihar And your head as well.

Murganah Yes, princess. There, that looks much better.

Nouronnihar (*anxiously*) Is it better? Does it look better?

Murganah You look ravishing.

Nouronnihar I'm so nervous. Why am I so nervous? An orange slice. Give me another orange slice.

Murganah Are you sure, Princess? You've had three slices this morning already.

Nouronnihar (*loudly*) I need a slice of orange. Give me one or I'll have your feet cut off as well.

Murganah Certainly, Princess.

> *Murganah produces the ornamental jar and opens it. Nouronnihar takes a slice of orange and gobbles it greedily.*
> *The Sultan enters with Salim.*

Sultan Where is she? Where is the bride? They're all waiting! Everyone's sitting there waiting!

Murganah She's ready, sire, she's ready now.

Sultan What is she doing? For heaven's sake, is the girl eating?

Murganah The happy bride is ready.

Sultan (*to Nouronnihar*) About time, too. Come, Salim, give the Princess your arm.

Salim removes one of his arms and offers it to Nouronnihar.

Salim Here.

Nouronnihar squawks and recoils in horror.

Sultan Oh, dear heavens, the man is impossible these days. (*proffering his own arm*) Here, Princess. Have one of mine.

Nouronnihar Thank you. (*She extends her arm. There is a ripping sound as her dress gives.*)

Nouronnihar Oh, no! What was that?

Murganah Nothing, Princess . . .

Nouronnihar (*hysterically*) It's split! My dress has split! My dress has split!

Murganah Keep calm! It's a tiny tear, Princess. No one will notice if you don't lift your arms. Now keep calm. That's better.

Nouronnihar calms down.

Sultan Thank you, Murganah! Someone at least with a modicum of sense. (*to Nouronnihar*) Now come along! And pull yourself together, girl.

The Sultan practically drags Nouronnihar off. Salim follows on, still holding his arm.

Salim (*as they go*) He is the man she must marry!

Murganah smiles to herself and follows them off. As she does so, the scene changes to:

SCENE FIVE

Paribanou's Mountain Palace.
Ahmed and Nasuh are preparing to fight. Paribanou watches them.

Nasuh (*shaping up to fight*) Alright. Once more. Come at me again but this time keeping your guard!

Ahmed hesitates uncertainly.

Come on, attack me! Lunge, lunge!

Finally, Ahmed makes a clumsy dash at Nasuh who easily evades the charge and helps Ahmed on his way with a kick in the pants. Ahmed sails past Nasuh and disappears off. A crash and a yell as he collides with something.

Ahmed (*off*) Aaaahh!

Nasuh looks at Paribanou and shrugs.

Paribanou (*concerned*) Oh dear . . .

As they go off after Ahmed, the scene changes to:

SCENE SIX

The Sultan's Palace.
  The wedding feast. Music. The Sultan, the Vizier,
Salim, Nouronnihar, Ali and Murganah are present.
  Murganah approaches the Sultan with a goblet of wine.

Murganah More wine, sire.

Sultan Ah! Should I now? I've had several glasses already.
The sooner we sit down to that feast, the better. Oh, it's a
wedding, after all. Why not? Thank you, Murganah.

Murganah It is my honour to serve you, sire.

Sultan Good, good. No, don't run away. You've grown
increasingly mature, Murganah, over these last few
months. I'm impressed with your progress. I have to say
that in the past, your conduct sometimes left a lot to be
desired. Running around the place like a savage.

Murganah I hope I have learned better, sire.

Sultan You've – er . . . You've also grown very beautiful.

Murganah (*humbly*) Thank you, sire. You, of course,
remember the ancient proverb. A woman is made more
beautiful when she stands in the shadow of a handsome
man.

Sultan (*embarrassed*) Ha! Yes. Very good. I like that.
Never heard it before. Thank you very much. I'll
remember that. Handsome man, yes

  He laughs some more. Murganah moves away,
  laughing too. The Vizier moves to her angrily.

Vizier Murganah! (*drawing her to one side*) What on
earth are you playing at, girl?

Murganah (*puzzled*) I'm sorry, father.

Vizier Do you realize what you are doing? Publicly disporting yourself like that? A mere servant, flirting with the Sultan himself! How dare you? I am speechless at your behaviour, Murganah! Absolutely! I would like –

Murganah places her fingers on her father's mouth.

Murganah And speechless you will remain, father. You will never speak to me like that again.

She moves away swiftly. The Vizier touches his mouth, startled. The music stops. A fanfare.

Sultan I shall now call upon the Grand Vizier to ask our young couple to commence the dancing. Grand Vizier!

The Vizier appears to find it impossible to open his mouth. He makes muffled sounds.

Grand Vizier!

More muffled sounds from the Vizier.

Sultan How extraordinary! What on earth's the matter, man?

Murganah Maybe he's eaten some toffee.

Sultan (*finding this very funny*) Toffee! Yes, very funny. Ah well. I'll do it myself. I call upon our beautiful young couple to lead the dancing!

Salim (*in a grand voice*) Highness His Ali Prince and Royal Her Princess Highness Nouronnihar – har – har – har – har –

Sultan Oh, do stop it!

The Sultan hits Salim. A piece falls off him. Ali and Nouronnihar step forward together and as the music starts up they begin to dance. Everyone claps. The

dancers twirl. Suddenly Nouronnihar's dress splits
completely. She screams and runs from the floor. The
music stops.

Ali (*hurrying after her*) Nouronnihar!

Sultan (*recovering the situation*) Alright! That's quite
enough dancing! Time for the feast! Bring on the feast!

Murganah I think under the circumstances, sire, that it
might be – inappropriate.

Sultan How do you mean?

Murganah The Princess seems rather distressed. Perhaps
it would be tactless to continue with the celebrations.

Sultan You think so? I suppose you're right. That's a
pity. Cancel the feast then. (*calling, as he goes*) Cancel
the feast!

The Sultan has gone off. The others follow him, the
Vizier making more muffled sounds. As they do so,
the scene changes to:

SCENE SEVEN

Paribanou's Mountain Palace.
Ahmed and Nasuh are still practising. Ahmed enters
with his sword, moving backwards as if he has been
given a giant shove by Nasuh.

Ahmed Aaaaaahhh! (*He sits with a bump*)

Nasuh enters holding a sword.

Nasuh How many times do I have to tell you?

Ahmed I'll never learn.

Nasuh (*fiercely*) You must learn!

Ahmed (*angrily*) I can't. I give up! Alright? I take back what I said. I'm nobody's Champion. I couldn't possibly be. If this was a real fight I'd have been dead twenty times over. What is the point? I'm sorry, I give up. (*He throws down his sword.*)

Paribanou appears in a doorway.

Paribanou Ahmed!

Ahmed I want to go home. I want to see my father. I want to see my brothers.

Paribanou Soon.

Ahmed Now!

Paribanou Please.

Ahmed (*weakening*) I – I – need to see them.

Paribanou Please. For me. My Champion.

Ahmed Your Champion? That's a laugh. I don't even know what all this is about. What I'm even training for. Who I shall even be fighting.

Paribanou All will be revealed in time. I promise.

Ahmed When?

Paribanou When the time is right. When the agent of Schaibar finally reveals themself. (*She picks up his sword.*) Please. For me.

Ahmed (*wearily*) For you. Yes. For you.

He takes his sword from her and makes another lunge at Nasuh.

The Champion of Paribanooooooo . . .

Again he is booted offstage.
Another crash.

445

Nasuh looks at Paribanou and shrugs hopelessly.
He goes off after Ahmed.

Nasuh (*as he goes*) Now, what did I tell you . . .?

Paribanou (*as she goes, worriedly to herself*) Oh dear,
oh dear . . .

The scene changes to:

SCENE EIGHT

The Sultan's Palace Gardens.
Nouronnihar, who has grown even larger than when
we last saw her, is unhappily walking in the gardens.
Murganah enters.

Murganah Excuse me, Princess. Breakfast is served.

Nouronnihar I don't want any breakfast.

Murganah Princess, you must eat. You had no dinner
yesterday and no lunch.

Nouronnihar I know that! I've had nothing to eat for
days. I'm starving. Nothing but those wretched oranges.
I should be as thin as a stick and look at me.

Murganah (*rather coyly*) Perhaps, Princess, we are
expecting a happy event.

Nouronnihar (*angrily*) No, we are not expecting a
happy event. There hasn't even been a happy event to
make a happy event. My husband hasn't been near me
for ages. (*tearfully*) He can't stand the sight of me.

Murganah Oh, Princess, that's not true. His highness
worships the very –

Nouronnihar Is his Highness having breakfast with me?

446

Murganah I fear he's busy with affairs of state, Princess.

Nouronnihar Is he expected for lunch?

Murganah A meeting with the Household, Princess.

Nouronnihar Or tea?

Murganah He's inspecting the Guard, Princess.

Nouronnihar (*getting increasingly hysterical*) Or supper?

Murganah A state banquet.

Nouronnihar Or bed time?

Murganah I couldn't possibly say, Princess.

Nouronnihar There you are then. He's as good as left me after three weeks. What am I going to do?

Murganah Might I suggest, Princess, that a little of this . . . (*She produces a small jar of cream.*) . . . could do wonders.

Nouronnihar (*suspiciously*) What is it? I hope it works better than those oranges.

Murganah A special face cream, Princess. It's miraculous for the complexion. I swear by it myself. See. How smooth it is.

Nouronnihar Yes. You have – lovely skin . . . Probably born with it. You're very lucky.

Murganah I assure you it's due to this cream, Princess. A little rubbed in, night and morning, is all that's required.

Nouronnihar Yes? (*She takes the jar.*) This had better work. If it doesn't I'll – I'll have your toes chopped off. One by one.

Murganah If it does not work, may I walk forever toeless, Princess.

Nouronnihar (*as she goes, looking back at her*) Yes. You do. You have lovely skin. Kindly put on your veil at once. How many more times?

Murganah (*curtseying*) Of course, Princess.

As Nouronnihar goes off, Murganah draws on her veil. As soon as she has gone, Ali creeps on.

Ali (*furtively*) Murganah . . .

Murganah Your highness . . .

Ali Has she gone? My wife?

Murganah The Princess has gone to her chambers, your highness.

Ali Stop calling me that, for heaven's sake. It's Ali.

Murganah I am only a servant, your highness. As the Princess is continually kind enough to remind me.

Ali Nonsense. You grew up with us. You're Murganah. You're a friend.

Murganah We all have our duty to perform, your highness.

Ali Murganah, I need your help. You see. I don't think I love my wife. Isn't that terrible? I don't think I ever did. After all, you can't really hope to love a woman you've won in a competition. Well, I didn't even win, I came second. It's not unnatural of me not to love her, is it?

Murganah It's not uncommon, your highness.

Ali No. Well, I feel terrible. I feel I've failed. It doesn't help that she seems to be – (*He indicates.*) – you know. I mean, strictly between ourselves, we've taken to separate beds. We had to, there's no room for me in

448

hers. What am I going to do? Help me, Murganah.
Please . . . Do you despise me for saying this? Look,
I wish you'd take off that stupid veil so I could see what
you were thinking.

Murganah I have been commanded by the Princess to
wear it, your highness. I am forbidden to remove it.

Ali Well, she hasn't forbidden me. I'll remove it.
(*hesitating*) May I?

Murganah You are my Prince. I am yours to command.

Ali Yes. (*He removes her veil.*) There. That's better.
(*He stares at her.*) You've grown even more beautiful,
Murganah.

Murganah Thank you, your highness.

Ali (*transfixed by her*) I – I – I could – if I wasn't –
I could almost . . . I think I'll go and have breakfast.
And a cold bath. Take my mind off things. I'll talk to
you again.

Murganah (*curtseying*) Your highness.

*Ali hurries off. Murganah smiles to herself. The Vizier
hurries across.*

Good morning, father. Lovely day.

*The Vizier makes a few muffled angry sounds and
goes off. Murganah laughs and follows. As she does
so, the scene changes to:*

449

SCENE NINE

Paribanou's Mountain Palace.
  Ahmed comes on slowly. He is listless and depressed. He sits. Paribanou comes on with Nasuh. They observe him anxiously.

Paribanou (*to Nasuh, quietly*) What on earth's wrong with him?

Nasuh He's lost heart completely. He's been like this all day. There is no fight left in him. I fear he will never become a Champion. It's as if his strength was draining from him minute by minute.

Paribanou What can we do? He's our only hope. Oh, of all the men the gods could have sent us . . . Is there nothing to be done with him?

Nasuh He – needs to see his family. To tell his father, his brothers that he's alive. He misses them.

Paribanou He must love them very much.

Nasuh (*sadly*) It must be good to have a family.

Paribanou (*affectionately*) Oh, poor Nasuh . . . Then there's nothing for it. He will have to return to his family, won't he?

Nasuh But how can he? Once he goes from here he –

Paribanou Ahmed!

Ahmed (*feebly*) Hallo.

Paribanou I have an offer to make to you. If you will continue to practise with Nasuh – prepare yourself to be my Champion . . .

Ahmed I can't. I'm sorry, I can't

Paribanou Wait, let me finish! I will allow you return to your family for one hour.

Ahmed (*brightening*) You will?

Paribanou Is it a bargain?

Ahmed I may see my family again?

Paribanou For one hour only. And there are two conditions, Ahmed. You must tell no one where you have been. If necessary, you must invent a story. Not a word about us. If the forces of Schaibar learn about our plan you will be in grave danger. Do you promise?

Ahmed I promise.

Paribanou Secondly, you will also swear to return to us after an hour?

Ahmed I promise.

Paribanou Then prepare for the journey. We will find you some fresh clothes.

Ahmed (*as he goes*) I shall be ready to leave immediately . . . (*He goes out.*)

Nasuh What if he is followed on his return?

Paribanou No one will be able to follow him, you know that. This Palace is invisible to all but him. And once he is close enough, he will become invisible as well.

Nasuh Not that he'll ever return.

Paribanou He'll return. He gave his word. His word as a Champion. Don't worry, Nasuh, he will return.

They go off. As they do so, the scene changes to:

451

SCENE TEN

The Sultan's Palace Gardens.
Ali creeps on. It is nearly dawn.

Ali (*calling quietly*) Murganah! Murganah! Are you there?

Murganah steps from the shadows.

Murganah Your highness . . .

Ali moves to her and takes her hands.

Ali Oh, Murganah. Thank heaven you got my message. I had to see you. I know it's wrong. I have a wife there in bed asleep. I know I should be faithful to her. But it's you I've always loved, Murganah. I swear it is.

Murganah What a shame you didn't show it at the time, your highness . . .

Ali I'll make up for it now Murganah, I promise. I'll take you away to a distant land where we'll –

A cry from Nouronnihar off.

What was that?

Murganah It sounded like your wife, your highness.

Another cry.

Ali It is my wife. Quickly.

He moves away from Murganah. Nouronnihar enters. Her face appears to have sprouted hair.

Nouronnihar My face! Look at my face! What's happened to my face? Ali . . .

Ali (*looking at her in horror*) Oh ! Oh! Aaaaaah!

He rushes out in horror.

Nouronnihar What am I going to do? Look at me, Murganah. What am I going to do?

Murganah (*coolly*) I would suggest you wear a veil, Princess.

A fanfare.

Nouronnihar Oh, no. People are coming. They can't see me like this . . .

Nouronnihar rushes off as the Sultan enters excitedly. He is followed by the Vizier, Salim and Ali.

Sultan Ahmed has returned. He has been sighted from the gates. Ahmed's returned, Murganah.

Murganah (*incredulously*) Ahmed?

Sultan Isn't it the most wonderful news? A feast! I must order a feast . . .

Ali (*indicating*) Father . . .

Sultan Mmm?

Ahmed enters. He is dressed in splendid new robes. Murganah draws on her veil.

Ahmed Father.

Sultan (*moved*) Ahmed!

They embrace. Ahmed then embraces Ali.

Ahmed Ali! So good to see you all!

Ali Ahmed! Where have you been?

Ahmed All in good time. (*looking at Murganah*) Murganah? Is that you?

Murganah (*curtseying*) Your highness.

Ahmed I'm home.

Murganah I am delighted, your highness.

Ahmed Murganah, it's me. Ahmed.

Murganah Your highness.

Ahmed (*a little confused by her coolness*) Where's my big brother? Where's Houssain?

Sultan He – he went away, Ahmed. When we thought you were dead, Houssain decided to retire with his books. We've not seen or heard from him.

Ahmed But I'm alive. Now he can return.

Ali He's gone to some remote place, heaven knows where.

Ahmed Oh. Well, we must find him. My lord Grand Vizier. I apologise for not greeting you sooner.

Muffled sounds from the Vizier. Ahmed looks puzzled.

Sultan The Grand Vizier has – developed some speech problems of late.

Ahmed Oh dear. I'm sorry to hear that.

Muffled sounds from the Vizier.

Special Emissary Salim! Greetings!

Salim (*singing, loudly*) I ride along the mountain trail on the Road to Samarkand . . .

The Sultan hits him. Salim stops abruptly.

Ahmed (*puzzled*) I'm sorry?

Sultan Take no notice. He's completely deranged. We still await the instruction booklet to repair him.

Ahmed I see. And the Princess Nouronnihar? She is well?

454

Ali Yes, she is – she is . . . She is now my wife.

Ahmed You're married!

Sultan Where is she? She should be here. Summon the Princess!

Murganah goes off to fetch her.

Ahmed Ali, I'm so thrilled for you! Are you happy, you lucky man? Is she as beautiful as ever?

Ali Yes, well, she's – Tell us about yourself, Ahmed.

Sultan Yes. Where have you been, boy? Where did you obtain these splendid clothes? Not from the top of a mountain, surely?

Ahmed Father, it is very awkward but I have been sworn to secrecy.

Sultan Secrecy? By whom?

Ahmed That's a secret, I'm afraid.

Sultan Nonsense! He's met some woman. That's what it is. We'll soon get it out of you, boy. Get you drunk over a good feast . . .

Ahmed Nor can I stay here more than an hour. I have been sworn to that as well.

Sultan What is all this about? Swearing this and swearing that . . .?

Murganah returns with Nouronnihar who is now swathed in veils.

Murganah Her Royal Highness The Princess Nouronnihar.

Ahmed (*turning to greet her*) Princess Nouronn – (*He stops at the sight of her.*) Princess?

Nouronnihar (*curtseying awkwardly, muffled*) My lord . . .

Ahmed (*to Ali*) Why is she wrapped up like that?

Ali She – she –

Murganah It is the custom in the Princess's own country to save her radiant beauty for her husband's eyes alone . . .

A muffled moan from Nouronnihar.

Ahmed I see. Well. Lucky man, Ali.

Ali (*unhappily*) Yes.

Ahmed And unless I am very much mistaken the Princess is shortly expecting a happy event?

Another moan from Nouronnihar.

Ali No. No happy events.

Ahmed No? I'm sorry.

Ali Not a single one.

Nouronnihar rushes out, weeping.

Sultan Come! Let us go indoors. At least we shall give you a breakfast feast. if nothing else. Everyone inside! Grand Vizier, write it to the kitchens. I want a breakfast feast for three hundred at once.

The Sultan, the Vizier and Salim, go off.

Salim (*as he goes, singing, loudly*) I ride along the mountain trail on the Road to Samarkand . . .

Ali Coming, brother?

Ahmed (*with a glance at Murganah*) Just one moment, Ali. I'll follow.

Ali (*reluctantly going*) This is all in your honour, you know. Don't be long.

Ahmed is left alone with Murganah.

Ahmed I may be wrong but I sense that in one area at least I am not welcome back at all.

Murganah Why should you think that?

Ahmed From your attitude towards me. It seems almost hostile.

Murganah Perhaps there's good reason.

Ahmed Why? What have I done?

Murganah Tell me.

Ahmed I can't begin to think.

Murganah You go away – for weeks. We presume you dead. Not a word. Then you return like some glorious prodigal son. Dressed like a – like a king and tell us nothing. That you've been sworn to secrecy.

Ahmed It's the truth.

Murganah Who is she?

Ahmed I can't tell you.

Murganah Then it is a woman?

Ahmed Possibly. Possibly not. How do you know?

Murganah Because you didn't choose those clothes yourself. That took a woman's eye. A woman moreover who loves you.

Ahmed Rubbish.

Murganah And I only have to look in your eyes to see that that love is reciprocated.

Ahmed You don't know this. How could you possibly know this?

Murganah (*violently*) Because I too am a woman, Ahmed. A woman who loved you, who would have readily died for you, who swore her life away for you. And you have betrayed me. And I will have lived for nothing.

Ahmed (*alarmed*) Murganah!

Murganah And I promise, Ahmed. I will kill you and I will kill her. And before I have finished I will bring down this whole kingdom. I will reduce it to ashes.

Ahmed (*moving to her and attempting to touch her*) Please listen to me . . .

Murganah Don't touch me! Don't ever touch me again!

Murganah produces a dagger and strikes at Ahmed. Ahmed manages to fend off the blow. But in the ensuing brief struggle Murganah easily overpowers Ahmed and holds the dagger to his throat.

(*laughing*) You could never beat me, could you, Ahmed? And you never will. And one day when I choose to do so, I will kill you as easily as this.

A second and she releases him. Ahmed realizes he has been within an inch of death.
The Sultan enters. Murganah steps back and hides the dagger.

Sultan Come along! We're all in there, waiting for you, Ahmed! Come on, boy, if you've only an hour then at least spend it with us.

Ahmed (*very upset*) I'm sorry, father. I cannot stop for a feast. I have no time. I'm sorry.

Sultan Can't stop? You mean we've got to cancel it?

Ahmed goes. The Sultan is about to follow him.

Murganah My lord . . .

Sultan Yes? Ah, Murganah . . .

Murganah May I have your permission to speak, sire.

Sultan Of course, only I'm just –

Murganah I will be brief, sire. I do not wish to alarm you but I believe the Prince's secrecy regarding his absence may have sinister implications for us all.

Sultan What on earth do you mean?

Murganah I will speak frankly. The Prince Ahmed is a dear friend. I would not wish him harm. But he is impressionable and easily swayed by unscrupulous people. He is a truly honest and honourable man and sadly men such as those are often the most easily led, for they trust everyone.

Sultan This is true. Only too true.

Murganah I think, even now, the Prince may have fallen under an wrong influence. One that means not only harm to him but to this whole kingdom.

Sultan You really think so?

Murganah There is something evil at work here. I sense it. I fear for him; I fear for you.

Sultan If you are correct, what are we to do?

Murganah Sire, when he leaves allow me to follow him.

Sultan You?

Murganah Please, sire . . .

Sultan But Murganah, this could prove dangerous, you're only a –

Murganah I am only a humble servant, sire, I know. But that is also my strength. I will pass unnoticed. One servant more or less. Who would know?

Sultan You're much more than a mere servant, Murganah, believe me. Very well. As soon as you find where he's gone, return at once and report to me personally. And to no one else.

Murganah Thank you, sire.

Sultan (*as he goes*) Murganah!

Murganah Sire?

Sultan Take care, won't you? I think you're rather – special. Hate to lose you.

Murganah Thank you, sire.

> *The Sultan goes.*
> *Murganah, pleased, prepares to leave.*
> *Ali returns.*

Ali Murganah . . .

Murganah (*irritably*) What do you want?

Ali I saw you there with Ahmed. Does that mean it's all over between us, now he's back?

Murganah What's all over?

Ali You're back with him again. Is that it? If so, what about me?

Murganah I am not back with anyone. I am free. As I've always been. I am not with him as you put it. And I am certainly not with you. Now leave me alone!

Ali Murganah, you can't do this. What am I going to do?

Murganah I suggest you go and try and cheer up your wife.

Ali (*in desperation*) My wife? I don't want to be with my wife. I want to be with you. I don't love my wife, I've told you. I can't stand the sight of her. I can't even bear to look at her.

Murganah (*in sudden anger*) Then don't! (*She gives a sudden violent gesture stabbing her fingers towards Ali's face. As she does this*) And stop staring at me!

Ali gives a cry and clutches his face.

Ali My eyes! What have you done to my eyes? Murganah! I'm blind! Murganah!

Murganah has gone. Ali staggers off calling her name as he goes. As he does this, the scene changes to:

SCENE ELEVEN

The Mountain of Storms
   The weather is as wild as ever. Ahmed enters, making his way to the top.

Ahmed How am I ever going to find my way back in this? It's impossible. (*He climbs a little further. He hears something below him and turns.*) Who is that? Is someone there? Is that someone following me? Come out, whoever you are?

Murganah appears.

Murganah, what are you doing here?

Murganah Ahmed, I'm sorry.

Ahmed I thought you never wanted to see me again. I thought you'd sworn to kill me.

Murganah I'm sorry. Forgive me.

Ahmed I do. I do forgive you. Now go back. Before you freeze to death. Go home.

Murganah I must come with you.

Ahmed Well, you can't. Now go back . . .

Murganah Ahmed!

Ahmed Go back! Back!

Ahmed starts on up the mountain. Murganah stares after him then contrives a fairly spectacular fall, crying out as she does so.

(*turning back to her, alarmed*) Murganah!

He scrambles back down to her. She is moaning in pain.

Are you alright?

Murganah (*moaning*) My leg! My leg!

Ahmed (*trying to help her up*) Can you stand?

Murganah (*crying with pain*) Aaaah! I think it may be broken.

Ahmed Oh, Lord! Here!

He lifts her and starts to carry her up the mountain.

There's the palace! We're nearly there!

As they continue up, the scene changes to:

SCENE TWELVE

Paribanou's Mountain Palace.
  Ahmed enters, still carrying Murganah.

Ahmed (*calling*) Nasuh! Nasuh!

  Nasuh enters swiftly.

Quickly, help me with her!

Nasuh Why have you brought her back here?

Ahmed I couldn't leave her there on the mountain, she would have died. Quickly, put her on the couch.

  Nasuh reluctantly takes Murganah from Ahmed and lays her on the couch. As he does this, Paribanou enters.

Paribanou What's happening? What is this?

Ahmed I'm sorry, she's a friend. She followed me. She's hurt. I couldn't leave her to die. How is she?

  Murganah groans and appears to recover.

Nasuh She's coming round.

Murganah (*weakly*) Where am I – ? Where – ?

  She sees Paribanou. They stare at each other for a moment.

I know you.

Paribanou And I you.

Ahmed You've met before? How marvellous!

Paribanou Have done. Or will do. Are you injured?

Ahmed Her leg. She's hurt her leg. She thinks it may be broken.

Paribanou Oh, I'm so sorry. May I see? (*She moves to Murganah*)

Murganah (*drawing back, warily*) No! It's fine. It was probably just a sprain.

Paribanou If I could just –

Murganah I'd sooner you didn't touch me. Please.

Paribanou (*smiling*) As you wish.

Murganah I will leave. I sense I am not welcome here. (*She gets up, limping only slightly.*)

Ahmed Murganah, wait! You can't leave yet.

Murganah Thank you for your hospitality. Fascinating to – recognize you again.

Ahmed Please. One minute. Paribanou, ask her to stay.

Paribanou Your friend apparently wishes to leave. Why should I stop her?

Ahmed Please, Murganah. One minute. Wait one minute. Please.

Murganah (*moving to the door*) I'll wait out here.

Paribanou Nasuh! Keep our guest company.

Nasuh (*grimly*) I will.

    Nasuh goes off with Murganah.

Ahmed What is all this? Have you both really met before?

Paribanou Not as such.

Ahmed I don't understand.

Paribanou Ahmed, she may have been your friend once but she has changed. Murganah has surely altered since

464

you first knew her. She is now a very dangerous person. I beg you, have nothing more to do with her.

Ahmed What are you saying?

Paribanou Do you love her?

Ahmed I am – deeply, deeply fond of her.

Paribanou But not love?

Ahmed (*angrily*) I don't know. All I know is Murganah is my friend and I will stand by her. And if you intend throwing her out, then I must go too.

Paribanou Ahmed! Listen –

Ahmed No, I'm sorry. Champion or no, there is such a thing as loyalty. She is my sworn blood twin. I will stand by her. I couldn't leave her to make that journey back on her own. What sort of friend would I be then? (*He starts to go.*)

Paribanou Listen to me! Ahmed! Come back here!

> *Ahmed has gone. Paribanou looks worried. In a second, Nasuh returns with a small glass jar.*

They've both gone?

Nasuh They've gone. I fear we may never see him again.

Paribanou Maybe.

Nasuh She – your visitor left you a small gift.

Paribanou What is it?

Nasuh (*examining the jar*) Oranges they look like.

Paribanou (*taking them from him*) How considerate of her. (*She holds the jar in her hands.*)

Nasuh Lady, I would advise you not to eat –

The jar turns suddenly into a small bunch of flowers.

Paribanou (*handing them back to Nasuh*) Put them in water for me, would you, Nasuh?

Nasuh goes off. Paribanou follows. As they go, the scene changes to:

SCENE THIRTEEN

The Mountain of Storms.
The wind is howling as usual. Ahmed enters with Murganah helping her down the mountain side.

Ahmed (*as he helps her*) Come on! Put your foot there, that's it. You're doing well.

Murganah (*triumphantly gripping his hand*) You chose rightly, Ahmed. Well done!

Ahmed How do you mean?

Murganah You chose me not her. I knew you wouldn't desert me. I knew you wouldn't.

Ahmed Of course I wouldn't.

Murganah And it's me you love?

Ahmed (*pretending not to hear above the wind*) What?

Murganah I said, it's me you love. Tell me it's me you love. Not her?

Ahmed Who? Paribanou? What makes you think I love her?

Murganah Then tell me you don't. Say you don't love her.

466

Ahmed Look, this is hardly the place, is it?

Murganah Say it!

Ahmed Can't we wait till we – ?

Murganah (*fiercely*) Say it!

Ahmed is silent.

You can't, can you? You can't say it? (*screaming above the wind*) You can't say it?

Ahmed I don't know. I just –

Murganah Then go back to her! Go on! But I warn you, you won't find her quite so pretty as when you left her. I promise you that.

Ahmed What have you done? What have you done to her?

Murganah Go back! See for yourself!

Ahmed If you've done anything to hurt her – ! I'll –

Murganah You'll what?

Ahmed Alright, I love her! Is that good enough for you! I do. I love her! (*He starts back up the mountain again.*)

Murganah Then die for love, then! Stay here and die! Die!

As she moves away, there is a great rumbling as of an avalanche. Ahmed throws up his arms in alarm. He cries out as the avalanche strikes him and he is bowled over on to his face. Murganah has gone.

Ahmed lies very still. The avalanche has passed. In a moment a figure, tall and angular, arrives. We dimly recognize that it is Houssain. He bends over Ahmed.

Houssain (*above the storm*) I say, are you alright?

Ahmed does not move. Houssain with an effort moves some rocks which are trapping Ahmed's body. He turns Ahmed over.

Ahmed! Ahmed!

Houssain starts to drag Ahmed clear. As he does this, we find ourselves in:

SCENE FOURTEEN

Houssain's Hut.
It is filled with books. Indeed, there is very little room for much else. Simple and spartan, as befits a hermit.
Houssain drags Ahmed into the middle of the room. He closes the door. The wind stops abruptly.

Houssain (*to himself*) There. Get you in the warm. Freezing out there. (*bending over his brother*) Ahmed! Ahmed!

Ahmed groans.

Oh, thank heaven.

Ahmed Houssain! How did you – ?

Houssain I found you. You were trapped by an avalanche. You're lucky I did. This is a deserted spot. I only went out for some firewood. Always forgetting to get it in. How do you feel? Are you alright?

Ahmed (*flexing his legs and trying to stand*) Yes, I think . . . I should be . . .

Houssain Careful. Don't try and do too much straight away. Sit down there. I'll get you some coffee. I make it with pine cones. It's very good. Wait there. There's always some on the boil.

Houssain goes off. Ahmed looks around.

Ahmed (*calling to Ahmed*) What is this place?

Houssain (*off*) It's my new home. Used to be a foresters' hut. Two rooms. This one and that one. Just enough for me and all my beautiful books.

Ahmed I've noticed them.

He opens a book at random. Something pops its head out and disappears immediately. Ahmed jumps in alarm.

What on earth was that?

Houssain What?

Ahmed There's something in one of these books. An animal of some sort.

Houssain returns with a dirty chipped mug.

Houssain Ah, that'll be Omar.

Ahmed Omar?

Houssain I named him that. I found him in one of the books. He's a Bookmarker.

Ahmed A Bookmarker?

Houssain I bought a load of books off a merchant from Samarkand. He threw in Omar. He's very handy. Eats a little waste paper, sleeps most of the time between the pages of your book and marks your place in the process. Here . . .

He hands the mug to Ahmed.

(*coaxing him*) Omar! Come on, Omar! Come and say hallo! Omar!

Omar pops his head out of the book.

This is Ahmed, Omar! He's my kid brother. Ahmed, say hallo to Omar.

Ahmed (*extending his hand, uncertainly*) Hallo!

Omar gives a squeak and disappears.

Houssain No, he's very shy. When I first got him it took months before he'd come out of the dictionary. How's the coffee?

Ahmed (*trying it, with ill disguised distaste*) Ah! Very. Interesting.

Houssain Come on then!

Ahmed What?

Houssain Bed. You can have my bed.

Ahmed But I have to get back –

Houssain Not tonight you don't.

Ahmed (*spilling out his fears*) Houssain, you don't understand. If I don't get back to her I fear that someone who is very – dear – to me, is in terrible danger. I don't know what I'm going to do, Houssain. I really don't.

Houssain Who are you talking about? Murganah?

Ahmed No! Not Murganah. Certainly not Murganah! Someone else.

Houssain My brothers and their women, really!

Ahmed I promised I would be her Champion, you see. Fight on her behalf. But you know me, Houssain. I'm no Champion. I'm hopeless, I can barely lift a sword. And now I think I know who it is she wants me to fight. And I'm not sure I can do it, Houssain. And even if I could, I'm not sure I could win. In fact I know I couldn't win. There's no way I could win against –

Houssain (*gently, under the last*) Ahmed! Ahmed! Ahmed!

Ahmed What?

Houssain Slow down. Please. Now listen. I have not been a good older brother to you in the past, I know. I could have been more help if I had chosen. Instead, I have selfishly stayed in my books in my own private world . . .

Ahmed No, you've not, you've been –

Houssain Listen. I too am no fighter. But I do know things about fighting. We need to talk. It's been long overdue –

Ahmed But what about – ?

Houssain But first sleep. You can return to your friend in the morning after we've talked. In fact, we can talk on the way. Come on. Big brother's telling you. Bed! You can hardly stand.

Ahmed (*sighing*) Alright!

Houssain (*as they go*) It's an interesting bed. I made it myself. Pine needles and then a layer of bracken. Very comfortable.

Ahmed (*alarmed*) Pine needles?
  As they go out, the scene changes to:

SCENE FIFTEEN

The Sultan's Palace.
  Murganah enters. She is dressed resplendantly, no longer bothering to maintain her role as a servant.

Murganah (*yelling*) I said I wanted everyone assembled here at once! Where are you? Where are you?

The pathetic survivors of the palace come on. The speechless Grand Vizier, the blind Ali led by a fat, totally cocooned Nouronnihar. Finally Salim looking terribly the worse for wear. They all stand reverently.

Salim (*singing*)
All hail the Princess, our lovely Princess.
We love our Princess. Long may she live.

Murganah Is this all of you? Is this all there are? (*She pauses.*) Somebody answer me. Quickly, I warn you.

The Vizier makes muffled sounds.

Ali This is all of us, I believe.

Murganah All of us – who?

Ali All of us, Princess.

Nouronnihar (*meekly*) All of us who can still move, Princess. If you will remember you lost your temper with the Palace Guard and –

Murganah I know what I did, thank you. I don't need reminding by you, you gross chimpanzee.

The Sultan hurries on.

Where have you been?

Sultan I'm so sorry, Princess. I had important matters to deal with –

Murganah Let us get one thing straight, shall we? When I give an order, there is nothing – nothing more important than that order. Do you understand that?

Sultan Yes. It was a matter of settling the budget for the –

Murganah (*yelling*) DO YOU UNDERSTAND THAT?

Sultan (*meekly*) Yes, Princess.

Murganah Then in future you do as you're told, you dismal old bat!

Sultan Now, now, now. Really! I must ask you not to – not to – talk to me in that tone. I am – I am – the Sultan – and as such I am owed a certain – I am your senior. You must surely respect your elders. Show some respect for age.

Murganah Age? You believe age gives you privilege? Automatic rights?

Sultan Well, surely . . .

Murganah And you demand those rights, do you?

Sultan I think it's generally understood that –

Murganah (*stretching out her hand as before*) Then if you value age so much, I'll give you it. Age then, old man. Age and age and – age.

As she speaks the Sultan ages visibly in front of her. He becomes a shrunken, helpless old man. The others stand by powerless.

Nouronnihar No . . .

Murganah Be quiet, chimp! Come along! We've all got duties to perform, haven't we? Then let's get on with them.

They all move off.

Salim (*singing*)
All hail the Princess, our lovely –

Murganah (*as she goes*) Shut up!

As they all go off the scene fades to:

SCENE SIXTEEN

Paribanou's Mountain Palace.
  Paribanou is standing sadly. In a moment, Nasuh enters.

Nasuh Lady, he has returned. Ahmed has returned.

Paribanou (*overjoyed*) He's alive?

Nasuh Alive and well. His brother found him and saved his life. The woman had left him on the mountain for dead.

Paribanou Oh, heaven be praised!

  Ahmed appears in the doorway with Houssain behind him. Paribanou looks at him for a second. They move and embrace each other. After a second they break apart, somewhat embarrassed.

Paribanou (*in confusion*) I'm sorry, I –

Ahmed (*equally flustered*) No, I'm – sorry I . . . I was –

Paribanou . . . pleased to see you . . .

Ahmed . . . glad you were not . . . I was frightened you might . . .

Paribanou . . . that you were . . . Oh!

Ahmed Oh!

  They embrace again. They part.

Paribanou and Ahmed (*apologetically, to the others*) Sorry!

Houssain I take it you two know each other?

Ahmed (*laughing nervously*) Yes. I just wanted to tell

you both that in the brief time I've been away – I know it hasn't been long – I have learnt certain things. One of those is that occasionally one must stand up and fight. Not always with swords but at the very least with words and thoughts. But if it comes to swords, then . . .

Houssain If it does come to swords, I have taught him a valuable lesson . . .

Nasuh *You* have taught him a lesson? To do with swords?

Ahmed Yes, Houssain has taught me the most important thing, Nasuh. To believe in myself. To believe that I can win.

Nasuh (*unconvinced*) We shall see.

Ahmed Try me.

Houssain Ahmed, be careful, you're still weak.

Ahmed Come on, Nasuh! Try me!

Nasuh Very well.

Paribanou Be careful, Ahmed. Being over-confident is almost as –

Ahmed Don't worry.

Nasuh has fetched the swords. Ahmed now takes his.

Nasuh Are you ready?

Ahmed Ready.

Ahmed and Nasuh fight. For a second it is evenly matched but suddenly Ahmed finds an opening and for the first time has Nasuh at his mercy. Nasuh is amazed.

Houssain Bravo!

Paribanou (*somewhat incredulously*) Bravo, indeed. Bravo!

Ahmed Am I a worthy Champion?

Paribanou Truly you are. Only I, too, have learnt a lesson whilst you've been away.

Ahmed What's that?

Paribanou That I wish it were someone other than you that has to fight. It would break my heart if anything happened to you.

Ahmed Then I must make sure that I come back, mustn't I? (*as he goes off*) Come on, Nasuh, let's practise.

Ahmed goes off. Nasuh looks at Paribanou.

Paribanou Teach him well, Nasuh.

Nasuh I'll do my best. There's little left I can teach him, I'm afraid.

Paribanou (*excitedly*) He did beat you, didn't he? He actually beat you.

Nasuh Me, yes. But I am not Murganah. (*He goes.*)

Paribanou looks worriedly at Houssain.

Houssain Keep faith.

Paribanou Yes.

Houssain He needs our faith.

They go out as the scene changes to:

SCENE SEVENTEEN

The Sultan's Palace.
  It is dawn. A great hammering on the gates. Ali comes on with Nouronnihar leading him, as before.

Ali What's happening? What's the noise?

Nouronnihar It's someone at the gates. Somebody said it was Ahmed.

Ali Ahmed? She told us he was dead.

Nouronnihar Apparently he isn't. And Houssain's with him, as well.

Ali What are they both doing here, the fools?

Nouronnihar Maybe they've come back to save us?

Ali Oh, yes. Very likely. An intellectual who barely has the strength to lift a pen and a coward with his head in the clouds. Very likely.

  More banging. Murganah enters angrily.

Murganah What is that noise? Who's woken me with that noise?

Ali It wasn't us, Princess.

Murganah I know it wasn't you, you fool. You're standing there. Who is it? Vizier! (*yelling*) Vizier! I thought I put Salim at the gates to drive people away. (*yelling*) Salim!

Nouronnihar Salim has finally broken down, Princess.

Murganah Broken?

Nouronnihar (*weeping*) You made him stand out in the rain and he fell apart.

Murganah Shut up, shut up, shut up!

The Vizier enters, apparently still struggling into his clothes.

Vizier! Find out who that is, at once.

The Vizier hurries off.

If there's one thing guaranteed to put me in a bad temper, it's being woken up from a sound sleep!

Ali Oh!

Nouronnihar Oh!

Murganah Be quiet!

The Sultan enters. He is now very frail.

Sultan It is rumoured, Princess, that it is Ahmed at the door.

Murganah What did you say? Did you say Ahmed?

Sultan Ahmed. And his brother Houssain.

Murganah You're senile, you stupid old man.

Sultan No, no, definitely Ahmed. Some people told me.

The Vizier returns hastily.

Murganah Is it Ahmed?

The Vizier nods.

Well, well, well. So he returns. Ahmed returns. We must welcome him then, mustn't we? Open the gates. (*yelling*) Open the gates. (*Murganah goes off.*)

A fanfare. Ahmed comes on dressed for a fight. He has his helmet and sword. Behind him comes Houssain.

Ali Who is it? Who's coming?

Nouronnihar It's Ahmed and Houssain.

Ali The fools! Why have they come here? Get away.
Tell them to get away from here!

The fanfare stops. A silence.

Houssain (*looking at them all*) What has been
happening here? Father?

Sultan Terrible things, my son. Too terrible to mention.

Houssain I cannot believe what I'm seeing. Ali?

Ali Houssain? Is that you?

Nouronnihar Yes, it's Houssain, Ali.

Houssain (*incredulously*) Nouronnihar?

Nouronnihar Yes.

Houssain Princess Nouronnihar?

Nouronnihar (*alarmed*) No, no! Not Princess. I am not
Princess. Please don't call me Princess. There is only
one Princess now. She who rules us all.

Ali And who will now rule you.

Houssain You mean Murganah? Are you talking of
Murganah?

*Another fanfare, menacing and bigger than before.
Murganah enters. She is now in her fighting clothes
and carries her helmet and sword. All but Ahmed and
Houssain kneel as she enters.*

Murganah (*nodding*) Ahmed.

Ahmed Murganah.

Murganah I see you and your brother no longer have
the breeding to bow or kneel before a Princess.

Ahmed We prefer to choose whom we kneel before.

Murganah I should value that choice whilst you have it. Why have you come here?

Ahmed I am the Champion of Paribanou who is your sworn enemy and rival. On her behalf I am here to fight you. And if necessary kill you.

Murganah (*laughing*) Big speeches. Big words.

Ahmed I am prepared to back them up.

Murganah I could melt that sword in your hand without moving a muscle. I could wither your arms and crumble the very bones in your legs. What sort of fight would that be?

Ahmed It would prove nothing, of course. Except that you lack the courage to fight me fairly and squarely. Without recourse to tricks.

Murganah You think I couldn't?

Ahmed I believe you may be frightened.

Murganah Frightened? Ahmed, we've known each other since we were children. I've always beaten you. Always. I beat you with sticks and later I beat you with swords. Why should things change? Put down your weapon and kneel and we'll forget it.

Ahmed I prefer to fight.

Murganah Then you're a fool. I will tell you this. I shall not enjoy killing you, Ahmed. I loved you but you scorned that love. You threw it back in my face. Not once but twice. Once with her – (*She indicates Nouronnihar.*) – and once with your so called Lady – Paribanou.

Ahmed I have behaved honourably.

Murganah (*angrily*) Well, I don't think you have.

Ahmed I behaved as my duty dictated that I should –

Murganah You've behaved like a traitor! A traitor to me! And you will die like a traitor! Very well. Let's finish this. I'm sorry. You leave me no choice.

Houssain (*softly to Ahmed*) Good. She's angry. It's good to get her angry.

Ahmed (*worried*) Good for who?

They prepare to fight. Both put on their fighting helmets, versions of the earlier ones but more ornate.

A drum beats. The spectators rise and draw back to the edges of the area to form an arena.

The fight begins. Evenly matched at first, Murganah is obviously a little taken aback at Ahmed's new found prowess.

Murganah Good, Ahmed! Good!

Ahmed, encouraged, almost makes a fatal slip.

(*laughing*) Oh, Ahmed. To fall for that. You always used to fall for that.

Murganah prepares for the coup de grâce. Ahmed somehow wriggles free.

The fight see-saws back and forth becoming more serious, more keenly contested.

At last Murganah appears to have the upper hand once again. But a burst of overconfidence proves her final undoing. Ahmed stabs her. She stares at him incredulously. Her sword slips from her hand and she slowly drops to the floor.

Oh, Ahmed. What have you done?

Ahmed (*kneeling by her*) Murganah. I will fetch a doctor. Maybe he can . . .

Murganah (*her voice growing weaker*) No, Ahmed.
You've done for me . . . done for me. Even in death,
I still love you. I'm sorry . . .

> *A strange sound is heard as the room grows darker*
> *and eerier. A cowled dark figure appears. Everyone,*
> *including Ahmed, draws back. It is Schaibar, returned*
> *for Murganah, as he promised.*

Schaibar . . . Schaibar . . .

> *Schaibar reaches Murganah. He slides back his hood*
> *to reveal the face of Death.*

Schaibar (*softly*) Murganah, I have come for you at last.
Take my hand, child.

Murganah (*taking his hand*) Schaibar . . .

Schaibar Come with me now. And I will give you peace.
Come now. Come.

> *Schaibar leads Murganah away. The sounds fade and*
> *the light brightens.*

Ahmed (*recovering first*) She's gone.

Ali Yes, I know I saw it. (*realising*) I saw it! I *saw* it.

Nouronnihar Ali, you can see?

Ali I can see.

Vizier Praise be to heaven! (*realizing*) Praise be to heaven!
Praise be to heaven! (*He laughs.*)

Sultan Well fought, lad. Damn good fight. Didn't know
you had it in you!

Ahmed Thank you, father.

Sultan I feel better as well. Twenty years younger.

Ali Oh, Nouronnihar! Forgive me. (*He reaches for her.*)

Nouronnihar (*drawing away*) No, no. Please . . .

Ali Come on! Take off that veil, I want to look at my wife . . .

Nouronnihar (*desperately*) Please, don't. Please I beg you.

Ali has grasped the edge of her veil. As she steps back the whole of her outer garment pulls away to reveal the former Nouronnihar.

Oh! Oh, goodness!

Ali Oh, my beautiful Princess!

Nouronnihar Oh, my lovely husband!

They embrace.

Sultan Very well. In honour of your victory, a feast! Grand Vizier. Tell the kitchens to prepare a banquet for a thousand. In honour of my gallant son, Prince Ahmed.

Vizier But, sire, the cooks. We have no cooks.

Sultan No cooks.

Vizier She exiled the cooks.

Sultan (*appalled*) No cooks? What are we going to do? Do something at once!

The Vizier goes off briefly.

Ahmed Father, in any case I cannot stay. I'm sorry.

Sultan Can't stay? Why ever not?

Ahmed I am the Champion of Paribanou. I must return to her and set her free.

Paribanou appears with Nasuh.

Paribanou No need, I am here. You have already set me free. And I in turn release you from your vow to me, if you so wish.

483

Ahmed For as long as you will permit me, lady, I will remain your Champion.

Paribanou (*smiling*) Very well. But I should warn you. It will be for ever.

Sultan Now what about these cooks? Who's going to cook?

The Vizier has returned.

Vizier Sire, good news! A cook has been found!

Sultan Splendid. Come on, everybody!

Houssain Not me, father, I'm sorry I do have to get back to my books.

Ali No, you don't, you're staying.

Ahmed You're staying!

Nouronnihar You're staying!

Houssain I'm staying.

Sultan Everyone's staying! At last, a feast! Ahmed, lead us in!

Ahmed (*proffering his arm*) Would you do me the honour, my lady!

Paribanou The honour is mine, Sir Champion . . .

Music as they start to process inside. Salim appears in the doorway. He is more or less reassembled. He has on a chef's hat and holds a covered dish.

Salim (*proudly*) Served is dinner!

He lifts the cover on the dish and is enveloped with smoke. They all laugh and go off to more music.
Blackout.
End.